LOVESIC
KY in TO

JAY CRYSTALL

with Catherine Lenox

IRONTWINE
— P R E S S —

Seattle, Washington, USA

This book is dedicated to all artists, musicians, writers,
entrepreneurs, adventurers, healers and teachers everywhere
who open creative pathways for themselves and inspire others,
and to anyone who musters up the guts to take charge of and
change their lives, not for themselves but for the good of humanity.
Keep flowering. You are changing the world.

LOVESIC in KYOTO

www.lovesicinkyoto.com

Published by Iron Twine Press
www.irontwinepress.com

Photos provided by Jay Crystall and Catherine Lenox

Cover and book design by Sonja L. Gerard

Back cover - "The Scarlet Fringe" (Fumiyoshi),
Oil on Linen by Phil Couture
www.philcouture.com

ISBN 978-0-9984808-1-7 (pb)

10 9 8 7 6 5 4 3 2 1

"Being creative means pushing open the heavy door to life. This is not an easy struggle. Indeed, it may be the hardest task in the world. For opening the door to your own life is more difficult than opening the doors to the mysteries of the universe. But the act of opening your door vindicates your existence as a human being and makes life worth living. To be human is not merely to stand erect and manifest reason and intellect; to be human in the full sense of the word is to lead a creative life."

- Daisaku Ikeda
– "The Flowering of Creative Life Force"
- April 18, 1974

京都物語

CONTENTS

PROLOGUE

I first saw Jay Crystall at a bohemian club in Kyoto called Urbanguild. My instincts told me I'd like him, and I was right. Jay and I "get" each other in terms of our love and fascination with the aesthetic and vibe of our adopted homeland. Both of us come from a sensory, musical, spiritual, artistic perspective. We work to build bridges between Japan and the West and open pathways for the flow of art, friendship, and philosophy between them. One of my favorite bands is The Church, from Australia. They have beautiful, insightful oral landscapes and textures but it takes a while for me to uncover them. Jay's music, however, is immediately "smack in your face cool," solidly rooted in Kyoto and psychedelic rock. I have an endless fascination with Kyoto, where just going for a walk fills me with a sense of wonder. Due to thousands of ancient temples here and the quality of silence they emit, there are endless pockets of divinity. Taking a meditative stroll along the Philosopher's Path in the Higashiyama District, where little temples are dotted along the way, is spellbinding. The nearly two-kilometer path begins around the Silver Pavilion (Ginkakuji), where my gallery is located, and ends in Nanzenji near my gallery, where I can climb up to the massive gate of Nanzenji Temple and watch the clouds float by. I never live in memory. I'm always present. An artist can be inspired anywhere, even in the dimmest places, if their senses are open. But in Kyoto, artistic excellence is everywhere. It's a city of inspiration. A person could spend three or four lifetimes learning about life here. Twelve thousand years of art and artistry can be found in the edges and center of Kyoto, right in the middle of the city's ultra-modern bustle. It's a place of endless contradiction, both ultra-modern and ancient. I like to support creative, living artists, which is what I do in my gallery in Kyoto. I'm happy Jay is sharing his observations in this book. He hasn't been in Japan that long, so he sees and tells about it with fresh eyes.

Robert Yellin, pottery journalist, ceramic specialist, and owner of Robert Yellin Yakimono Gallery has lived in Japan for 34 years. He writes regularly on Japanese pottery for numerous publications. The author of *Yakimono Sanka*, a book about saki utensils, he has also written for *Daruma* magazine, *Honoho Geijutsu, Asian Art Newspaper, WINDS* magazine, *Ceramics, Art and Perception*, and the Japan Ceramics Society publication, *Tohsetsu*. To learn more, please visit *JapanesePottery.com*.

INTRODUCTION

In April 2014, I went to an art show opening at a new contemporary art gallery in Kyoto, Japan owned by Yoshitomo and Miyuki Yokomizo. They were my English language students and had graciously invited me to attend the reception. As I swept through the room admiring the abstract LED sculptures, funky metallic etched mirrors and otherworldly landscape photos on display, I couldn't help but notice a woman who looked noticeably out of place in that sea of Japanese artists and friends. Standing in one of the concrete cube rooms in the stark white gallery, a good head taller than most of the other people there, she was blond and speaking English to a shorter Japanese woman. I soon found out the Japanese woman was a gallery owner from Kitakyushu, Kyushu, located in the southwest of Japan, and friend of the Yokomizo family.

To my surprise, the taller, blond woman bounded enthusiastically up to me and said she was pleased to see an American, especially a New Yorker. Startled, I'd asked her if it was that obvious. Laughing warmly, she'd said yes, that she loved New Yorkers. As we toasted champagne, she said her name was Catherine Lenox. We immediately recognized each other as friends with a common appreciation of Japan and friended each other on Facebook. Little did I know at the time that my Buddhist practice, founded in the concept of being in rhythm with the universe and of what I call "Original Good," was already at work toward writing this book. The essence and meaning of Original Good, a phrase I coined twenty years ago for a song, is based on the Buddhist concept of seeing the essential goodness and potential in ourselves and others. If we stay true to it, see and feel it, and consciously exert ourselves to draw out the innate goodness in everything around us and in us, we connect directly to a divine force for good. Wonderful things happen.

Fast forward to a year later when I posted a 30 second iPhone video on Facebook. Taken from the window of my school, the WAVE Center for Language and Culture, it featured the *Aoi Matsuri* (Aoi Festival) parade procession. Oxen-drawn carts loaded with flowers and offerings to the ancient emperor were followed by men on horses clad in Heian Era (794-1185) garb. White-powdered, sullen-faced, costumed women silently walked behind them in loose formation, ancient and exotic. A creaking of huge wooden-spoked wheels and clod of hooves on the pavement provided the soundtrack. A few hours later I received an out-of-the-blue Facebook chat message from Catherine asking if I'd ever thought of writing a book. She'd seen the video and thought my school, music and the journey that led me to Kyoto would make a fascinating story. Coincidentally, I'd just been talking with a friend the night before who suggested that I write a book. My friend said in response to me complaining about how busy and complicated my life was, "you are a complicated person, so naturally you have a complicated life. In fact, you probably should write a book about it."

Lack of time, however, due to my work at the WAVE Center, teaching at Doshisha University, and fighting for my dream of being a successful musician, made writing a book next to impossible. I was so damn busy at the time. Should I write a book? I had only one answer for that question. Hell Yes.

Frankly, I never entertained the idea. But now, suddenly in its perfect way, Original Good, conspiring with the mystic workings of the universe had catapulted it right into my life. To my amazement, Catherine told me she had a passion for telling other people's stories. When she suggested we write a book together, I knew immediately that nudge from the universe was too timely to ignore. The seed for *Lovesic in Kyoto* had been planted.

But, write a book? I'm a songwriter. I can write melodies and hooks that people, especially me, remember and sing in their sleep. I've never written a book, and I sure as heck can't write a self-help book. I'm most often the one who needs the help. So, don't look to my book to give you any answers. But it's important to me to not keep my realizations to myself. They're a celebration of what makes my world grow, and it also helps me remember what I've learned. So, to the best of my ability, I'm going to share them along with what it's like for me to live in today's Kyoto.

If you're expecting an academic historical perspective on Japanese history, you might be better off poking around on Wikipedia. I can't sequence the respective historical eras of Japan any better than I can name more than two French Impressionist painters, Monet and Chagall. If you want an accurate cultural perspective and analysis of Japan, there are some great BBC documentaries such as *The Art of Japanese Life* and *The Idea of*

Japan. They brilliantly and eloquently illuminate some of the principles and aesthetical connections that keep me from leaving Japan and, in their own way, inspired me to buckle down, expand my creative reach and write this book.

If you're privy to fact checking and have a lot of time on your hands, go for it. I make no apologies. I don't have a PhD in Asian studies or Japanese culture. In my life, I have owned two Toyotas, a Mazda pick-up truck and sold my beloved black Honda CRV the week before I moved to Japan seven years ago. I haven't even begun to master Japanese language. I can get around, or some might say, even thrive with my survival Japanese. I know enough Kanji characters to find the exit of a parking lot and not walk into the ladies' side of a public bath, or *sento*. I adore, respect and admire traditional Japanese art forms and practices but am confused by the *urasenke* tea ceremony style as it compares to others. I once dropped and broke a cup, spilling hot tea across a table onto mine and two other laps, which in Japan with its civility culture of etiquette, was something close to unthinkable. The first time I really looked at traditional *shodo* (calligraphy) on a scroll, I might well have been looking at the daily specials on a menu in a fancy Chinese restaurant.

My credentials? I have drummed "serious" roots reggae Nyabinghi rhythms on a djembe in a smoky shanty shack as Rastafarian priests chanted ancient verse to the rainy sunset perched on a cliff above the sea in Jamaica. I have a degree in civil engineering, and can, and have held my own when discussing the Superstring Theory of the universe with a visiting Moscow University professor in a 15-minute ride in my taxi, back in the day. I can repair a leaking toilet by perfectly fitting it onto a new wax floor ring, with a few beers in me. I can entertain a crowd with just a guitar and a mic. I'm able to elicit gushing reviews on a song I've written and recorded from somebody I'll never meet who lives halfway around the world. Speaking generally, I'm confident that I know how things work and, by and large, can troubleshoot them if required. People too, for the most part.

As a devoted practitioner of Nichiren Buddhism for more than 25 years, I am constantly racking my brains to figure life out, the how and whys of the causes and effects that move in, through and around me. What should I say? Why did they do that? What's wrong with him? Or is it me? I am obsessively and almost annoyingly aware of my responsibility to elevate myself and others, to dig deeper to find the hidden gems and kernels of truth in every situation, and act in a way that creates true value.

You may ask how this former civil engineer, New York fine art management specialist, advertising hack, and event production manager whose background was more given to setting up razzle-dazzle sales presentations and schmoozing art gallery curators in Chelsea than teaching English in Kyoto ended up in Japan. Who would have thought that the further I moved away from the U.S., the closer I would get to my real home? The truth is, I believe I was always destined to be in Kyoto. Every step of my life in New York paved the path to my new creative world in Japan. The glue binding everything together is most certainly the 20 years I spent practicing with the Soka Gakkai International Buddhist organization (SGI-USA). There, based on the spiritual practice of Nichiren Buddhism, I learned how to overcome problems. Through honest dialogue, friendship, musical performance, leadership and life skills training, I was without a doubt being primed for life in Kyoto. Besides that, I have a big mouth and an expansive heart. Couple that with a residual Jewish guilt complex, and I have all the makings of a tortured "sushi-knish, dangerously dipped in a wasabi smile."

I'm one of those idiots who never holds on to the roll bar at the top of the rollercoaster, flailing my arms wildly above my head, thinking it might be more fun this way. Certifiably willing to kick wildly and splash if called for, this propensity for big, emotionally impulsive dreaming is what led me to living, teaching, and making music in Kyoto, Japan. For the past seven years, I've carved out a niche in Kyoto as an English teacher, combining multimedia and interactive activities with textbook learning, role play, drama, and music. My school, the WAVE Center of Language and Culture, immerses Japanese students in English through unique methods and programs that culturally assimilate them with the world at large.

Sigmund Freud says the id is the only part of a person's personality that is unconscious, instinctive, primitive and driven by pleasure. Truth is, I wouldn't know how to change my id filter even if I could find it. Also, maybe I have an off switch, but I haven't been able to find that either. Put simply, the flow from my brain to mouth has no governor, let alone mayor. This almost reckless bravado helped me gain the fortune and sparkle to own a business, work at a great university, and pull my heart, kidney, and spleen out to mash them into original music, all within my third year in Japan. I feel justified to write a book about Kyoto and Japan simply because I'm actively watching and observing it with the gazing eyeballs of a recently landed Martian and am not an expert.

Sitting at my computer, I'm noticing the obvious squiggly, red correction lines underscoring the word, lovesic. "WTF!" spell check scolds me. "I thought you're supposed to be an English teacher. Write like one!" I grin impishly. The fact is, I've misspelled lovesick intentionally. Why? Merriam-Webster defines love as a strong affection for another due to kinship or personal ties, sexual attraction, tenderness, fondness based on admiration, benevolence, or common interests, a warm attachment to an object of devotion, and an assurance of affection, deep loyalty, and concern for another. Or, a score of zero in tennis. Trust me, my relationship with love runs this entire gamut, including the occasional zero scores. Love is wonderful, messy, unpredictable, and often completely perplexing and complicated, and that's just as true in Kyoto as anywhere, even if you dress it up in ancient samurai traditions and a colorful kimono. [Sic] is also an editing term used to point out grammatical errors, misspellings or misstatement of facts. [Sic] means "the content was quoted as said, despite its mistake." The Western misconception of life and love in Japan is often painted as a constrained, delicate, orderly affair when, in fact, relationships here are every bit as scrambled as those in the U.S., often in quirky, edgy ways inexplicable to Western minds. Hence, use of the term "sic." But more on "lovesic" later.

Finally, poet E.E. Cummings was famous for never using an uppercase "I" in his poems. Convention prescribed he use capital letters, but he chose not to. By doing so, he explained he "took his ego out of his poems." In a letter to his mother in 1925, he wrote, "I am a small 'i' poet." He pushed convention because he knew the rules and chose to break them anyway, with purpose, and he could. Or, maybe he just wanted to create something unique. For whatever reason, he was a rule breaker. Let's be clear from the start. Like E.E. Cummings, I am driven to break rules and push convention. My brain is just wired that way.

How am I going to share my story? I'll share it through the lens of Buddhist wisdom, backlit by the myriad lessons of the colorful and twisting life path I took that led me to Kyoto. In this book, I hope to convey my fascination with the beauty and contradictions of modern-day Japan (particularly Kyoto) as I struggle to create a new life and begin to realize my lifelong ambition of impacting culture. Japan today is balanced on a precipice between a mindset of ancient Samurai attitude and traditions and the drive for technological, new innovations. This study in opposites, an oddball intersection between old and new, is where life here gets interesting...

IT'S MY BEST HOPE TO MAKE KYOTO, WITH ALL ITS QUIRKINESS AND BEAUTY, MORE ACCESSIBLE AND UNDERSTANDABLE TO WESTERNERS. TO THAT END, I OFFER YOU THIS BOOK.

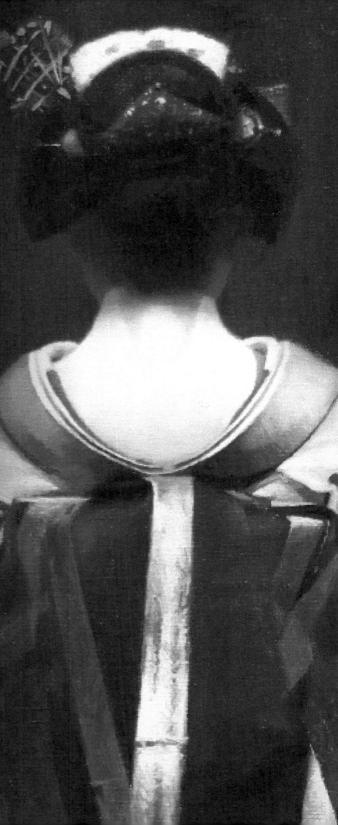

WHY KYOTO?

*"I loved the quiet
places in Kyoto,
the places that held
the world within a
windless moment.
Inside the temples,
Nature held her
breath. All longing
was put to sleep
in the stillness, and all
was distilled into
a clean simplicity.
The smell of
wood-smoke,
the drift of incense;
a procession
of monks in
black-and-gold
robes, one of them
giggling in a voice
yet unbroken;
a touch of autumn
in the air, a sense of
gathering rain."*

- Pico Iyer

"The Scarlet Fringe"
(Fumiyoshi),
Oils on Linen by Phil Couture

京都物語

CHAPTER 1

KEEPING THE BEAT

"Broken dreams simply don't exist when you're in the land, when you live in the land, when you're building the Land of Tranquil Light."

- "Bubblin' Up"
– Jay Crystall
(Kansai Rocks!
Changing Poison into Medicine)

There's something different about Kyoto, Japan. Everyone who has ever visited or lived here knows that they can never say good-bye for good. You know you'll be back someday. It's the jewel of the Kansai region which many people feel embodies the very heart and soul of Japan. Surrounded by green foothills, as if cradled in the hands of ancestors and protected by ancient gods, Kyoto is the cultural mecca for all Japanese, and at the same time the must-go destination for visitors to Japan from around the world. Tradition and beauty pulse vibrantly in Kyoto as they blend with modernity. Proud temples and shrines stand amidst trendy cafes and modern art galleries. This is the place where Gucci meets geisha. It is a truly international city where the rhythms and flavors of the world are distilled and refined into cuisine, fashion, music, and higher education, giving it a refreshing and distinct personality that is both familiar and fascinating. But beyond that, it is also the lesser-known underbelly of Japan that draws me to Kyoto. It is the people's human vulnerability and quirky response to change that intrigues me. Through the lens of an expatriate, I want to share observations about this beautiful, somewhat peculiar Land of the Rising Sun to dispel age-old Western attitudes about Japan. It's my intent to show how modernization has infiltrated the culture here, both positively and negatively, and welcome you to the new, vibrant swirl of today's Kyoto.

At my English school, the teaching style and methods I've created have made the school successful and somewhat of a landmark in my neighborhood. I had chosen to call it The WAVE Center for Language and Culture because I discovered teaching culture was just as important as teaching language, and a lot more fun.

At the same time, I'm also continuously recording and releasing my original music. Who knows, with the right mix and a ton of luck it might possibly change the world profoundly and forever! Might I be remembered as a Bob Marley-esque cultural ambassador or even memorialized in elevator muzak?! At the least maybe I'll help someone to reconsider committing suicide. Even making a few thousand people smile might do the trick. I would categorize it as "poppy, alternative, conscious world-music." My first CD, *Kansai Rocks! – Changing Poison into Medicine*, a collection of original and positive world music and acoustic reggae, has received great reviews internationally. All thirty-seven people that bought it loved it! [available on iTunes and most other platforms.]

Additionally, I regularly attend Buddhist meetings and often speak, sometimes in English and sometimes with my own mixed dialect of "semi-enlightened toddler-Japanese." Although Buddhism has generally moved East to West, from India through Thailand, Myanmar, and Japan before being seeded in Europe and the Americas, I'm bringing it back from America to Japan, sending those waves back East. But now I'm infusing it with a new perspective.

Why else am I so drawn to create a life in Japan? There are countless reasons. One is that decades ago, a seed was planted by Huey Ueda, a New York-based Japanese newspaper correspondent and SGI Buddhist leader. Walking slowly with the measured gait of someone who overcame polio as a child in Japan forty years prior, he told me with a slow smile that I "get" Japanese people and they "get" me. That rang a bell deep in my heart and mind that resonated for years. You might, then, expect this book is primarily about my school and music. In part, it is. But the stories that burst from these pages paint a much broader picture. More deeply, the endearing, often contradictory contrasts in Japan that Westerners don't typically ever see tell the real story. These are the true quirky eye-openers, those unexpected moments that often fill me with humor and edgy surprise.

My simple, gut-level perspective of Japan may be mocked by scholars or even by some of my most seriously Japanophile friends. But, as a musician, being transplanted into this land and experiencing it and having to navigate the confusing maze of cultural wrongs and rights is both stimulating and disorienting at the same time. It's the perfect blend of stimuli to keep me off balance and help me grow every nanosecond as a person and artist, as a global citizen and human being. Kyoto is and always will be a living, dynamic, astoundingly beautiful, historical city. I am continually moved to call Japan my home. I will probably die here. I revel in its beauty and intrigue. I'm starting to understand how a small island nation goes from militaristic imperialism to getting their asses kicked by the stupendous force inside the atom, and in a few decades, becomes the third largest economy in the world. I see the struggles. I admire the work ethic. I benefit from the fact that 100-percent of the population has national healthcare, and I'm paying half of what I was paying in the U.S. for great, quality care. Plus, I pick my own doctors. I'm a feral advocate as well as observer in this land of contradictions. This is a land where people pay exorbitant amounts of money for the most finely-sourced foods presented in meticulously concocted arrangements in which the very order and ritual of eating them makes a Passover Seder plate look like a McDonald's Happy Meal. But, this is also the place where the pendulum swings effortlessly over to the nonsensicality of a potato salad sandwich on white bread or yakisoba sandwiches (i.e. soy-flavored spaghetti on a hot dog roll).

One morning I was drawn to the window by the most exotic soundscape I'd ever heard. Coming from two or three different directions, guttural, otherworldly tones sang from the throat chants of young Buddhist monks in training. Dressed in dark-colored robes and large conical straw hats, the young men were performing, or perhaps re-enacting, an ancient call-and-response walking ritual in my neighborhood near the former Imperial Palace, *Gosho*, which has been in the same location since the 1200s. As the sound of one of the monks got louder, I heard the clucking of his *geta* (wooden sandals) stop. I timidly peeked outside of the 2nd floor rear window of my school, which faces a quiet back street, and remained silent and motionless. I certainly didn't want to interrupt this solemn centuries-old training ritual, performing a mere 20 feet from me. In perfect synchronicity, it was his time to stop and wait for the call of one of his fellow acolytes positioned a few blocks away, somewhere amidst the maze of homes, small shops, and apartments. This pause was just enough time for him to pull his iPhone out of his robe pocket, check for text messages, and reply to one. Then, without missing his cue, he started chanting and walked out of view. (Seeing it is believing it. Visit https://bit.ly/lovesicinkyoto1)

These contradictions abound in Japan. Walking through Kyoto, you'll see the profound simplicity of precisely manicured and obsessively maintained gardens in its temples, each painstakingly perfect element symbolizing the sea, mountains or other aspect of nature. In contrast, if you look down any city street, you'll see ugly, twisting black power and phone lines dangling overhead, obscuring sky views. Everything in Japan is generally very buttoned up and trimmed. But these wires, even in upscale neighborhoods, seem to be connected by a haphazard "make it up as you go along" design. The civility, bowing and formalized politeness in greetings at the doors of clubs is expected and genuine, and no more so than in the foyers of clubs in Shibuya, Tokyo where gift bearing businessmen pay money to flirt with and hope for the best with short-skirted high school girls working part-time jobs after school.

To this day, I perceive myself as a mish-mash of two polar-opposites twisted and intertwined like the red and white in a candy cane, my feet comfortably straddling the curved center line of the yin-yang fish symbol. To "normal" folks, it may seem extraordinarily contradictory to have two sides seemingly at cross-purposes pulling a person in opposite directions. But it's perfectly ME! On the one hand, I'm the brightest star in any galaxy with a genuine, sincere smile and the confidence to elevate any person or unify any group I'm engaging. On the other hand, I can be a sad and lonely, broken-hearted father and husband, crumpled up and sobbing in the fetal position on the carpet. I can be a university teacher leaving the front of the classroom, excitedly pacing through the aisles of desks, and coaching students with tears in my eyes. Then, at 1:30 AM that same night in my darkened school with headphones on, I'm frantically singing the same five-seconds of a lyric over-and-over again into a recording mic. In a dangerously high pitch, I'm desperately trying to find that sweet spot between a scream and falsetto. I can be blissfully engorged in the smoky experience of a high-end *Yakiniku* shop, or DIY BBQ grill-in-the-center-of-the-table shops. But the next morning I'm risking life and limb on a speeding six-minute bicycle death ride, weaving around pedestrians on the sidewalk past the Imperial Palace to get a Sausage McMuffin meal with the extra hash browns before McDonald's stops serving breakfast at 10:30 AM. These truly aren't self-conflicted contradictions. They're just two sides of the same coin.

So, I am well suited to living in a land of contradictions. I might even be thriving in it. In fact, I take pride in being a walking, breathing, arms-flailing-in-the-air contradiction. My chanting of "*Nam-myoho-renge-kyo*" is directly linked to balancing these contradictions. The more I do it, the brighter the fire that burns inside my life. Day by day, year by year, that white-hot flame manifests as a dynamic, exhilarating experience, revolutionizing my character. Chanting makes me focus and extends my gaze over and beyond the visual horizon. This self-generated, controlled cosmic fireball emanating from the depths of my life is hot enough to smelt everything together. It provides enough momentum to ensnare and harness the seemingly repelling forces so that they swing wildly and erratically in tandem. It's like two weighted balls attached by a rope, swung with might and then let go. Through complicated relationships of kinetic energy and momentum transfer, they feed off each other's energy and fly much further than if they were slung alone. "*Nam-myoho-renge-kyo*" means to connect or fuse with the "mystic law" of the universe that encompasses everything, including these laws of physics. I have come to realize that my truest identity lies at this junction of opposites and contradictions.

Why does a practice that centers on daily repetitive chanting of the Chinese Sanskrit phrase "*Nam-myoho-renge-kyo*" that's done in my socks at a home altar so deeply affect my life? Why did the Buddhism born in India travel East across Asia and evolve into the essence of the Buddha's teachings, distilled into an accessible practice by the Japanese monk Nichiren on Mount Minobu in the 1200's? Why has this practice become a worldwide religion that's practiced in every country by people of varying intellect, economic and social status? Why has it manifested in universities, museums, cultural exchange organizations, and a United Nations NGO? My short answer is because it's not dogmatic; it's rooted in moment to moment reality shaping. It's based on the principle that everything is rhythm and light, and when science and philosophy don't contradict, I'm in!

In Kyoto, I've been highly fortunate to have many opportunities to employ this spiritual mechanism which has catapulted me creatively, professionally and intellectually to new heights. I may spend an hour teaching a researcher who specializes in fertility treatments. While I'm teaching him or at least helping him refine his technical English, I'm also learning about the intricacies and advances in in vitro fertilization (IVF) while broadening my own horizons. How could my life have been complete without knowing that when choosing a sperm cell for IVF you must select one with a well-defined head and tail? The lucky contestant should exhibit a "spunky" attitude, be a good swimmer and NOT swim in a circle. Then you chop off the tail with a pipette so it can't swim away and touch it to the egg and...Hello Kitty!! I'm not sure how, but I sense that there will be some way to put this tidbit of information to use in my life. (Oh wait! I just did.)

Another example of where the truth lies for me happened in my Wednesday morning ladies group class, where I taught three wealthy Kyoto women who are in their sixties. They paid me the equivalent of one hundred dollars for a 90-minute "group conversation lesson" class for two reasons. One was to hone their already advanced English language skills developed through decades of world travel throughout their privileged lives. The other was they had a chance to see each other and socialize. They'd been friends for over forty years. Why not do this in a comfortable room in the presence of an interesting, educated foreigner?

These women were well-accomplished English language speakers long before they met me and had already lived full lives by anyone's standards. Harue is simply elegant and fashionable with silver, shoulder-length hair that compliments any Chanel outfit or kimono. Her husband is the president of one of the top urasenke tea ceremony schools in Japan. Their family business helps other tea ceremony teachers advance in the traditional art of preparing and serving tea. Her family also owns a musical theater company in Tokyo and Yokohama.

Another student, Ms. Oka, is plump and jolly with long hair that ends at her waistline. She fills up a room with her boisterous laugh and smile, which is accentuated by her colorful print-flowered hippie dresses, oversized glasses and large costume jewelry necklaces. She's collected them over the years from all corners of the globe. A piano teacher, she must have married or been born into wealth. Ms. Oka periodically travels to Milan with the Kyoto City Choir to accompany them during Sister City cultural exchange ceremonies. She also trains gorgeous, white Labrador puppies to become sight assistance dogs. I had the privilege of meeting a few of them, but especially liked the loveable pup, Freud. However, Freud was later banned from attending my school because he repeatedly sneaked off to pee on my carpet during lessons.

The third woman, Ms. Yagu, is a short-haired, sixty-something Aikido (modern Japanese martial art) teacher who has a gorgeous home centered around a Japanese garden designed by Japan's master gardener Mirei Shigemori. The cost of this garden alone, and its annual upkeep, could easily pay for an entire family's small home.

In addition to travel role play and grammar drilling, our lessons delved into a wide span of foreign culture. I remember a particularly interesting class where we dissected a modern ballet piece performed over projected 3D mapping, splashed on my huge cinema-style multimedia setup with my studio monitors blasting out the futuristic soundtrack. Sometimes we just talked about George Clooney roles in movies.

After a few months, as these women became more accustomed to me and the classroom, our lessons took on an entirely new dimension. To consummate our dynamic student-teacher relationship, a kind of friendship drawn from explicitly different worlds, and to take their understanding of culture to a new level, I introduced them to rhythm. Whereas Japanese love to communicate verbally through carefully chosen words capturing the perfect tone, I wanted to shake things up. So, I used African drums. I handed them shakers, a djembe and a log drum that I'd bought from a craftsman at The Saratoga Springs Jazz Festival in Upstate New York when I was in college. I also had a cajón wooden box drum on hand. (On a side note, I am currently working with a team of technologists to develop and market a cajón-playing percussion robot.) After a few minutes of showing them basic technique, I started a simple rhythm. They slowly joined in. As I watched them, I noticed that the smiles had turned to focused expressions. The laughing and familiar chatter of friends of forty years turned into pure, primal rhythmic communication between Harue on the sofa and Ms. Oka who sat a few feet away on another sofa in my conversation-promoting L-shaped furniture arrangement. I looked up after a few minutes from my Persian doumbek and saw Ms. Yagu's eyes close as she belted out a perfectly metered steady rhythm on the cajón. Time stood still. I was in my school, my little cultural center with three older Japanese women. We had travelled back in time. Regressing through two-thousand years of lingual development and four hundred years of proper and accepted Japanese women's behavioral codes, we passionately beat these drums together in perfect synergic cross-cultural unity. At that moment, in that place, in my school which happens to be situated on top of a "power spot" above the ruins of an ancient temple, the joint was rockin' at 10:00 AM on a Wednesday morning.

That space in time, the experience of jamming out with these Japanese women on African drums, was one of the dots that Steve Jobs talked about in his legendary "Stay Hungry, Stay Foolish" speech. He said when you trust your gut, you know the dots will connect in your future, and you can only connect those dots by looking back through your life. In that moment, I could see with absolute clarity the underlying pattern that led me to that moment with those women in that classroom. I knew this was exactly where I was supposed to be, doing precisely what I wanted to do. I was bridging culture and informing people on a level beneath the differences of language, age, gender, cultural, and religious backgrounds. This blissful confluence of energy is what I deem as one aspect of enlightenment, a manifestation of perfect convergence. I knew I was profoundly advancing their understanding of "cultural English." I felt it keenly, and it was wonderful.

When I was fourteen, I'd taken drum lessons in the basement of my house in Tappan, New York a suburb about a 20-minute drive from New York City. My father had played drums in his ship's small jazz band on a Navy destroyer during the Korean War. My guess is the closest he ever came to combat was when he and his drunken shipmates got into it with locals at a bar near the Brooklyn Navy Yard. Because I never heard him speaking about it, I assume my father's ship never made it into hostile Asian waters, let alone the Pacific.

But the saxophone player in his quartet was a guy named Cannonball Adderley. That name alone would raise an eyebrow in any conversation about jazz. It was my dad's dream for that one full sentence of bragging rights to live as a legacy through him to me, the younger of his two sons, and the musician one. In short, he just wanted me to be happy and maybe that could be through playing drums.

As a fourteen-year-old, though, hormones and emo-physio growing pains contorted any sense of steady rhythm from me. Trying to keep a solid, simple drum beat going was as if someone was purposefully twisting the tempo knob on a drum machine while grinning. My drum teacher would say, "Jay, if you think too hard, you'll lose the beat."

Neither of us realized at the time that those words uttered from a drum teacher's mouth to a boy who would one day dream of becoming a world-famous musician (or something resembling it) would become a bit of a life mantra. Unknowingly gifted to me a year into my teens, it was the pubescent Zen maxim that would drive me to make every important decision throughout my life and ultimately lead me to Japan. And it came imbedded with a concise answer, fully-assembled, with batteries included.

Think too hard and you'll lose the beat. Pure brilliance!

After basking in that euphoria, it was then time for me to prepare for the kids' classes. The ladies paid me a 10,000-yen bill and left, happily chatting in Japanese.

CHAPTER 2

LISTENING TO LIFE

"With our thoughts, we make the world."

- Gautama Buddha

There is rhythm all around us. It flows in and out of our lives and affects and defines us, whether we are sweating and twerking on a dance floor or lying next to a snoring partner who's sound asleep. This musical rhythm weaves in and out of life in infinite combinations. It impacts us in myriad ways whether we are the transmitters or the receivers, or both. Take for example the recurring melodic patterns of notes expressed by Mozart 250 years ago. "Baby Mozart" DVDs are played the world over by tired parents trying to stimulate their infant's minds while simultaneously lulling them back to sleep. When I listen to Mozart's Horn Concerto #4 in E minor (YouTube it and play it loud), even after 500 listens, I feel alive! After a few cycles of being swept up by the bopping French horns, I am jolted skyward as the whole orchestra kicks in with basically the same melody. If you are human, your brain's highly stimulated aural processing center is firing on all cylinders too. Is it entirely possible this even exceeds the level of exhilaration that Amadeus felt when he was writing it? Then there's thousands-year-old rhythms that have been played by African tribesman on drums made of wood and animal skin that are still being played in our 21st century digital world. The beats are powerful ancestral calls to the spirits, entrancing the entire village in primordial chants and frenetic dancing around the fire, hypnotizing and entraining everyone to the exact same rhythm. The group is unified in purpose, making an offering to the gods, hopefully to be repaid by a successful hunt the next day.

Mozart connects us more cerebrally to a place where melodies and harmonies are processed, understood and noted by the brain, while African drums connect us to the body and appendages in a less "executive thinking" part of the brain. The drums and bass make you move your waist. Both are comprised of an array of frequencies delivered in rhythmic waves that are essentially nothing more than compressed, moving air. Only those who are physiologically deaf or floating in the vacuum of space cannot experience the sound made by our ear drums vibrating and tweaking specialized nerves.

We see and hear the rhythm of waves washing up on the beach in tides twice a day, pulled by a moon that revolves around the Earth approximately every 30 days. The sun rises every day whether you do or not. The earth rotates on its axis once every 24 hours. Would we even be here if it spun once every seven hours? A perfect natural, fundamental pulse drives and underlies everything. Out in space, the planets of our solar system run their respective years orbiting the Sun ranging from 88 days for Mercury to the Neptunian year which is 165 of our years. The absurdly precise vibration of the Cesium atom is the reason why the clock on your iPhone is in perfect synch to the atomic clock in the Royal Observatory in Greenwich, London. The music of the spheres all functions according to some sort of incomprehensibly integrated rhythm.

Back here on Earth, there are the rhythms of nature. The seasons, if you're lucky enough to live in a place that experiences them, are, by definition, cyclical even though they are likely being altered by human impact. Salmon migrate thousands of miles every year and are programmed by DNA magic to find the mouth of that same river that they go up to spawn in every year. Migratory birds, whales and caribou have regular cycles. Maybe you are aware of it, but don't try to convince me that you GET it. This is beyond logical reasoning and comprehension.

I'd been in Kyoto for a few months when I came across some new rhythms that changed me while riding on a bicycle. As a busy, employed adult, I rarely rode a bike back in New York and New Jersey. In fact, I hadn't owned one since college. Maybe I was just lazy. I preferred sun-roofs and air-conditioning. Plus, cycling was dangerous in the city. But in Japan, bicycles are practical and essential. A week after arriving here in 2011, cycling soon became part of my daily commute. They say you never forget how to ride a bike, but I beg to differ. I had a few close calls in my first few months navigating driveways and slaloming around utility poles, jutting out of sidewalks in unexpected places. On rainy days, there were medieval-like jousting events which took place every few minutes on the sidewalks. It was me versus university students, both of us holding open umbrellas and coming at each other from opposite directions. It was an unfamiliar landscape to relearn evasive maneuvers and short stops.

I would often ride my bike home late at night after work. One night I picked it up where I parked it early that morning at the Matsugasaki subway station, about a 10-minute bike ride from my home on the northern edge of Kyoto City proper. It would be a six or seven-minute ride home if I rode on the sidewalk of the busy Kitayama Road (Kita =North, Yama = Mountain), but I would opt for the darker narrow backstreets. Some of the streets are so narrow that they probably weren't meant for cars, as it seemed that only bicycles and motorbikes could get through them. It was an adventure taking different routes home each night, turning down different alleys or streets and sometimes winding up in dead-ends. It felt mysterious and at times even scary, but this was a good neighborhood in a safe city. The occasional joyful confusion of getting lost among the quiet, closely arranged homes and red-gated temples with little gurgling streams running along the roads would always pay off. They all seemed to lead into a narrow-paved path that coursed through a small field near my home. My bike wheels hitting this homestretch signaled the end of a long day and late night, and that I would be home in two minutes. The 50-yard, twisting path was a homemade sidewalk of black pavement that bisected a flooded rice paddy. It was located at the base of a small mountain, overlooked by an old graveyard made of a few dozen granite, obelisk monument stones. One miscalculation or one too many beers would send my bike and me tumbling off the path into the dark and murky, shallow, mysterious rice paddy, which was a scary ecosystem of rice seedlings, algae, bugs (both flying and swimming) and likely snakes, salamanders, and other swampy critters.

It was on this path in the middle of the rice paddy that it really hit home that I was "not in Kansas" anymore. I was in a far-off exotic land, a universe away from Jersey City. But then suddenly, after taking this route home for a few months, something happened. I heard that sound. It seemed like it came on immediately but maybe it was more gradual over the course of a few days. It was hypnotic, melodious, pulsating and mesmerizing. It was a symphony of frogs in the swampy paddies, dozens of them croaking to mark the mid-Spring season. The sound was loud, but not deafening. It was truly mood-altering. It was hard to tell whether there was coordination between each creature or if it was completely random and amorphous. Was this a slimy collaboration of amphibian windbags playing off each other in a competitive, sexually-charged rhythm section or was it a cacophonous, unmathematical, Caligulan orgy? I think the answer is that it was just so damned arrhythmic that it was a perfect, natural rhythm. It's analogous to how we're taught that white is not really a distinct "color" but a combination of all colors, which in my experience has never worked with crayons or paints. [Visit https://bit.ly/lovesicinkyoto2C to hear what I heard.]

It was on this path a year later, when at 1:30 AM on a dark night void of moonlight, I convinced myself that I was being watched by a ghost that suddenly bolted into the darkness rattling some nearby bushes in the direction of that graveyard. The frog symphony was the second closest thing to what I imagine an LSD flashback would be like. But, the winner of that title, that perfect mind-altering rhythmic sound in nature in Japan comes in late summer at the onset of the daytime deafening, chirping of *semi*, (pronounced SEH –mee) or cicadas. The multilayered mating call of thousands of wings rubbing against thoraxes coming from the trees creates tones and frequencies that are truly otherworldly, a perfect soundtrack to a science fiction movie [visit https://bit.ly/lovesicinkyoto2D]. The timing and cyclical accents of cicada tones are like an alien DJ slowly riding the volume faders and FX knobs on a mixing board while the echoes of a nitrous oxide (laughing gas) high is billowing out of speakers directly into your brain. It could easily be amplified and put to effective use as a dry waterboarding torture technique in extracting important information from detained terrorists.

This pulsating, rotating, vibrating, swimming, croaking universe is an amalgamation of everything moving in concert. Matter and energy are bound in an infinitely meticulous intertwined dance that is tonal and rhythmic. In many ways it's measurable and predictable by physics and math and biology. But for all intents and purposes, its complexity, continuity and very essence exceeds our understanding of the universe.

On a guitar, the open E minor is a chord that any novice or child can strum. The fingering is simple and accomplished by pressing the two adjacent strings, the A and D string, onto the second fret. It is the base chord of many songs from descending do-wop progressions to hard rock. No matter who plays it, so long as the guitar is in tune, it fills up the room with resonance and energy. It tweaks those aural nerve centers in the brain and brings a smile and maybe the hope of becoming a great and famous musician to anyone who strums it. Naturally, an instrument must be tuned to itself as well as to all other instruments in the orchestra, jazz trio or rock band. The resonance of harmony and unison in perfect rhythm is uplifting and produces energy and emotion greater than the sum of its parts. The dissonance of being off pitch, out of key or off beat hurts.

THERE IS RHYTHM WITHOUT, THERE IS RHYTHM WITHIN.

Years ago, I was in the Lower East Side of Manhattan visiting Stephen, someone I had just met a few days before, in what seemed to be an unsafe, somewhat foreboding neighborhood, even though it was close to an old Orthodox Jewish neighborhood. Other than seeing a few bearded Hasidim dressed in black walking home from a bus station, it was dead silent at 11:00 PM at night. This was the easternmost side of the Lower East Side and Stephen's building was next to a small, poorly-lit park that butted up against a highway which ran along the East River. It was a creepy, deserted park that seemed a perfect setting for any imagined shady scenario. No one in their right mind would jog there at night. The East River is a dark, muddy, fast-moving tidal river that forms the east side of Manhattan extending uptown through the Bronx and Queens and to the south joining the Hudson River to form the New York Harbor. It's the kind of river that on the evening news in the 1980s you would see police boats with scuba divers trying to navigate tricky currents while attempting to fish cars or bodies out of it.

I was visiting Stephen that night because I was on a mission to enshrine his *Gohonzon* (Buddhist scroll) and encourage him. He had received his *Gohonzon* the night before, and I wanted to help him set up his altar and set him off on the right track with his new Buddhist practice. After ten minutes of chanting and going through the basics of the ritual of daily chanting and altar maintenance, we chatted. As I dug into deeper detail about stoking that fire of Original Good (i.e. our innate Buddha nature) and other basic concepts about this philosophy, his eyes widened. After fielding a few of his questions, I watched his smile morph into something grander, his sparkling eyes were now fireballs, throwing off flares of uncontainable excitement. He insistently wanted to share something with me.

Abruptly ending the conversation, he fished in a box and pulled up a cassette with some scribbled words on the label and rammed it into his old stereo system. [note to millennials, a cassette is like a large USB flash drive with two spinning spools of thin magnetic tape, please Google "cassette tape" for a picture] At first, it blasted out a blazing wild Latin percussion jam. He said it was three percussion players, an African djembe player, Cuban conga player and a jazz drummer. After a few minutes I was moved but gave him a puzzled look as to why he felt compelled to make me listen to this at midnight on a weeknight. But he was determined and fast forwarded it to the start of the interview with the jazz drummer. The interview conversation was between a very well-informed, intelligent public radio DJ and Dr. Milford Graves. Stephen felt strongly that there was a connection between chanting and the new Buddhist practice he was about to embark on and what he had heard on this cassette tape a decade before encountering Buddhism. He couldn't quite explain it but insisted that we should listen to it together.

At first listen, I was drawn into and soon ripped out of my seat by this middle aged "Dr." as he giggled in eloquence, enthusiastically responding to questions about the nature of rhythm. This 30-minute interview clarified and expressed many inklings and notions I've had about beats and music. But beyond that it has become to me one of those unexpected treasures that serendipitously changes one's life. In addition to being one of the pioneers of "free jazz," Milford Graves is also a revered music instructor and has taught at universities. But in that taped interview, he spoke with the honest, imperfect grammar and drawl of an elderly brother from the countryside. I later found out he was from Queens like me! As far as his musicianship goes, he is a world-renowned, polyrhythmic genius, meaning he can play different time signatures simultaneously with different appendages, which is akin to walking and chewing gum on a tight rope over a windy Grand Canyon in the dark. It's near impossible for the rest of us common mortals. But it's his words that changed my perspective on life and further reinforced why I kneel on the floor in my socks every morning in front of my altar for 30-minutes of chanting before work and find time in my busy evening to do the same.

He spoke about the multitude of natural rhythms that occur in our bodies. In addition to the beating of the heart, he spoke of the corpuscles and white blood cells coursing through our arteries and capillaries, complete with comedian-like vibrating tongue and lip sound effects. Humans, he observed, have complex, interconnected body systems like breathing, glandular secretions, twitching digestive system, nerves firing signals to muscles and the brain, and more. All these things happen because we are ALIVE. They work independently and often in tandem in such a way as to sustain good health. Of course, we define life, at least medically, as a heart that is beating regularly. Sometimes the heart fails or goes into the spasms of arrhythmia which signals imbalance and is truly an emergency. But he said underlying this there is a more fundamental pulse that triggers the heart, and everything else for that matter. It is a signal sent from the brain which really controls everything that happens in our bodies whether we think about it or not. He refers to it as "the real man in charge." This basic, foundational pulse energizes and informs our lives.

Milford described how he had worked with djembe drum players in West Africa, and the rigorous manner by which they are trained. A group of drummers, including amateurs and elders, would stand in a circle keeping the same beat in a steady, common rhythm for two or three hours at a time with no deviation in tempo or beat. During these sessions, that beat would have to become deeply solidified, fusing to the life of each drummer. Only then did they have the "right" to take a turn and solo, each improvising and expressing whatever came up from their lives for a half hour or so. They would take turns soloing before falling back into the group and giving someone else a turn. They did this day after day.

It took a second listening to this interview for me to realize that he was expressing the very essence of why I was practicing Nichiren Buddhism. This somewhat eccentric, superhuman percussionist, this "Doctor of Biorhythmic Physiology," helped me realize that we have the responsibility to self-activate and nurture this primordial pulse in our lives. The stronger the effort to jumpstart it and maintain it, the closer it brings us to the "universal rhythm." Applying these musical concepts to human life effects a continual deepening of the spirit. That's how I endeavor to approach every day of my life in Kyoto.

CHAPTER 3

TAIPEI
BAR MITZVAH

Some people are fortunate enough to have the time and money to travel at will, to explore this world to their heart's desire. They save up for that once-every-three-year, cheesy norovirus-laden cruise and approach nirvana floating on an air mattress in the pool with mojito in hand watching a movie. Or they languish over romantic dinners in Paris and haggle with vendors in the markets of Marrakech over a metal lantern light fixture with the star cutouts that would look so cool in their home. Or, they ride a raft made of rope-tied logs down the Amazon wondering whether the squawking birds and screeching monkeys are greeting them or scolding them for intruding on their turf. The thrill of riding a camel a scorching hour across the desert pays off as the pyramids come into view over the horizon. Some are lucky enough to have taken a dip in the Devil's Pool which hangs precariously over Victoria Falls in Zimbabwe. My cousins in New York City, who are comfortable, to say the least, celebrated a birthday sleeping in furs in their all-ice room at an "ice hotel" in Iceland. It may or may not have been the same trip where they raced and spun around wildly across a frozen lake in a BMW after a tour of the automobile plant.

But however extensive or limited our travel experiences have been, we all have cardboard boxes filled with oversized albums and loose, semi-sorted photos of where we've been. For the not-so-old, our laptops and smartphone memories are clogged to the gills with thousands of photos, sometimes ten shots of the same pose or the same view of the ocean from that scenic lookout. And, did I mention the videos? We all have great stories we love to share or remember. "I think of Misa and I, New Year's Eve 1999, lost in a sea of thousands of drunk and stoned revelers in Rembrandt Square in

Amsterdam watching Prince perform [Party like it's] 1999 from a scaffolding stage, 100-feet in the air before the countdown. Dangerous fireworks were coming from every direction." Everybody has their stories. Often the details fade or morph for dramatic effect. [It was really a Prince imitator. But who cares? Everybody was so stoned.] These experiences are indelibly printed and embroidered in the fabric of our very being. We wear them proudly for the rest of our lives to parties or reunions and think about them when a commercial on TV reminds us of our memory or it pops up in a conversation. "Remember that time" can be a handy and effective ice-breaker in a relationship gone silent. Those memories, those cardboard boxes, those videos transferred from iPhone 4 to iPhone X can be big splashes in your "bucket list" bucket.

It's a given that each time you travel to another country something beyond the mere experience of a physical change of scenery is given to you. Whether profoundly life-changing or more sublime, the corner poles of your "tent" have been extended and moved outward, and your "life photos" are enlarged. Maybe it reaffirms why you're proud to be an American, French, or Japanese. Or it might instill the determination in you to change your lifestyle or your job. Or, you may begin to think, "I have to be more like the Spanish and take a long nap in the afternoon and eat dinner and drink with my friends after work no earlier than 9:00 PM." But when you're a kid dealing with school, friends, pre-pubescence and related concerns, the whole travel experience can be like one big sensory acid trip that doesn't quite sink in until you've had a chance to digest it many years later.

I was twelve years old when I travelled to Asia with my family. It wasn't a typical family trip like the ones that I see every day outside of the WAVE in Kyoto, where small groups and families, guidebooks in hand, block the sidewalks while scratching their heads trying to figure out posted routes at a bus stop. Nope. It couldn't be a normal trip to an exotic beach or a photo op with the Leaning Tower of Pisa for me and my family. Not a chance. For this episode in my life's cosmic TV show, my first trip overseas had to be a three month trip combined with my bar mitzvah to the ultimate spiritual pilgrimage destination for a Jewish boy's ritualistic passage into adulthood. Not Jerusalem but the other one, Taipei, Taiwan. Like most Buddhists who have spent decades developing their lives, changing themselves from the inside

Still shell shocked by the whole overseas bar mitzvah experience, the not quite 13-year-old stands somewhere in the sun-drenched back streets of Taipei.

and devoting a big chunk of time toward helping others get their acts together, I was bar mitzvah'd in Taipei. Of course, I jest. Chalk that one up in the "anything but normal" column. Somewhere I have a newspaper clipping from the only English daily newspaper in Taipei at the time. The fact is, it could not have been less predictable. But in the complex, mystical pretzel logic of the law of cause and effect, it follows that I would have crossed this spiritual milestone in Taiwan, especially now that I'm living as a Buddhist musician in Kyoto.

I am often amazed at how things connect back and forth through time. Now, when I hold that hand-carved animal-horn Siamese Buddha-head sculpture that I took from my mother's apartment the day after she started the phase of her life which would be lived out in a bed in an elderly care home, it makes perfect sense to me. That six-inch statue sits in my school in Kyoto on the same table where I set up a mini-altar and chant before and between classes. I shook it and made it dance in front of my computer's camera to look like a primordial alien in the music video I made for the song, "2Kool4Mars," that's on my new CD [watch at https://bit.ly/lovesicinkyoto3]. The past, present and future all meet here in one life moment. My life, in many ways, has come full circle. It all makes sense now.

It wasn't my choice to be bar mitzvah'd in Taipei, but it seemed like a very cool idea to my parents, family and grandparents, Helene "Nanny" and Barnet "Poppy" Grossman. Why not give the young man a once-in-a-lifetime experience and plant the seeds of foreign intrigue in his skinny 12-year-old body? Then, after the Bar Mitzvah, go off to Hong Kong and Bangkok.

Some of my earliest memories are of my grandfather's shop in New York

City. I don't know specifically where it was, but it was a small dress-cutting factory in the old Garment District in New York City. That means it must have been located somewhere between the mid-20s to 30th Street, between 5th and 6th Avenues. At that time, the garment district had the highest concentration of garment manufacturers in the world. That venture somehow turned into his later life career consulting for textile companies in Asia, and after a long stay in Hong Kong, my grandparents wound up in Taipei for fifteen years. My thirteenth birthday would be in six or seven months, the time when "boys become men," according to Judaism.

My family wasn't anything close to being religious, let alone orthodox Jews. Scripture was no match for bacon cheeseburgers, and spare ribs were like my mother's heroin. We did, however, observe the "High Holidays" and a Bar Mitzvah (or Bat Mitzvah for the girls) was as much a social ritual as it was a religious one. I'd spent the previous year or two attending my friends' and schoolmates' rites of passage and my number was coming up. One day my parents dropped the bomb and said, "Let's do it in Taipei."

When I think about it, I had no say in the matter. I do remember crying for a few weeks when informed of the unthinkable suggestion. In theory, it may have seemed like a great idea. It would be different and cool. But, there was a big downside. Other than the fact I wouldn't get to celebrate this important event with my friends and most of my family in New York, there was the money. This is typically the first big windfall in a just-turned-13-years-old Jewish kid's life. I knew I would take a huge hit financially having a Bar Mitzvah in a place where no one close to me and my family other than Nanny and Poppy could attend. But, it turned out to be a great experience.

There I was trying to memorize the melody and phonetic pronunciation of Hebrew prayers that I was supposed to half chant/half sing in front of dozens of strangers that would be attending my once-in-a-lifetime auspicious spiritual rite of passage. Add to it the fact that I had jet lag and was experiencing culture shock. With just a cassette tape, I was tasked with memorizing and mastering the 20-minute *Haftorah* that I started learning in New York, uncoached and on my own in Taiwan. What a relaxing summer vacation!

We spent the entire summer at my grandparent's house. It wasn't located directly in the sprawling sun-roasted city of Taipei, but in Yangminshan, an upscale neighborhood community overlooking the city. My grandparents lived in a huge rented mansion with a swimming pool, surrounded by a tall stucco wall and iron gates situated on the side of a mountain providing a postcard view of the city. A maid named Ah-Lin, and another maid dressed in white, served and cleaned up after us. I sometimes saw the unnamed maid, who was a part-timer hired to help carry the load of a visiting family from New York, walking off the property looking behind her with towels in her hands. Who knows what else she had scoffed from those elderly, rich Americans with the swimming pool?

Back then, the American presence in Taiwan was mostly tied to the U.S. military base and a variety of export trading companies. We often had lunch at the officer's club where the food was safe, the air conditioner rocked, and American TV was broadcast on monitors in the hallways. There was a thriving community of foreigners that gathered in this club regularly to eat, attend parties and events and just mingle inside, away from the bustle of the busy sweltering city. Middle Eastern traders, European salesmen, and other businessmen with their English-speaking Taiwanese buddies or young, hot, girlfriends all met there forming a colorful social community of borderless ethno-harmony. My grandparents were a little older than many of their friends but were a well-respected couple at the core of that community.

I'm not going to say that the Bar Mitzvah was a disappointment, but it bore no resemblance to the lavish, pull-out-all-the-plugs, DJ'd, over-catered white-linen affairs that I had been attending in New York. There was no Electric Sliding, (a diddly group dance), no cutting of the traditional *Challah* bread, and I was not lifted overhead on a chair by my friends on the dance floor. But it was different. Instead of the ceremony being conducted in a synagogue with all the traditional elegance and symbolism of Judaism, it was held in the uncarpeted All Faith Chapel in the U.S. Army base. What I do remember is that VIPs, Nanny and Poppy's best friends, sat in the front row of the ceremony. There was a Samir from Syria, along with an Oaf and his wife who were German nationals, an Abdul from Jordan, and Pierre, a rich businessman from Lebanon. They were all wearing *kippot* or *yarmulkes* out of respect for my parents and grandparents. I thought, well, I may not make the money that I would have in New York, but I have Arabs attending my Bar Mitzvah wearing yarmulkes. My father joked to them that the photos of them could be used for blackmail if the need ever arose.

After I struggled through my Haftorah in a cracking, high-pitched voice that hadn't changed yet, we had a big party. The party was at my grandparents' estate and the furthest thing imaginable from a catered banquet hall spread. It was a Mongolian barbecue with people lined up on two sides of a long buffet bar placing all kinds of meats, noodles, vegetables, sauces, and indiscernible ingredients in a bowl. The bowl was then given to a chef who would dump it on a large, circular, super-heated metal grill and dramatically stir-fry the crap out of it. Then, with lightning Ninja dexterity, he'd deftly swoop it all back into the bowl and hand it back to you. This, and the dancing of the Middle Eastern traders' short-skirted, inebriated Taiwanese girlfriends, all took place on a huge terrace overlooking the city of Taipei. I may have missed out on the joy of celebrating it with friends and relatives in New York, and the windfall was more like a breeze-fall, but I couldn't ask for anything more interesting. It left a lifelong impression on me.

At that time, Taipei wasn't quite the super-developed, modernized city that it is now, especially in the surrounding mountainside communities. Yangminshan was a tropical suburban community of a few thousand homes with a twisting network of roads that were as much potholes as pavement. We were told to watch out for slithering little green bamboo snakes because they were highly poisonous. I had seen them in the night market in Taipei, hanging live by their necks while some sort of medicine peddling shaman cut them open with a razor blade and watched them writhe in a most inhumane fashion. He ripped out their gallbladder, then squeezed it open into a shot glass. Apparently, that part of a bamboo snake's physiology brewed a supplement that was supposed to help you with your own "bamboo." It was a fresh shot of reptile Viagra, which fascinated me. But, I wasn't interested in adding it to my spiritual rite of passage of becoming a man. In fact, I still felt like a boy. We were informed that the bamboo snakes only came out at night. So, herein lay a dilemma for my brother, Gregg, and me. He was fifteen at the time. We were told that there was a large estate down the hill from us in easy view from Nanny and Poppy's yard. This sprawling, gorgeously landscaped crib served as the site of weekly debauchery, drinking and dancing for the young international community every Friday night. We were told these parties invariably turned into open-air orgies. You can imagine Gregg and my intrigue and curiosity at the idea of viewing this diverse group of drunken Arabs, Germans, and Israelis with a contingent of sexy Taiwanese girlfriends that regularly attended these all-night parties. But, we had to weigh the pros and cons of, "do we go out on a Friday night and try to get a view down the mountain and see what's happening and risk being bitten by a bamboo snake or not?" We erred on the side of caution and never got to see that debauchery. But we know there were, in fact, orgies.

Weeks later we attended a dinner party in Pierre's home. Pierre was an older, charming, super-rich Lebanese businessman. He was somewhat swarthy and heavy with long, wiry gray and black hair. That same hair in short version covered his arms and overexposed chest and peaked out of his ears and nostrils. His hearty laugh and sophistication filled his home, which was loaded with antiques, rugs and artwork, and, of course, his hot, young Taiwanese wife. While giving us a tour of his home, he proudly pointed out the orgy room, a hexagonal mirrored chamber with dozens of shiny, embroidered, tasseled pillows arranged neatly against each other like falling dominoes in still frame just after the flick of a finger. Anyway, I was too young to really appreciate all of this at the time. This was a super-sized serving of new possibilities and boundaries for a 12-½-year-old's mind and libido to digest. With grit and a cracking voice, I did make it through the whole Bar Mitzvah ritual and party and found myself getting used to life in Taipei.

But one afternoon I got extremely sick with a fever, diarrhea and nausea. It wasn't anything too outrageous, just the normal stuff that might invade the body of a middle-class American teenager with a wimpy air-conditioned, water-filtered immune system dropped into a tropical third-world, bacterial Disneyland. Rather than go to a hospital or clinic, Poppy called a local doctor. The house call, if anybody can remember what that means, consisted of a two-or three-minute peripheral examination. I blinked my eyes and realized that the "doctor" had left the room and headed outside with my Poppy to a field along the road outside of the estate's iron gate. You know, the place where the little green bamboo snakes probably spend their days basking in the sun and plotting their lethal night time bites on horny little foreigners. As they were walking back into the room, I noticed the "doctor" was tearing apart some fresh picked leaves into tiny little pieces in his hands. Poppy signaled Ah-lin, to get some water. Ah-lin had by now fallen in love with me, or rather, emotionally adopted me in the two or three weeks I'd been there. You see, she was childless, and I was cute and the personification of innocence and naivete.

In the mornings, she would come into the room where Gregg and I slept and say in smiling, melodic yet pulverized English, "Jay-Jay, you wan' eat egg?" She'd then look at Gregg and say quickly in monotone, "How 'bout you?" Anyway, the voiced concern of my mother at her baby eating some leaves from the field outside was squelched by the confident, strict, former-dressmaker-turned-senior-executive-international-consultant who straddled continents as a lifestyle. It would be futile to challenge Poppy. I was up and running in an hour. No kidding.

There were many such eye-opening experiences in Taiwan. One day Gregg and I took a walk up a potholed excuse for a road to have a baseball catch. It turned into an impromptu four-way catch with two smiling, crewcut local teenagers closer to my brother's age of 15. I realized in a few seconds that what I thought was America's past-time had become the love and pride of many an Asian boy. It started off as a casual, slow lobbing of the ball back and forth between two sets of boys from opposite corners of the Earth, with contrasting socioeconomic circumstances. They had crew cuts, we had '70s Beatles' cuts. I was Paul, and Gregg was George. It was a sort of nonverbal international athletic summit and it was downright fun! But after 15 or 20 cycles of crisscross back and forth, the throws got harder...and harder. It became more of a "who's got the more accurate fastball" pitching contest between Asians and the true inventers of baseball; a proxy World Series between the Chinese All Stars and the New York Yankees. (Though being from Queens, we were really New York Mets fans.) There were all sorts of xenophobic and foreign intrigue emotions at play in this simple game of catch. I submit that somewhere in there was also a dash of hormonally charged "alpha male gets to have sex with the female lions" competitive strength posturing. The blissful danger and excitement ended when I insisted on catching that Taiwanese *protégé's* errant fast highball. It was high, and I had to reach for it, but I got it. My dad, the coach of my Little League team, had always assigned me to left field, as I was quick and agile. But the shear momentum of that whizzing blur of a ball hitting the pocket of my baseball mitt in a mid-air jump, and the transfer of kinetic energy to the future engineer's preteen frame, sent me spinning and tumbling. I landed on the one piece of intact pavement between the potholes, knee first. But, I caught it, and the game was over. That international summit ended with Gregg and the two future Cy Young pitching award winners laughing hysterically together in true global harmony as I was crying and brushing sand out of a bleeding knee. Poppy later cleaned the wound with peroxide and dressed it with something he picked from the garden.

Our three-month Asian vacation was only a month old, and although I didn't consciously perceive it, my inner world was changing deeply, and much more rapidly than my voice. I was not that well-developed physically and emotionally, I was very much still a work in progress. Even though I was now religiously certified to be an adult, technically I was still twelve and that all important ½ year. It soon became time for a family trip to Bangkok. Is there any place that can turn a preteen's confused, sexually unaware hormonal blender on the frappe setting better than Bangkok? Even saying the words "bang cock" made Gregg and I giggle. I remember walking with him, maybe fifty-steps ahead of my family, down a back street in that mysterious sun-scorched city. Rounding a corner, we made eye contact with a beautiful girl in full afternoon lingerie and garters, drenched in makeup standing atop maybe five or six steps leading up to a neon club. Aside from her bright lipstick, all I remember is that the club had a slutty type of name, like "The Pussy Club." As we walked by this silk clad goddess of the midday sun, she said to us, probably more to Gregg than me, "You come back later, we have 'paw-ty'." What kind of party I wondered? I didn't quite catch the meaning of this until Gregg put it together for me a few steps later. Again, this kind of ritual isn't usually included in a young man's coming-of-age life phase. Also, I doubt the money I got gipped out of not having a Bar Mitzvah in New York City would have colored my perspective in quite the same way.

At that time in Bangkok, anti-West rallies were being held, big violent smoky rallies that closed the streets. Fortunately, for our one-week trip there we had a taxi driver tour-guide who knew how to stay away from those places. But a few days in, at my grandparents' suggestion, we found ourselves on a quest to buy this must-have bamboo-shaped silverware at Bangkok prices. So, we went to a famous silverware district to shop in the stores there. I remember on the ride out of the neighborhood hearing yelling and seeing much commotion outside. Suddenly, there was yelling and smoke and people running crazily in all directions up ahead. Immediately, the taxi driver stopped the car and pulled some sort of wild maneuver to turn the car around amidst the fast-coming onslaught of chaos. It was a jagged and wild perfectly executed turn. I wouldn't call it a U-turn by any stretch of the imagination. It was more like one of those squiggly Thai characters that we saw on the signs of the stores. I remember the sound of a fist pounding into the side fender of our car as we bolted out of there. The taxi driver might very well have saved our lives. The depth and profundity of being caught in the rage of a third-world uprising of the pissed off and disenfranchised didn't really sink in. It was just a cool experience for me, and a story to tell my friends back home aside from being imprinted forever in my psyche. That bamboo-shaped silverware we risked life and limb to get tarnished a few months after returning to New York. It was all fake silver. But, we were compelled to eat every meal with it until I went away to college six years later.

My grandparents' adventures also brought them to El Salvador. During unrest there, Poppy was held hostage along with the entire management staff of a textile company in the industrial district of San Salvador. It was a labor dispute of some kind. He was literally held in a non-air-conditioned back room for three days with army and police surrounding the factory outside. Poppy was negotiated out by saying that he had a heart problem or some serious medical condition, which he didn't. Everything did resolve peacefully in a few days.

This zest and openness to the world, a world way beyond the shores of America and far removed from my comfort zone delineated by the borders of New York and New Jersey, was implanted early on by my bold grandparents. It made the life-changing jump of pulling up the roots of my entire life with proximity to adored friends and relatives to move to Japan a no-brainer. It was an almost expected spin of the dial on the game of life. That same hand-carved animal horn Siamese Buddha head sculpture makes another cameo appearance in my new music video for the song *SUGE!*. As it beams out over the airwaves into ears and eyes across the world I can only smile at how everything I have done, am doing and will do seem to interconnect, right here, right now!

Somewhere in my brother's garage in New Jersey, in a big cardboard moving box, is my treasured "Princess Throne." It's made from panels of a demolished temple, crafted by a furniture maker in Taipei, too big and fragile to bring from my penthouse loft in Jersey City to a small apartment in Japan. I haven't simply retained an emotional connection to the Orient and Asian culture, I've turned it into a life. I was fortunate enough to encounter Nichiren Buddhism decades ago in New York, and through that have developed the heart, spirit and path of fortune that ultimately lead me to Kyoto. My draw to Japan has been the culmination of decades of developing appreciation for the world in all its gorgeous and confusing diversity, and my confidence that a life well lived is one that, as Joseph Campbell says, should be based on the motto "follow your bliss." I am thrilled to say, I could not have written a better script if I wanted to. What a life!

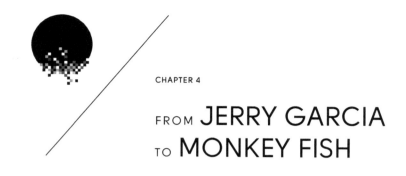

CHAPTER 4

FROM JERRY GARCIA
TO MONKEY FISH

As I zig-zagged through my formative years into college, I discovered myself, spread my wings socially and culturally, and had many vibrant, sometimes psychedelic-fueled, extracurricular experiences. Lucky for me, New Brunswick, New Jersey, where I went to Rutgers University, was in the shadow of New York City. There was a thriving, edgy, alternative music scene in New Brunswick, a true artistic community that I quickly bound myself to as a music lover, and in a few years as a young performer. I was tapping into previously unmined creativity, learning cool cover songs on guitar, attending nitrous oxide "laughing gas" parties in dorm rooms and gaining many colorful friends. I was feeling the music I was listening to and starting to develop my voice. Although I was still learning to play guitar, I realized at heart that I was a percussionist and drummer. Finally, I knew how to not just keep a beat, but create one with my hands and feet, and even more so with my personality. I also had the life vest of being a 90-minute drive from my parents in my home town of Cinnaminson, New Jersey but I was living entirely on my own. It was a 20-year-old's dream life of independence.

I spent much of those life shaping years focused on my real major, listening to all kinds of great music. But where does a college student go after experiencing the Grateful Dead, Neil Young, Little Feat and other cool bands? What could possibly follow those years of listening to hundreds of Grateful Dead bootleg concert recordings and discussing with friends the best Jerry Garcia guitar solo from that unbelievable version of "Saint Stephen" which then morphed into "Not Fade Away" and then back into "Saint Stephen" at that Anaheim Auditorium concert in 1981? What was the next progression from that amazing musicianship, songwriting, cultural coolness and social consciousness? What would come after the Grateful Dead? The answer was obvious. Bob Marley and reggae music. The message of unity, love, and peace and all the distorted psychedelic ideals of the Grateful Dead movement fit so neatly into reggae's one love and no-problem kind of culture. Reggae's seven-pointed leaf seemed to seamlessly connect Grateful Dead culture with reggae culture. I dove into it, lungs first, so much so that my second year of college I knew it was time to go to Mecca (i.e., Jamaica). With my friend Jared, the son of a rabbi from North Jersey, we got on a plane to go to Jamaica. Just think of it. The excitement was beyond comprehension! Tropical beaches, sun, seafood, an unlimited supply of ganja, reggae music, cool people with dreadlocks, and our first real trip as an adult without family.

On the airplane, Jared sat in the window seat, I was in the middle, and sitting next to me in the aisle seat was a tall well-dressed black man with a beard and glasses. He was as charming as could be, dressed in a pristine suit and shiny patent leather shoes. A half hour into the flight, he reached into his carry-on bag and pulled out a dozen or so Rolex watches. Pulling them out of their plastic display cases, he dropped them loosely into his jacket pocket. It was a real conversation starter. With a sly glint in his eye, this distinguished-looking stranger started a conversation. "Where you from? What kind of music do you like?" I didn't realize it at the time, but we were being vetted. The conversation was quiet, congenial and funny. His manner was warm and genuine. We immediately made a great connection. So much so, that before landing a few hours later, he asked us about our plans in Jamaica. I explained to him that we were on our way to Negril, a resort town 45 minutes from the Montego Bay airport, to stay in a campground. He said, "Forget about the campground in Negril. Stay in Montego Bay in a nice hotel. Just follow me." So, we followed him off the plane. To our surprise, without a single break in stride or conversation, let alone a stop at a security checkpoint, he walked us right through Customs. His Chicago accent turned into true Jamaican patois as he greeted airport staff and fist-bumped them while handing out Rolex watches to men in uniforms. We were in the tow of some rich VIP businessman as he swaggered down restricted airport hallways. Excited as can be but not quite sure who he was and what was happening, we knew we were in the presence of somebody truly important, and that we were now his "friends." It didn't dawn on either of us what may have been lying ahead until he pointed out a window to a mid-sized silver and blue commercial jet without any airline markings on the fuselage or tail, baking alone on the tarmac and boasted, "Hey, that's my plane." Next thing I knew, we were sitting in a rather nondescript Toyota Camry with shaded windows heading out of the airport into Montego Bay to the Ritz Carlton.

By now, our host with the amazing suit, who was sitting next to us in the back seat of his private car, had told us his full name, Angus Carlton. He was an American citizen with some deep connections in Jamaica. The driver's name was Walker and, seated in the front seat, was another guy named Monkey Fish. When Carlton introduced them to us, as they turned their heads toward the back seat, I was struck by their huge, yellowed, toothy smiles. These were not the well-cared-for, distinguished Rolex teeth of our host. These smiles had missing teeth and shiny gold implants that beamed in the mid-afternoon under the Jamaican sunlight sifting through the car's tinted windshield. Their wide-gapped grins glinted on the upholstery. It was obvious how Monkey Fish got his name. He had a round, dark brown, complicated face with a protruding forehead and large, droopy, yellowed eyes that cascaded into a flattened, glaring nostril snoot, situated on large fleshy lips. He was a personified Monkey Fish with gold teeth. Walker apparently was the driver's last name. They both wore polo shirts. The acrid smell of a long, sweaty Jamaican workday carried by the AC wafted to Jared's and my nostrils in the back seat. The picture was starting to become clear. These two were Angus Carlton's guys; his workers and, if provoked, his bodyguards.

In less than five minutes, we pulled into the Montego Bay Ritz Carlton where porters and bell staff carried our luggage into the lobby, but we were kept away from the front desk. While Carlton was speaking to the front desk staff, Jared and I were looking at each other thinking the same thought, "If we're paying for this, our week camping in Jamaica has just turned into a one-night stay. We're fucked! What's going to happen next?" But, in an instant, we were whisked up to an amazing suite in the Ritz Carlton with no bellman and no mention of having to pay for it. Carlton gestured to Jared and me to sit on the bed as he walked over to the window and closed the curtains before sitting down in an armchair. This was not the time to gawk at the breathtaking blues and greens of the Caribbean cut by white lines of small waves breaking on the offshore reef we'd seen a half hour earlier on the final descent into the airport. The curtains were closed. Carlton, still impeccably dressed from head to toe, leaned back further into his chair and put his polished shoes up on a low, round table. Mr. Monkey Fish and Mr. Walker stood quietly and unmenacingly between us and the door. Were they friends or just bodyguards? Were they here to protect Carlton from the two 20-year-olds in shorts and Bob Marley tee-shirts sitting on the edge of the bed? That would have been laughable. We didn't know what to expect. The jovial discourse that had started on the plane now took on a more serious tone as Carlton asked us in more detail about our lives. Did we belong to a fraternity at Rutgers University? Did we have a lot of friends and did all our friends smoke pot? Where do we get it from? And, the clincher was, "How do you feel about making a lot of money?" Without details, he began laying down a proposal, suggesting that Jared and I could be his New York - New Jersey "partners." We realized we were in way over our heads. We'd been in Jamaica barely a half-hour and Jared, the son of a rabbi, and me, a budding guitarist and civil engineer student, were being propositioned to be distribution agents in some large marijuana trafficking ring. It goes without saying, we were both a little fidgety, nervous and uncertain of what giving an answer of no or yes would entail.

Suddenly there was a knock at the hotel room door, the room for which we hadn't paid. Monkey Fish jumped up and stood inside the open-air closet by the door and pulled out a large knife, wielded in a way that only somebody who knows how to use one does. There, sitting on the bed of the Montego Bay Ritz Carlton in the presence of another high-priced Carlton, I was all but freaking out. My mind was overcome with the flashing red lights and screeching audio alarm of a spaceship in a sci-fi movie as the last 10-seconds are being counted down before its nuclear reactor core reaches critical mass and explodes. Frozen, I realized this may have not only been the end of my Jamaican vacation but maybe the end of my life or at least the life I was striving to know and was just starting to make for myself.

Walker opened the door. A serious, beefy hotel security guard at the door looked in, wanting to make sure everything was okay. Carlton responded to his query with smooth perfection and a controlled laugh that morphed into elegant Jamaican patois, telling the security guard we were just a bunch of friends hanging out. Monkey Fish was in the closet with his knife, ready to go. The security guard smiled back and said in similar melodic patois, "Alright then" as he turned around and left. Standing up from his chair, Carlton swung open the curtains and made a gesture, putting his two fingers up to his lips. Walker pulled out a huge Jamaican ganja cone spliff and handed it to me. They left a few seconds later, with a promise of being back the next day before the 11:00 am check-out time to pick us up and continue the conversation.

Trembling in the room, Jared and I decided to go outside to the beach, get some drinks and smoke that spliff. We didn't know what to make of that afternoon's adventure. Should we get out of there immediately? Could we milk this opportunity for another night at the Ritz Carlton without committing to accepting his unfinished proposal? Our conclusion was, we had no conclusion. We were clueless! Even if we wanted to salvage our planned one-week beach vacation in Negril, could we?

By 11:00 AM the next day our phone wasn't ringing, so we nervously checked out. To our relief and delight, everything was pre-paid. We walked to a nearby car rental agency thinking, "We've gotta figure out what's going on or simply get the hell out of Montego Bay." Carlton had mentioned on the plane that he'd just purchased a new, hot disco called "King's Aquarius" in Montego Bay and that he was also an investor in the Jamaican National Soccer League. We were impressed and mystified by what had transpired on the first afternoon of our dream vacation. Take curiosity, mix it with bold, brazen, blind stupidity and stir in some slightly distorted logic from the tail-end of that cone spliff, and a plan seemed to congeal as we took off in the rent-a-car. We needed more information. Clearly, we should investigate. As our bloodshot eyes saw it, the "natural thing" to do would be to drive through the streets of a third-world country and find King's Aquarius disco and go poke around to see if we could find out something about our new friend. What could possibly go wrong?

I'm not sure how we found the disco amidst the narrow winding streets that crept up the hills just outside of downtown Montego Bay, but we did.

Propped up over the roof on a metal truss was a large black wooden sign framed by a hundred lightbulbs that by nightfall would be flashing "Kings Aquarius Disco" in red, yellow, and green letters with hand-painted, big-booty dancers on a black background. It was a smaller building than we expected and being that it was before noon, it wasn't exactly hopping. But the half-opened screen door, with a booming reggae bassline drifting through the warm, late morning air to our open car windows, invited us in.

We entered an empty, customer-less room with a man cleaning up and organizing bottles behind the bar. He was dressed in the same stained-polo-shirt fashion that Monkey Fish and Walker had worn, and they must have also had the same dentist. The glinting, gold-smiled bartender thought we were tourists popping in for drinks. We sat down at the bar and before we could even order, there were two bottles of Red Stripe beer, without glasses or coasters, placed in front of us. In terms of a cultural experience, drinking the iconic Jamaican "national" beer in authentic room-temperature presentation in an un-air-conditioned musty room with a ceiling fan was high on my list. But trying to convince my mouth that this was truly thirst-quenching and refreshing, was a stretch. After some small talk, I decided it was time to mention "our friend Carlton" to him and see if we could find out anything helpful from him. Surely, with tactful banter we can find some missing piece of this puzzle and anything to help us figure out what it is we were being pulled into. Or, what our next step ought to be.

While we were talking to the bartender, a Giant Water Bug, the fierce flying cockroach of the tropics, flew into the bar, buzzing over our heads like a World War II Zero fighter plane making a beeline for the mirror behind the bar. The bartender reached out with one hand, grabbed it, and smashed it down on the counter in front of us. With the back of his hand, he brushed it off the side of the counter onto the floor where it lay upside down, it's legs wriggling in near-death. All of this was done in one fell swoop, with the bartender barely breaking smiling eye contact with us.

I realized I was in the middle of a Spaghetti-Western James Bond movie and it was getting more interesting by the moment. Five minutes went by. Continuing the narrative, I mentioned Carlton a few more times saying we'd met him in Chicago years ago. Our bartender didn't buy it for a second and seemed to be getting a little suspicious of us. When he left the bar to make a phone call from a back room, we realized it was time to go. So, we hastily just threw some money on the bar, jumped over the still-twitching Giant Water Bug and sprinted out, almost certain that we were going to be chased. We leapt into the rental car and drove through some narrow streets and alleys in downtown Montego Bay. Our brains were screaming, "Let's get the hell out of here! Let's bolt to Negril!"

Not knowing exactly where we were going, and driving a little fast while buzzed, we still hadn't mastered the traffic scheme of this former British colony. The odds were stacked against us as we pondered, in motion, from the unfamiliar side of the road, "What the hell is a roundabout?" I found out. They only flow one way and not the direction I was driving in, which nearly ran me headlong into another car driven by a local who clearly knew the rules of the round. We bumped, but suffice it to say, it could have been much worse. We were a good distance away from the disco and the other car had no damage, barely a scratch in the paint. After a short scolding of rapid-fire, indiscernible, angry patois, the other driver drove off. Our car bumper, on the other hand, was smashed in. Through the grace of *Jah Rastafari*, there was a guy nearby in a little garage full of motorcycles who had tools. For seventy-five dollars, he banged out that bumper, and in what seemed like an eternity but couldn't have been more than a half an hour, we were on our way.

We had wild adrenalin gushing through our veins. That, combined with the hot Jamaican sun frying our pale, unprotected skin and hatless heads, was enough to dissolve the confidence of our convictions that drove us to investigate and decipher this mess in the first place. We weren't sure if we were experiencing the wildest, weirdest vacation ever or if we did truly just escape with our lives. But somehow this story was just beginning, as two "unwilling, not-ready-to-be-international-pawns-for-some-international-smuggling-business" spent a delightful week in Jamaica in a cheap villa in Negril, all the while looking over our shoulders.

All in all, it was a wild adventure in a tropical paradise. The danger, the mystery and uncertainty of what was around the corner was nothing short of exhilarating to my young, untethered mind. The improvised make-it-up-as-you-go-along survival instincts, as off-target as they might have sometimes been, were starting to take root in me. I went back to Jamaica in less than a year and continued to go back once or twice a year for the next six years. I was intrigued by how different life was there from my life at home, which had been entirely lived in the northeast corridor of the U.S., from New York City to the suburbs of South Jersey near Philadelphia. It was easy to become addicted to the serene natural surroundings, the gentle trade winds barely rippling the shallow, glassy water of Negril's Seven Mile Beach, and a daily diet of fresh fruits and fish. Rasta culture, unlimited ganja, and drum sessions on the cliffs overlooking the ocean were imprinting themselves in my soul. The steady repetitive pulse of the reggae bass and drums are said to be the sound of a contemplative heart. My spirit was entranced by it back then, and still is.

On subsequent trips, I would sometimes exchange the magnificent sunsets of the beach for week-long "National Geographic" excursions via motorbike to explore the island's interior. Way beyond being a tourist, my urge was to live like the people of the island and feel what inspired and informed them. Why was it that most Jamaicans seemed to be smiling and good-natured all the time? I had stayed with a family in their home in a remote little village and almost fell in love with the eldest daughter, C.H.A.R.M., as she spelled her name. The word "charm" did no justice to her manner and beauty. Her voluptuous proportions and graceful, well-mannered demeanor stoked the possibility that maybe this, by then 23-year-old, could fall in love and live there "up in the 'ills" forever, until I found out that she was only 14. I remember mistakenly riding my motorbike up a road that must have been a long private road to a huge home. My eyes were drawn to a man yelling and flailing his arms wildly on a wrap-around third-floor terrace. I didn't quite understand what he was trying to communicate to me, until the gunshots from a pistol aimed up into the air made his point very clear. No trespassing! I made a quick skid to a halt and zipped down the mountain.

Little did I know at the time that my trips there and this wide-eyed civil engineer-turned-taxi-driver's spiritual quest would be another cog in the spiritual wheel that was leading me to Japan. Deep inside, the thrill of exploring culture and music, especially this new culture that I had latched onto, was working itself into me. I was bound to embrace something different in the future. I'd been given a taste of it, albeit a dangerous and edgy one. A natural attraction to a life based on culture, adventure, and "natural mystic," as Bob Marley had called it, had already begun nibbling away at the wooden ladder of an anticipated, corporate "normal lifestyle," from the inside out. Having abandoned my engineering career by age 24, my life was precariously straddling Jamaica and New Brunswick, New Jersey, my college town. In New Jersey, I was driving a taxi, playing percussion and singing in a reggae calypso rock band, The Deed. We opened for Living Colour and Fishbone, two well-known international acts, and were a solid member of the New York City-based "Black Rock Coalition." On one of my extended trips to Jamaica, I became known by locals as the "white boy" in the band Children of Jah, playing percussion and singing at night. I paid for my room by renting jet skis to tourists in Negril.

Knowing I couldn't stay forever in Jamaica didn't strike me as a bolt of lightning. In fact, it came on gradually over the course of a year or two. I started realizing that I couldn't find true happiness on the beaches there, at least not the kind of sustaining happiness I wanted, despite the fact I was having the time of my life. I had begun chanting *Nam-myoho-renge-kyo*" as part of my Buddhist practice and was starting to develop a deeper sense of purpose for my life, one that extended well beyond my own hedonistic tendencies and selfish desires. I thought, "How can I really impact the WORLD by just standing with my feet in the sand looking out on the beautiful sunset?" I had lived five crucial years of my 20s firmly wrapping myself around the reluctance of sliding into a real working lifestyle. I couldn't part with the notion that <u>music had to be the vehicle for me</u>. Music was the answer. At this time, as self-assured as I was in my unique musical taste and ability, I was simply a backing vocalist and a drummer/percussionist who played a little rhythm guitar. Although I knew how to play a lot of other people's songs, I couldn't write a melody or a lyric that would move ME, let alone change someone's life or make me adored by the masses. But I was utterly convinced that music was my destined calling in life. I was sure I belonged to the select group of humans that I'd read about in mythologist author Joseph Campbell's books. I was a "Shaman of the 21st Century." This was how the well-respected mythologist author referred to artists of all shapes and forms. He proclaimed that they are the ones who have the responsibility of driving culture and informing and energizing society to better itself and develop to a higher level of harmonious existence. For me, music had to be the vehicle for accomplishing this profound mission. I was now a budding Nichiren Buddhist and was feeling that my success in music was as much for others as it was for me. Reggae and Rasta culture had become an important part of my psyche. But philosophically, I felt Rastafarianism only went so far into lifting the individual or the society up and out of smallness. A major theme of reggae was expressing the heavy weight of oppression by fighting against "Babylon" in all that it stands for and eventually being repatriated into Africa. I thought, "Who would want to leave Jamaica, this land of beauty, kissed by the pristine sea and cool natural vibes to go back to Africa?" In my eyes, the Rastafarian "holy trilogy" of Marcus Garvey, Haile Selassie and Bob Marley seemed a super-cool version of what other religions had, with the added attraction of the "sacrament" of ganja and the soundtrack of reggae. It was also exclusionary and somewhat protective in its ideals and strictly espoused that its purity not be tainted by outside or modern, reformist viewpoints.

As I came to understand and exert myself more deeply in my newly adopted Buddhist practice I realized that, just as with many religions, Rastafarianism didn't focus on the most important concepts to which I ascribed. Among those were the necessities of breaking the shells of the smaller self (i.e. ego) and dissolving the barriers between peoples and tribes. I felt Buddhism aimed higher and gave practical tools to ascend beyond the lesser "selves" of complaint, fears and division, both internally and out in the world. I realized I now had access to a philosophy that, for me, was more universal and powerful than any I had previously known. Buddhism could quite possibly bring out the capability, karmic circumstances and fortune to make a more expansive, purposeful life possible. Decades later when my life steered me towards Japan, I felt I was on the vanguard of much-needed cultural change in The Land of the Rising Sun, boy bands and anime music. In Kyoto, I would take the reggae message and vibe and stretch it across a broader philosophical framework.

CHAPTER 5

THE
ANCIENT CITY

"How much of the color and wonder of life would be lost if it weren't for our differences?"

– Daisaku Ikeda, founding president of the Soka Gakkai International (SGI)

To say that Kyoto is rich in culture does not come close to doing it justice. It is a multidimensional mashup that churns and bubbles with everything from boutique video gaming companies to acclaimed ceramic artists creating works for their exhibitions at New York City's Museum of Modern Art (MOMA). There are treasured, traditional Ikebana flower arrangement schools and 400-year-old tea houses sharing the same sidewalk, where a few meters away a moving projected logo on the pavement gestures for you to come inside to sample signature drinks and worldly tapas. "Avant-gardens" of LED-illuminated sculptures stand under rooftop all-you-can-drink-and-eat summer beer gardens where you can indulge and engorge for two hours at a cost of around $30. You'll also see the occasional sweet deal in the maze of confusing alleyways throughout the city where a tiny karaoke hole-in-the-wall whiskey bar that can barely squeeze in eight guests abuts an all-night Turkish kebab and hookah bar. Turn the corner into the next alley and the inviting street-facing windows suddenly morph into upscale architectural facades of stone and old wood. The lights dim and the mood changes as the formal, orchestrated rituals of the city's elegant debauchery can be observed with much bowing and ceremonial introduction, as young consorts ease into black limos for the night. It's all very dignified and civilized. These are but a few of the many faces of Kyoto.

Even Kyoto's geography, its very location, eases one's senses into complete, safe immersion and the freedom to experience and take in the delights the city has to offer. There is an unacknowledged soothing safety in the fact that the city is situated inland, far away from any shorelines capable of a devastating storm surge or tsunami. It also rarely seems to take a direct hit from the strong typhoons that generally come from the south and east in the late summer. Plus, Kyoto is an epicenter of thought and culture, but almost never one of earthquakes. Its seismic insignificance rarely even shakes a playful jiggle, let alone a major earthquake. There are also no nuclear power plants anywhere near the city.

The depth of Kyoto's intrigue can be seen in the little treasures you find scattered along its mountain paths. A one-hour hike into the woods along a desolate path that connected dozens of small shrines revealed these old stone and bronze statues.

On the elevated, landscaped banks of the shallow, wide Kamogawa River (Kamo= duck, Gawa = river), riverside drum circles beat while kimono-clad "old money" women have reunion parties on *yukas*, or wooden restaurant terraces. They eat ridiculously priced *kaiseki* course meals, the iconic haute cuisine of Kyoto, while beneath them, groups of loud university students work on perfecting their amateur drinking skills, laughing into the night, and sometimes wading into the river in their underwear.

It's hard to imagine Kyoto without the ancient neighborhood of Gion in Spring, the fragrance of cherry trees in bloom, or the plethora of shrines and temples within the city. During the 13th and 15th centuries, Kyoto was strongly influenced by religious traditions and became a center for new forms of Buddhism. Many temples were built at the foot of the Kitayama (north), Higashiyama (east) and Nishiyama (west) mountains. Daikaku-ji Temple was built in the 9th century as a palace for the emperor and later made into a large temple, Kinkakuji (Golden) Temple belonged to a shōgun, and in the 8th century, Fushimi Inari Shrine was built to pay homage to rice and sake, to name a few. You can spend an entire day walking through its 10,000 *Torii*, or bright-orange wooden gates, that form shadowy, mysterious tunnels connecting many small sub-shrines in paths up and down the Inari mountain. These are but a few of the dozens of priceless treasures in Kyoto's living, ancient history.

To give you an idea of the scope of Japan's long and ancient history, my friend and co-author, Catherine, once soaked in a cast-iron tub at a farmhouse outside of Kyoto that was nearly twice as old as our United States' entire history. In the U.S., we'd have put that tub in a museum and labeled it an "ancient soaking tub." But in the Japanese farmer's mind, the tub, resembling a giant cast-iron cooking pot encased in wood, was just another place to soak. That it was 400 years old at the time was immaterial. It wasn't considered ancient. The farm itself was that old, and the brandy Catherine drank that night close to it. This was a special, historic event to be celebrated but not because of the tub. It was due to the person soaking in it. Acting as a student ambassador of peace between Japan and the U.S., she was the first American to ever visit that farm. Peace between nations marked the moment's significance, not the antiquity of the tub. Ancient artifacts are commonplace here.

Most foreigners come to Japan to walk through these temples, shrines and gardens and eat artisan-created concoctions. They entertain themselves by trying on kimonos and "playing Japanese" for a day. They also bathe in hot springs or experience the sometimes-quirky electricity and energy of night life in cities like Tokyo, Osaka, Nagoya, Fukouka or Kobe. Others come to study for a few years as an undergraduate or post-graduate. They might land a dream job as part of a research team at a university or join a high-tech start-up developing fuel cells or something similar, often changing their long-term plans to make a lifelong career of it.

Others come to Japan because they fall in love with a Japanese girl or with the culture, and sometimes not in that order. I came to Japan for some of these reasons and more. Girding this midlife pivot was the confidence I'd developed in trusting my gut. The guidance and inspiration of Daisaku Ikeda, the third president of the Soka Gakkai, had instilled in me the importance and timeliness of becoming a truly Global Citizen. "Sensei" has and always will be my mentor in life. Besides that, I was getting sick of New York and wanted a change.

Many other foreigners who come to Kyoto fall into the last category: those who've aborted their previous life of hum-drum mediocrity, those who seek to make amends for unrequited love or those looking to satisfy an ungratified libido. Perhaps it's a combination of one or more of these, or they've simply lost their direction and never managed to assemble a cohesive, fulfilling career path. When the winds of fate deposit these seeds of unexceptional capacity into the fertile soil, streams, rivers, and English-parched population of Japan, they wind up carving out a niche teaching English. Japanese people are desperately itching to further engage the world community and survive their decades-long economic downslide from the "bubble" of the 1980s. Just by the virtue of being a foreigner, the "average Joe or Liam" from any city in the U.S. or Britain can become a neighborhood celebrity.

Male-pattern baldness, age, or lack of ambition are overlooked because you can help them connect to the world, give them then an edge, and help nudge them up the ladder of success. Besides that, you sport different DNA. So, it's not surprising to see a man who might be considered only mildly appealing to be walking hand in hand with a Japanese woman of such physical beauty that back home she might have been "out of his league." For women, if your hair is light with natural curl, you become irresistible. Your big, hooked nose, which may have been a liability back home, is now referred to as a "tall nose," and makes you desirable. It's a mecca for the disenfranchised.

Although Japan is growing up and changing little by little, this land of intrigue is deceivingly fragile in many respects. There is the life-critical need for, but often reluctant drive toward modernization - not of technology, but of thought. As Japan wrestles with the complexity of defining its destiny, it could get it all wrong and possibly collapse from within. Like a termite-infested floor, Japan may be undermined by institutions run by historically validated male domination. Or, due to too heavy a focus on formality over substance, tribalism over globalism, and consumerism over spirituality, it may chug along too slowly to compete in the Pacific Rim arena, or even suffer a cultural downfall. There is even the possibility that Japan may self-destroy, not by design, but by manmade accident or natural disaster. The national debit is double the U.S.'s in terms of gross domestic product. China is continuously knocking on the door militarily and economically in the middle of the night. Kim Jong Un likes to shoot off big, scary, metal tubes into the Sea of Japan and more recently fly them over the island into the Pacific.

On the banks of the Kamogawa near the popular Sanjō Bridge, lovers cuddle, families gather for picnics, musicians practice music, and tourists take it all in. For all it's a reprieve from the busy city. Photo credit: Yoko Matsuda

Sometimes it's easy to forget you're in perhaps the most traditional city of Japan. All are drawn to the tranquility of the Kamogawa river.

During World War II, the U.S. considered bombing Kyoto because as an intellectual center of Japan it was thought the impact would be more deeply felt by the Japanese. Thankfully, due to the mindset of a few U.S. military leaders who recognized its precious historic value, Kyoto was spared the bombing devastation of most major cities and removed from the list of targets. Ultimately, we can be grateful to Henry L. Stimson, Secretary of

War in the Roosevelt and Truman administrations, who protested the idea. Having weathered the harsh impact of World War II, present-day Kyoto has grown in ways that define its unique stature amongst the dozen or so large, busy cities in Japan.

In the seven years I have been living here, I have developed a deep connection to the community that has embraced me, forming myriad relationships with people. They are entire families of three generations, shop owners, university students, government workers. There's even the occasional loner freakazoids I encounter who, if you let them, can absorb you into their twisted sociopathic inward spirals. But, my exhaustion is often due to my subpar Japanese skills more than anything else. Honestly, I view my relationship with Japan as a perfect joining of destinies with every possibility of a mutually successful, beneficial relationship, one born countless eons ago and formed in previous lifetimes. I can sense the spirit of Kyoto deeply imbedded in the depths of my being, threaded and coiled in my DNA. In the ever-transforming former ancient capital city, there is a thriving international community, and I'm thrilled to be a part of it. I feel I fit in. There is no better suited, more livable situation for me to try that one last push. Kyoto inspires me to attempt to reach for the rope that will swing me into a soaring life of musical glory, to reconcile the sacrifices I've made in career and relationships and finally launch my lifelong assault on "dreamlightenment." I feel that I was deposited here by forces well beyond myself. If I can put Kyoto on the map as a place from which cool international music emits and help construct that international bridge from both ends, then I can die with an eternal smile on my face. There's a reason I came here when I did and why I choose to stay. If I hadn't come here, well, I don't want to think about it. Thank God we found each other!

CHAPTER 6

KANSAI ROCKS!

It was Friday afternoon, January 26, 2011. A wild blizzard was blowing outside JFK International Airport as I attempted to leave New York and join my family for good in Kyoto. But the planes were delayed for several hours. So, I signed on to a Wi-Fi network that popped up on my MacBook, paid $2.99 and spent a few hours emailing my bosses and sending goodbyes to some of my clients, as I was still partially employed by Mana Contemporary Fine Arts. Gene Lemay, the president, had given me an iPad as a goodbye gift and asked me to stay on and continue prospecting and communicating with my clients, amongst them the Guggenheim Museum. A few days later, my second day of living in Japan, I noticed that someone had wiped out $1,700 dollars from my Visa ATM card. I'm certain a scoundrel had been sitting near me in that JFK Departure lounge and grabbed my information.

I set foot unceremoniously in Japan on January 27, 2011. Although it took weeks for my jetlag to wear off, (there is a 14-hour time difference between New York and Japan, and 13 when daylight savings is in effect), I still wasn't feeling quite up to speed even by March. I had an on-and-off, persistent, low-grade headache that seemed to last all day long. I Googled the symptoms and was relieved to find out that I wasn't alone, and I wasn't experiencing some minor stroke or migraine. It was the result of some change in amino acids in my new diet or something to that effect.

I started working at Velco English Schools on March 3, 2011, all the while determined to jump in as soon as possible to begin my real new life of music. Just days after I started, during my second week at work, on March 11, 2011, an earthquake shook the Tohoku region north of Tokyo. It sent a 45-foot tall tsunami through the Fukushima Daiichi Nuclear Power plant, triggering the second worst unintentional nuclear disaster in history. I was on a train to the Velco Osaka school when the great Eastern Japan earthquake and tsunami struck. I remember gasping on my iPad at the live news feed of massive floodwaters carrying buildings and tossing around cars with four or five fellow commuters standing around my seat. One man kept saying in utter astonishment, "*Sugoi! Sugoi!*" I knew this word meant "amazing" since I first heard it in New York years ago. But now I became aware that it was not only used in positive situations. A few days later, at the Kyoto branch of Velco, I stood with students around the reception counter. We were staring at my iPad in disbelief as smoke billowed from the Fukushima Daiichi Nuclear Power plant reactor #2 building. I remember assuring them that it wasn't an actual full-scale meltdown and to not worry, that we were far away. We were in Kansai, eight or nine hours away by car from the devastated region. Still a sense of uneasiness underlay every conversation lesson I gave at these schools for the entire week. [Milas News: https://bit.ly/japan-tsunami-2011]

As bad went to worse, for the next month, everybody constantly checked the direction of the wind on their smartphones. One month later, the nuclear power plant was still spewing out radiation and spreading fright throughout Japan. A dozen friends on Facebook insisted that I come back to America. But my brother Gregg, a seasoned environmental scientist, said not to worry, but it would be a good idea to keep an eye on the wind. Wind patterns generally don't come from the East and blow south towards Kansai in West Japan. To some extent we felt generally safe in Kyoto.

I had heard for decades that there was something special about the Kansai region of Japan, and not just because I was married to a Kansai woman. I sensed that the revered "Kansai Spirit" would play an important role and have a big impact on my life. Kansai is the heart of western Japan and is comprised of seven prefectures. The three core cities of Kansai are Osaka (the third largest city in Japan), Kobe and Kyoto. Each is distinctly different in tone and in their overall mission for Japan. In short, I was told by students that Kobe is the bastion of fashion and international trading, Osaka is the big city business hub with hundreds of distinct neighborhoods and zillions of eateries and drinkeries, and Kyoto keeps the traditional culture real and intact.

Back in New York, I thought a good way to start the musical and spiritual transition between my old life and new life in Japan would be to write a song and call it "Kansai Rocks!" It would not only bridge and connect New York City and Kyoto for me, but how could I go wrong branding my music towards the tens of millions of prideful Japanese who lived in Kansai? It became the theme song for that transitional period of my life expressing the excitement, energy and personality of Japan and my anticipation in moving there, as well as a shout-out to the vivacious character of Kansai. All of this would be recorded in relatable, cool English blended with Japanese. With a catchy hook and a reggae vibe, surely it would translate into thousands upon thousands of iTunes downloads. In the unbearable freeze of January in Chicago, on my final business trip, I recorded the vocals on "Kansai Rocks!" in a hotel room at night with a microphone hanging from the shower bar. I uploaded it to iTunes and certainly wouldn't call it a big hit by any stretch of the imagination, but it's cool and groovin' and it's out there in the universe. My life in music, every step of the way emotionally churning inside of me, available for digital download only as I transitioned to a new life in Japan.

KANSAI ROCKS!

By Jay Crystall © 2013 Jay Crystall

I get the job done and go through the city
....and even if I wanted to, I won't...STOP!
Just pack and go away, make it shine, make it shine, make it shine
Take the Shinkansen to Kyoto Station.
Hold your baby's hand going up the escalator,
All the time, always, all around, motivated by Jah Jah Love
All the kids in town, all the funky styles, all the colored hair,
rub it up, rub it up, rub it up
Everybody's cool, everybody's cute, everybody cares
Kansai Rocks and everyone knows that the fire burn brighter
when the strong wind blows
You gotta change Poison into Medicine.

Although it would be two-and-a-half years after arrival before I would release my debut CD, I knew I had to plug immediately into the scene and start making musical causes of my own. I looked through some online postings in English. I believe it was in *Kansai Scene* where I saw an ad for Harmony Music and Dining Bar in Osaka that had a few small acts on their schedule. The posting listed "the blues of Mojo Jones" and a small jazz trio and an email address of a Bobby Something at gmail.com. I sent a message to the effect of, "Hi. I'm a singer songwriter from New York City who just moved to Japan. I play original and covers of mostly reggae and rock. Can I get onto your schedule? BTW, I don't mind playing for free." He quickly replied. I would consummate my musical relationship with Japan as a solo act on a Sunday night in April during a torrential downpour. I spent the one-hour train ride from Kyoto to Osaka standing in a crowded car going over a set list in my mind for what would be my first overseas performance. Upon arriving at the train station, I found myself lost in the catacombs of Osaka's Umeda train station. It was not only located dead center in that city of eight million people, to make it even more confusing, there were two Umeda stations, one for the Hankyu train line and another for the larger Japan Railroad (JR) Line.

I had to find my way through the South Gate building to the North Gate building, navigating a crowded complex of busy shopping malls, endless escalators and sublevel passageways containing five or six Macy's-sized department stores. I lugged my acoustic guitar and a heavy shoulder bag through this ant farm of tens-of-thousands of people walking in every direction with gyroscopic navigation skills, miraculously not colliding with each other. Did this skill come from those amino acids that gave me a constant headache for my first five or six weeks in Kyoto? I was lost and starting to get a little nervous, so I picked up my pace. As I emerged from behind a large column, my guitar case nearly took the head off a little boy whose father grabbed him and pulled him away at the last moment, giving me a scolding with his eyes that was louder than anything that could have been yelled.

The huge maps over the ticket machines were not the geometric, sharp-angled, color-coded spaghetti that guide travelers in New York's Grand Central

Station or Madrid's metro. They weren't logical like the Paris Métropolitain, where the line's name is also its final stop. These were luminescent tentacles of a Portuguese Man-of-War that had been put in a blender and dropped on a child's spin-art canvas. There wasn't a smidgeon of English on them except for the absurdly obvious and bold OSAKA jellyfish eye. Come on Osaka! Kyoto is much more tourist-friendly. I could make out the "loop line" which I was informed of by Google, but I wasn't sure which way to take the loop.

By some small miracle, I made it to Harmony Music and Dining Bar which was down a narrow back street and a five minute walk from Tamatsukuri Station. But five minutes in a torrential downpour without an umbrella is all it takes. I was soaked. This dark backstreet was home to four or five little *izakayas* (small boozy eateries) and snack bars. Snack bars or snack clubs are a more member-oriented izakaya with local girls serving and flirting with the guests. I still to this day don't quite grasp the difference between a snack bar, a hostess club, a boys' club, a lady's club or a few other variations of liquor, food, service, and role play that I'm sure have special off-the-menu services and hidden rooms. I came upon a sandwich board with handwritten English "From New York City! Jay Crystall performing Original Reggae and Rock." It was five minutes until the advertised 8:00 PM show time. I climbed a steep, narrow wooden staircase to the second floor and shook hands with a smiling but somewhat concerned Bobby. Walking quickly behind ten people chatting in groups of two sitting at the long bar counter, I plugged in my guitar and raised the mic on the boom stand to my mouth. I didn't have a sound-check and I was dripping from my hair to waterlogged shoes. I gave a quick, "*Konbanwa Minasan* ("Good evening, Everyone"), two of the twenty words in my infantile Japanese lexicon. Forgetting to introduce myself, I broke into Bob Marley's "Redemption Song." I had played it hundreds of times in America, studying and entranced by Bob Marley's voice and how it cracked with human frailty on high notes. I did my best to cop his patois and prophetic presence in this now worldwide iconic, soulful expression of hope and "rising up." In the song Bob Marley almost pleads with us to not allow our minds to be controlled or owned by anyone or anything. He then reassures us that even in the remote possibility of a nuclear disaster, humanity will endure as nothing can stop the flow of time. It was my hope that the people there could understand these English lyrics and feel his wisdom and compassion.

At the Harmony Music and Dining Bar in Osaka, the venue of my first overseas solo performance, where I still regularly perform.

"Everyone was just staring at me."

It was April 2011, and the Fukushima Nuclear Power Plant was continuing to emit radiation and induce alarm across Japan as headlines reported that radioactive iodine had been detected in Tokyo's drinking water. Halfway through the song I got the nerve to open my eyes and look up and noticed nobody was talking to each other. They were staring at this dripping foreigner, standing in a puddle with his eyes closed. I was transported back to a smoke-filled shanty shack in Jamaica overlooking the sea, to that rainy evening of drumming with the Rasta priests. But now my first Japanese audience, ten silently staring souls, were there with me. It was clear that beyond the spectacle, they sensed something genuine and honest going on, and that I was not there simply to provide entertainment. A bold, reassuring feeling started to well up inside me. It was the notion that this whole "leave my career and comfort in New York to start a new life in Japan chasing a musical dream thing" just might work out. As I approached the last verse of the song, with my voice and soggy guitar-locked hands on autopilot, I was deliberating on whether I should follow this with one of my songs, written before I came to Japan, "Whappy Now," a fast, original ska song or a Beatles tune.

WHAPPY NOW (We Happy Now)

By Jay Crystall © 2008 Jay Crystall

Oh, see mountain and ya run to the top
Oh, see money and ya chase it up
Ya get so used to strugglin it gets you off
So just step up and forward now
There's a rhythm... to the Flow.... And it goes, and it goes, and it goes
Oh, somebody come over here we got so much love today
Oh, Jah Jah give us these hills of green
Him gurgle up from a mountain spring
Him'a go boom, boom, boom in stormy surge
Me give ya love that you ...uuhhh deserve

I left that show wet, drunk and beaming with confidence, determined to make my live act better than anything I had ever done in New York. It was never clearer that this was my calling and now was my time. I had an entire country at my fingertips, an audience of millions hungry for authenticity and original music. Delivered from a foreigner that had taken up residency in the homeland, the odds seemed stacked in my favor. Everyone knows that Japan has its own rich culture, but there's also a reverence and craving for western music. A large swathe of Japanese, if not half the population identify and connect more with the mindset and culture of Europe and the Americas than they do with that of their Pacific Rim neighbors. That includes movies, baseball, celebrity culture, to name a few. Except for the K-pop (South Korean) soap dramas and music, and cuisine from India, China, Viet Nam, and Thailand, the rest of the Asian continent don't have much influence over most people's lives in Japan.

It dawned on this foreigner singer-songwriter that I needed to learn at least one Japanese cover song, and a cool one. A few months into Japan, I was taken into a quiet room during a small party by my wife's long-time friend, Morin San. He wanted to share something with me from YouTube that he knew would inspire me. I watched a video of a song called "Sayonara Kara." (Sayonara Color) written by Hanaregumi, who was the lead singer and guitar player of eighties band, Super Butter Dog. Sitting on a stool in jeans, a big white hat and glasses, in a darkened TV soundstage with thousands of twinkling lights in the studio sky, he strummed an acoustic guitar and sang a simple, soulful song. He was joined by a standing, twitching freakshow of a human being playing harmonica. Dressed in a black and white polka dot shirt and tie-dyed pants, with makeup and wispy graying hair sprayed into the shape of an overhead flame, this apparition looked almost inhuman. I felt as if I was watching the lovechild of Ziggy Stardust and Joe Cocker. At first, I thought it was a woman. I later learned it was Kiyoshiro Imawano. He laid back on the harmonica, tastefully embellishing Hanaregumi's warm melodic ballad, which in pure, bittersweet verse conveys the wisdom and new opportunities born of saying goodbye. Suddenly during the second verse, Kiyoshiro broke into harmony singing in a shrieking, but soft and gelatinous tone unlike anything I've ever heard before. It wasn't an in-your-face scream or super-human American Idol voice, but something comfortably weird, perfectly unrehearsed and a hair out of time. I was penetrated to the core by the song and the synergy between these two Japanese performers, as is every one of the hundreds of people I have turned on to this song (listen at: https://bit.ly/lovesicinkyoto6A).

A week later I came across the English subtitled version and fell in even deeper. If I was to move on with my life I had to learn this song first. It became an obsession. I listened to it several times a day, usually sitting on a train staring out the window. I had to pursue and pocket this "master's degree" in Japanese pronunciation and genuine alternative rock as soon as yesterday. I was studying how NOT to squeeze too much of a phrase into a few notes. Generally, it takes longer to say something of complex emotion in Japanese than in English, just ask Google translator. For example, "I'm too deeply in love and it hurts" can be said in English in two beats. Try it. The Japanese equivalent, depending on the translator, can have two dozen characters including five kanji and take up to six beats to say or sing. But this song, "Sayonara Kara," was perfectly phrased and gorgeously sung. For months, I wracked the multilinguistic synapses of my brain to learn how to perfectly pronounce it and sing it like they do. As a foreigner, I successfully defend that thesis every time I play it live. It gives me instant "cred" with any

Japanese audience and more importantly it draws those who haven't heard it into the deeper end of the J-pop cultural pool.

By this time, I had joined Izah Blu and Hi-Intenzion reggae band playing keyboards. I'd struggled for a few months with Izah's band to connect with the lyrics which were great and true-to-the-colors reggae meditations but couldn't help flashing back to the realization I'd had standing on that beach in Jamaica. I needed to aim and reach higher with my creative impulse. This meant stepping beyond reggae conventions and planting the seeds of thought I felt were needed to change consciousness in the listener's microcosm, and in turn, society. I had spent half of my life developing perspective and abilities to create something that was uniquely my own.

When a teacher from New Zealand walked into the Velco English School in Kyoto one night late in my first year in Japan, I knew instantly something was about to change.

In Solomon, I knew I had met a true brethren and kindred spirit. This charming, wild-eyed, intelligent being from another part of the world, with geometric, organic Maori tattoos running up and down his muscular arms would become an instant friend and musical partner in crime. He held it down with the responsibility of supporting a family with three kids. He also played percussion, guitar and ukulele and loved reggae. Jah Rastafari!!! I soon found out that this undiscovered talent had some serious pipes too, a sensitive voice that could reach high registers I couldn't even dream of. We immediately started jamming together and booked a few gigs as a duet. Solomon drummed the crap out of that wooden cajón percussion box and hit perfect harmonies while I strummed and sang reggae covers and some of my originals. Sometimes we switched, and he would sing an Etta James blues song in a solid, sexy falsetto while I kept the beat. Other times we just jammed on hand drums and brought the jungle into the middle of a Japanese city (listen at: https://bit.ly/lovesicinkyoto6B).

We'd rehearse at night in the basement bomb shelter of Kyoto International School where he worked. Soon we were joined by Taketo, one of our students at Velco English school. He was a cool, debonair, well-traveled young man who happened to be a seasoned melodic bass player with great instinct and ability. Shortly thereafter, his former bandmate and buddy, Masafumi, joined us, wailing on the sax. We were playing ska and reggae cover songs, and rock songs with reggae beats, sometime with three-part harmonies. They loved my original material and eagerly learned the songs. Finally, I had a chance to hear my songs played with a full band, the way I had envisioned them. We naturally took on the name Kansai Rocks! With a built-in audience of students from our English school we began to play clubs. There were incredible nights of fun and audience sing-a-longs at Irish bars in Kyoto and small clubs in Osaka. Sometimes we would just jam down by the Kamogawa River at night as people gathered around (listen at: https://bit.ly/lovesicinkyoto6C).

The energy and freshness of this brand-new band of four, two foreigners and two Japanese called Kansai Rocks!, fit nicely into the CD I'd already been creating. These songs were my "babies," the first things I'd written that I really liked since my days with Orchid Room ten years earlier. Finally, I was able to turn my deepest impulses, my years of developing songwriting and production skills, and my voice into a finished product, of which I could be proud!

I named the CD *Changing Poison into Medicine*, after the Japanese phrase of "changing poison into medicine," or *hendoku iyaku*. A Nichiren Buddhist concept, it expresses the strategy of using the heat that comes from the friction of difficulty as fuel for personal betterment and practical problem resolution. By confronting obstacles head on, embracing them, mining the depths of your wisdom, employing courage, creativity, and boundless compassion girded in common sense, you can extract real value that can take on the form of newly-acquired perspective. Essentially, it means regarding and using everything that happens to you as your teacher and converting all of this into greater momentum for growth and attainment of unshakable resilient happiness. It can take painstaking effort. In the last few seconds of the track, "Kansai Rocks!," I whisper the phrase *laboremus*, Latin for "Let us do our work!" (conveyed by Dr. Arnold Toynbee as his life motto in a published dialogue with Daisaku Ikeda).

In case you're interested, the entire album can be found here: https://bit.ly/kansairocks.

CHAPTER 7

IZAH BLUE
INTO THE WAVE

So here was my plan: Move to Japan and carve out a niche as the foreigner who would lift audiences up by writing and singing conscious reggae music. I was certain I'd have them dancing to my vibes and meditating on my lyrics across the entire Land of the Rising Sun in few years at most. On a previous trip to Japan with my family, I remember how in an *Okonomiyaki* restaurant, we'd sat on *tatami* bamboo mats around a hot, rectangular flat grill in the center of a table, flipping thick, shredded cabbage pancakes topped with pork, beef, shrimp or squid, or sometimes all four together. The signature shaved bonito flakes that were sprinkled on top of these concoctions were mesmerizing as they danced and swayed to the music of Bob Marley wafting over the restaurant PA. Now, as I squiggled mayonnaise from a squeeze bottle all over these high calorie, nutritious, steaming UFOs, it all made sense to me. I would hail that banner as one of the new voices of international reggae, a New Yorker living in Kyoto beaming my positive message and hooky melodies out to the world.

Two months prior to my move to Japan, I Googled the words "reggae + Kyoto" and up came a name, Izah Blue. Huh? There was a foreigner already doing the original reggae thing in Kyoto?! I wouldn't be the first?! There he was: a tall, handsome white man with chiseled features, a squared chin, cooler than cool Rastaman with blue eyes (aka, eyes of blue). Upon deeper inspection I found out his real name was Aiza Hartman, which sounded Jewish to me. I gazed at videos of shows in Osaka featuring this tall man with blond dreadlocks dancing in a steppin' out reggae style and singing original music in small clubs. Leading his band, Hi-N-Tenzion, Izah Blue was giving a spectacularly great time to all, proved by the many hands

---

thrusting into the air over the dance floor. As I poked around a little deeper on Facebook, I saw that this foreigner with the blond dreadlocks came from Hawaii, where twenty years ago he'd had a band, Roots Natty Roots, that, at the time, was considered Hawaii's biggest reggae band. About four years prior to that late night when I was spying on him from my laptop in Jersey City, he had moved to Kyoto, apparently due to having married a Japanese girl. It was plain to see that this guy was the real deal, a true Rasta man; living, breathing, and sending out reggae vibes from Kyoto throughout the Kansai area. It was inevitable that I would eventually meet Izah, for he seemed like he was a true brethren and kindred spirit. "He'll be my best friend, Or, maybe he'd become something of a rival." I thought this because what he was doing was supposed to be MY original plan. Two weeks after I arrived in Japan, having reunited with my family after almost a year alone we finally found an apartment to live and settle down in. I contacted Izah through Facebook. He returned my message immediately with a phone call. He sounded like a nice guy. I was to meet him at the Aiza Aloha English school located near *Gosho*, the former Imperial Palace in the center of Kyoto. With much excitement, I walked down the sidewalk and came upon a four-story triangular-shaped building with three big Japanese *kanji* characters in the window that I would come to learn said *Eikaiwa*, or English conversation school. The doorway to the building was marked with a tall, hand-painted, wooden sandwich board sign with a drawing of a globe and a few English and Japanese characters on it. The sign was obviously homemade and aged, with gray paint chipping off it, and a plastic Ziploc bag with some bright, red-colored tri-fold school brochures for curious passers-by to grab.

As I climbed up the stairs to the second floor and opened the door, I was greeted by a big, bright smile and a loud hello followed by a friendly Rasta fist-bump handshake. I never did get that fist bump right since there are a few variations depending on mood and person. As I walked into that place, it immediately changed my conception of how a school is supposed to look and feel. There were tropical plants and trees along a wall of windows and a big, colorful surfboard suspended on the wall. A poster of Haile Selassie, also known as Jah Rastafari, the messianic King of Ethiopia, hung on the wall. There was a poster of Bob Marley. Tropical island paraphernalia hung everywhere. Surfing and ukulele-playing Santa Claus Christmas ornaments were suspended from air-conditioning units. There were large, black speakers on the floor and a keyboard on the stand. I was standing in some unique vortex in the universe, a joining of Hawaiian culture and reggae music in the heart of a busy Japanese city of one-and-a-half million people. As I looked deeper, I could see there was a school in the middle of all this culture. On one side of the room, there was a huge flat screen TV flanked by two large speakers that might've seemed more at home shaking the rafters at a small dance club. Situated in the back of the room was a computer workstation and mixing board. Atop a high stool, like a pilot in his cockpit, this English teacher reggae man would control an audiovisual wonderland, which I later would realize played an important role in some of his lesson plans. There were homemade "kids learning" posters on black cardboard strategically placed on easels or suspended from cabinets. I could sense all the work that he had put into designing this visually stimulating center of learning, such as the colorful 12-months of the year poster formed by laminated cutouts on black poster board. Ice skating bears were pictured on the calendar in January, smiling sunflowers in August, and feisty squirrels raking leaves in October. There were ABC posters on the walls and long skinny white metal tables lined up along the windows. Tucked under these tables were a dozen simple wooden stools with round, circular tops painted in different colors. Two puffy cushioned gray sofas (that I later realized became trampolines for sugar-buzzed kids) sat across from waist high bookcases filled with textbooks, which stood next to cabinets filled with games. About a half-dozen long, dual-fluorescent light fixtures dangled overhead, exposed. This English school was like no other. It was most certainly not your grandmother's English classroom. A mix of pure culture and eccentric vibes, it was way bigger than the sum of its parts. I felt immediately right at home.

The man with the piercing blue eyes, big smile, and perfect CAD-designed (computer-aided-drafting) nose tucked his short dreadlocks neatly into a hat. Sitting behind that MacBook Pro workstation techno cockpit, he looked like a handsome British model in some edgy YouTube ad, that is until he talked and laughed. Somehow that Hawaii accent sounded very Californian to me. When he laughed, it wasn't a little laugh either. It was a bellow. Haw!

Haw! Haw! I was in the presence of a real character; a man of reggae vibes, a teacher, an entrepreneur of sorts, who had put all of this together. Sitting comfortably in this happy man's domain, I reached out and picked up a nearby guitar and started to play an original reggae song of mine. I chose "Soon, Soon, Soon," which would be on my yet-to-be-released debut CD. I wasn't sure if this was some sort of audition or just two brethren hanging out and enjoying each other's presence. But I was driven to sing that song as I never had before, because, again, I sensed I was in the presence of greatness. Izah Blue, my soon-to-be brethren, a light-skinned Rasta man from Hawaii, owner of an English school in Kyoto, Japan, had already built the first few floors of what I thought was supposed to be my tower.

The next weekend, I went back to the Aiza Aloha English School. This time, I lugged my 60-pound Roland Fantom X6 digital keyboard workstation, the one I'd bought a decade earlier with my cashed in 401K. On noisy casters, I rolled it in a six-foot long rectangular, hard flight case from my small apartment in Matsugasaki in North Kyoto into the train to get to the "rehearsal." Mine wasn't the only knee that was bruised from lugging this expensive, cumbersome behemoth on the Eizan Light Rail Line. I got one of those silent, scornful looks which, in Japan, is louder than a New York City "WTF!" It was from a young man who happened to be slouched on a subway bench seat with legs extended a little too far into the aisle. Huffing and puffing after climbing the steps, I nearly fell through the door of the Hawaiian reggae English school, dropping a bag of percussion instruments on the carpet. That's when I met the band. First, a guy named Rootz walked up to me, a young Filipino guy, in his early 20s, with dreadlocks halfway down his back. With him, I nailed that fist bump. A good sign. He was skinny, borderline scrawny and exuded a mix of positive, Rasta-energy along with a gnarly, mischievous smile. Then I met Tsubo, gentle and messy-haired in a Thai shirt and batik pants. Charmed by his *genki* (happy and smiling) demeanor, his masterful reggae skanking-style guitar would make it onto my own CD a year later. Masa, the very normal, late-20s bass player from Osaka was an artistic, alternative rock bass player who was apparently now going through forced "reggae conversion therapy."

There I was, three weeks after arriving in Japan, learning and playing simple percussive reggae chords on piano and organ patches on my oversized, overpriced, overweight keyboard workstation. I was rehearsing backup harmonies singing on Izah's songs like "Go to Zion" and "I Love I Sensi," This was not a reference to sensei as in a teacher, but rather to sensi, as in sensimilla. These songs were true-to-form, real reggae with lyrics sung in English and Jamaican-style *patois*. The reggae bass, harmonious chant and praise of Jah booming from the large PA speakers, barely muffled by the large windows, sent waves across the streets and through the neighborhood of Japan's former Imperial Palace. With strategically placed incense and exhaust fans to cover measured little puffs of ganja, I was delighted to spend my Sunday afternoon rehearsing with Izah Blue and Hi-N-Tenzion. I had barely recovered from jet lag at this point and all I could think was, "what a cool country!" And, I was playing in a reggae band in it!

Watch at: https://bit.ly/lovesicinkyoto7

After three or four of these rehearsals and a sidewalk photo shoot, I was playing in clubs like The Safari in Osaka and Trinity in Kobe. We would start our second set at midnight as the animated audiences, a mix of Japanese and foreigner inebriates, would dance and sing to Izah's masterful call-and-response reggae. I enjoyed my role as the white boy from New York, playing reggae keyboard and picking up a djembe in the middle of a song banging out a rootsy niyabinghi riddim' while Izah did the reggae improv toasting. I was lovin' it!

People loved it, too! It was a blessing from the universe, a gift bestowed on me from Jah to have this much fun and cultural realness in my second month in Kyoto. Sometimes after these gigs, I was handed eight thousand yen, which was about eighty dollars at the time. Other times, well, maybe our pay was in free drinks.

But the dark side of all this fun was that the trains from Kobe and Osaka to Kyoto generally stopped running at midnight. So, by the time the music stopped, the equipment was unplugged, and the sixty-pound keyboard was packed in its hard flight case, we had long since missed our only way back home – and, the trains didn't start running again until five o'clock AM. The next day was a work day, mind you, and there was nothing else to do but find some all-night *izakaya* or chain restaurant and continue eating and drinking until the metal-shuttered outdoor gates of the train stations opened.

When the clock approached 4:50 AM, the Kyoto contingent, Izah, Tsubo and I would walk toward the train for the ride back to Kyoto. But on the way back, our bandleader would duck quickly into a convenience store to grab one last beer for the hour-and-a-half train ride back to Kyoto. That happened after being up all day, playing music all night, and then plopping our sweaty asses down in an izakaya for the wee hour after-party. On the train to Kyoto, school children and *salarymen* (i.e. blue-suited businessmen) and other assorted early birds would be embarking on their regular Sunday morning routines. Picture uniformed school kids on a train at five o'clock on a Sunday morning sitting on the bench across from a messy-haired, tie-dyed Japanese guitar player and two weary-eyed foreigners. One was struggling to steady and keep a huge keyboard in a hard case from tipping over and the other asleep and snoring with an open beer in his hand.

After I got off at the last connecting train, it was time for the ten-minute walk to my house in North Kyoto while wheeling that sixty-pound keyboard in front of me. Surely the screech and grind of those noisy, self-installed casters that I bought from the Home Depot in Jersey City reached through every open window in my neighborhood of Matsugasaki, stealing the quiet of the early Sunday morning. I'd arrive home at 6:30 AM. My wife, Misa, would have a warm bath waiting for me because naturally I would have texted her about the entire odyssey. Those were the days.

That's how I spent my first summer, playing in Izah Blue and Hi-N-Tenzion reggae band in clubs in Kobe and Osaka, having a blast and getting into trouble, not much trouble, but often missing the trains. It was great fun. But great fun can be addictive and self-limiting. More often than not, great fun has a ceiling. Can great fun be a final goal? Not for me. It was clear that there were a few built-in defects in this phase of "*irieness.*" I was now part of something that, although brilliant and wonderful, might just prevent me from reaching a higher level of "*higher ites*" (higher heights) in my dream trajectory. There was the fact that there isn't much of a reggae scene in Japan. Sure, there were a few national festivals headlined by touring international bands, and a select handful of famous reggae artists in Japan that played them. But, it was a very small niche contingent of fans that went to reggae clubs to dance and have a good time, and only a fraction of them would buy reggae music. Radio play? No way. So, making the leap from "*nice'ing up de place*" in small clubs to becoming a successful moneymaking act with national reach seemed all but impossible. In my eyes, I thought a big part of the reason that this might not be the right vehicle for me was because all these songs were sung entirely in English – and, where were we? Oh yeah, in the middle of fucking Japan! Yes, the vibes were cool, and they preached allegiance to Jah Rastafari, goodness, positive energy, ganja and Rasta culture. But they really didn't reach out to anybody except that small niche of reggae lovers in Japan, or to those reggae fans from abroad that might somehow come across this music. Plus, as much as I liked the music, it was somewhat standard reggae to me in terms of production. Some of the grooves that this band's songs were built around we artfully copied from cool, produced DJ tracks that were traded around the world. On these downloadable grooves people of wide ranging talent and diverse origins sang their hearts out and popped them online in hopes of catching viral gold. I didn't feel the vibes were provocative and new. "*Kultcha I!*" was my unspoken calling in life! (a proud and loudly stated vocal proclamation in Jamaican vernacular: "I live and breathe culture") I needed to blend culture and create something new and *crucial*. Aside from that, the message being projected was not mine. My message was rooted in the Buddhist philosophy of self-empowerment, of Original Good. And yes, I strived to pay homage to and reflect on all the emotional entanglement of being lovesick, all the ups and downs and ups again of life. Plus, although I have always devoted a big chunk of my life towards feeling and supporting others, often sacrificing my own comfort to a fault, I am as narcissistic as any lead singer-songwriter and think that the world needs to hear the music that comes out of MY heart and MY mouth. After a few months Izah sensed this and was generous enough to let me open our shows with a set of me playing my stuff. An Izah Blue and Hi-N-Tenzion's evening's live concert would start with me singing some original songs and a few cover songs on acoustic guitar. Little by little, the band joined in on percussion, backing vocals and guitars until the full band was on stage. Then, with the pump primed, we would launch into Izah's songs and his music. It was a great formula and it worked well. Izah was open to letting me audition a few of my songs to the band for possible inclusion into our live sets.

One summer night during rehearsal in August 2011 at the Aiza Aloha English school, I tried to teach everybody a fast-paced ska-rock song. Inspired by positivity and my excitement about life, I'd written a song in New York called "Juvenation." I'd had some great jams with this runaway-roller-coaster, high-energy, high-speed-yet-soulful groove among some of my fellow musicians in the states. I thought it would add a little pep to the slow tempo sets we were playing in Kyoto. But, frankly, it was a bit too fast for the drummer, Rootz, to handle. Truthfully, at the time he wasn't all that skilled at being a rock solid, tight, Rhythm-Meister although he certainly had the vibe. His sense of meter reminded me of my teenage days in my basement in Tappan, New York. The "think too hard and you'll lose the beat" days. Izah told me a week later, very tactfully and sincerely, that Rootz had wondered or complained to him, "What's "Juvenation" song about?" He just didn't connect to the message of juvenation because it wasn't about or seemingly endorsed by Jah. Ironically, it really was since I was using juvenation to mean that we are already good, so we didn't need to be re-energized or rejuvenated. If only he would have dug deeper.

Six months after joining Izah Blue and Hi-N-Tenzion as a keyboard player, it was apparent that there just wasn't enough room for two lead singer-songwriters, two big egos, as big hearted as they were, to be in the same band. I was sent a long, beautifully written email from Izah explaining with the utmost sincerity how he thought maybe I needed to "pay my dues" a little bit before I could be the lead singer of a band, and how he had been paying his dues to get where he was. I was a little taken aback and thought, "well, I've been paying my dues for twenty years, often bleeding from it." I'd gone from being a percussion player in a reggae calypso band to a drummer in a quirky pop band to a singer in an industrial alt rock band in New York. On the spiritual side, I'd spent years visiting young men and families whose front doors had bullet holes in them from stray bullets of gang violence, encouraging them to overcome their difficulties through practicing Buddhism and helping them get their lives together. I'd driven a taxi cab for five years through the night until the morning light, singing at the top of my lungs to develop my voice and learn about melody and hooks from the radio. I'd come to Japan to pursue MY dream, not to sing somebody else's songs in their band.

We parted ways and there was a complete cessation of any communication between us. This true brethren and man of great spirit, talent and positivity that I had felt was not just my new best friend, but a big brother of sorts, had certainly put together a great thing. But, it was time for me to go. I would focus on my songs and my mission in Japan. In a few months, the universe would respond in kind, eventually giving me my band Kansai Rocks!. I wouldn't call us rivals, but the fact was there were now two reggae bands in Kyoto, Izah Blue and Hi-N-Tenzion and Kansai Rocks!. The synergy of testosterone and a lingering, childish, competitive side naturally led me to believe that Kansai Rocks! was the better of the two bands. We had a sound that was more pertinent to Japanese ears and Japanese themes – and, beyond that, some of my lyrics were in Japanese. We would "rise up" over the land like that red sun on the flag!

For the next year, Izah and I bounced off each other a few times, and positively. We were both foreigners and singer-songwriters. In Kyoto, frankly there weren't many of us and we were both making a living teaching English. Izah was the owner and charismatic teacher of an English school with a lot of kids and adult students while at the same time leading the life as a highly spirited, musical troubadour. I shared that calling. In terms of sustenance, I was beginning to build up a patchwork of teaching jobs in Japan, mostly at private schools. I had also started working at a university and taught privately at a few companies. I remember Izah asking me how I got so busy after less than a year in Japan. The answer had partly to do with the fact that I had a technical university degree, which looked better on a resume than not having one. Also, I'd like to think that it was the way I carried myself in a society governed by "proper" behavior and decorum. But the bulk of it, I am convinced was due to the fortune I'd developed in my life through my Buddhist practice.

Importantly, Izah and my friendship endured these differences. By my third year in Japan, I could sense that he was starting to burn out a little bit in what was now his fifth year in Japan. When your true calling is original music, it's difficult to teach, especially kids, let alone run an entire language school. Plus, there are all the temptations and distractions that a foreigner in Japan is confronted with, which I'll expand on later. Any weakness in the fabric of one's character can easily tear living in Japan. Izah was trying to sell his school and go back to Hawaii and reform Roots Natty Roots. His marriage also may not have survived much longer in Japan since his wife really wanted to go back to Hawaii, where they'd first met. He had developed a fun and powerful English teaching style by using music, culture and physical movement around the classroom. He was the first to walk past those floor-to-ceiling windows "like a robot," with kids in tow and loud music booming on the PA. He told me a few times, "Brethren, you're the only one who could really take over the school and understand what I've been doing. You're a musician."

The kids, and many of the adult students that he had put his heart and soul into teaching, would certainly quit the school if he sold it to the Indian school owners from Tokyo who had expressed interest in it or the low energy guy in Osaka with the unkempt hair and potbelly, who had recently gone through a traumatic divorce. Izah really took pride in and had deep affection for his students. Occasionally over the next year or so, he pitched the concept of me buying his school from him. But, I had a new professional life approaching stability that consisted of managing the Velco English private schools in three locations, along with my other 47 jobs. So, I would have nothing of it, that is, until I had an epiphany on my birthday, October 17, 2014, when Izah took me out for drinks.

We were at a *hyakuen* (¥100) *Standing Bar*, a tiny open-air watering hole in the busy Shijo Karasuma neighborhood of Kyoto. One hundred yen, or about a dollar, can buy you a small cup of beer. This place was always teeming with after-work locals and was a gathering place for foreigner English teachers who'd finished their evening classes. As we walked in through the tented entrance, we were greeted with inappropriately loud hellos, red-eyed smiling faces and boisterous handshakes from six or seven of his friends. There were guys from England, Italy, Australia, and America standing elbow to elbow around two tables covered with dozens of plastic beer cups that ranged from uncollected empties, to full ones waiting on-deck, to disgusting floating ashtrays. The flow of conversation sloshed back and forth between the two banks of "relief that we could put our guard down and speak colorfully without risk of offending anyone" and "the challenges, tribulations and meandering career paths of foreign English teachers in Kyoto." In slurring cacophony, they spilled their stories of triumph in education as well as in successful "bird hunting" (a British term for promiscuity). A year later, I would learn the phrase *furyou gaijin* refers to foreigners who are exploitive, womanizing assholes who just take up space and oxygen and don't contribute much to Japanese society. At one point in the evening, I found myself getting sucked into this mindless banter of little or no value. I nodded silently, staring at a fellow English teacher's face. I remember wondering whether someone in their mid-thirties is too young to have what I perceived as a cauliflower nose; a swollen, reddened pock-marked Winston Churchill badge of alcoholism. In my silence, I panned across this group of drunken Gaijin (foreigners) and observed what may have once-upon-a-time been an array of well-intentioned life paths. But now they all seemed to be in or approaching a dead-end. I saw what happens when an exciting and gutsy plan veers off the side of the road and tumbles down the mountainside, giggling and holding a bottle of booze to break the impact. I saw a shiny, heart-shaped, foil helium balloon two days after being left in the room after a party with the words "Welcome, Sensei!" sadly shriveling and barely able to stay afloat.

Once again, after the third or fourth birthday *kanpai* (cheers, as in making a toast), Izah pitched the idea of me buying his school. I had for a year-and-a-half always rejected the proposition as I thought I could not imagine myself teaching kids. I had no training, nor did I have the patience or desire to engage a group of kids. I'd been experiencing the delightful joy and love of raising my daughter, Mimi, who was in the middle of elementary school at the time. That was all the kid I needed. Another reason I'd paused was it would be an expensive investment to buy the business that I simply didn't want to take on. I had a good thing going and the momentum of my new two-year career was steadily building up steam. But the image of that triangular room with the sunlight beaming in on tropical plants, with the huge TV in the great location seemed like a rare jewel waiting for a craftsman to turn it into a priceless brooch. Plus, when you throw in the all-important premium feature of being able to handle loud noise at any time of day or night, that jewel exploded into rays of light dispelling any doubt that it was meant specifically for me. It could serve as my home base for both work and music. It would be the perfect place for me to further develop and enact the life play that I was writing and starring in.

My soul is anchored in the belief that everything happens for a reason, and that past, present and future all converge in a single moment. I was led to my school. I knew if I reached deeper inside myself that I could find the passion and desire to teach kids instead of just focusing on adults. I started to grasp the importance, the very necessity, of helping to shape the minds, hearts and communication skills of these little people who would lead our world into the future. I'd climbed steeper mountains. My spirit screamed to me, "Buy it! Buy it! Just do it and you'll figure out the rest."

CHAPTER 8

TRIANGULAR FISHBOWL

Almost all the city streets in Kyoto run east to west and north to south, forming a nearly unbroken, rectangular grid. This geometric design most believe derives from the practicality and protective energy harmonics (i.e. Feng Shui) of the old Chinese capital, formerly Peking, now Beijing. Wider streets are busy and noisy. I happen to live on Marutamachi Street, one of Kyoto's widest and busiest. A ring of small mountains encircling the city forms a basin that holds moisture in, making the weather unbearably hot and humid in July, August, and September. The winters are cold, wet and penetrating. If you can't stand the extreme swings of temperature, Osaka is an hour way by train and situated on a bay. You can live there comfortably and more cheaply if you don't mind sharing your home with 8,000,000 neighbors.

I spend most of the day and much of the night on the second floor of a four-story, small triangular building in the WAVE Center for Language and Culture. It's a small building with only four business tenants. A vertical four-story painted metal sign on its side, proudly marks that corner in English letters, "Yoshinari." The building owner, Yoshinari-san, or Tak, as he likes to be called, is a charming, well-cultured man, probably around 80-years-old. He's wealthy as can be and owns several buildings in Kyoto. Tak spent many years consulting with Disney and is a fabulous English speaker. There's a lot of large, black Mercedes in Kyoto but only one has a driver wearing a bright-red Mickey Mouse logoed sweater topped with a luxurious "do" of wavy white hair.

The building is in the Gosho Minami neighborhood, which in English means "the area to the south of the former Imperial Palace." It's the "former" Imperial Palace because, after around 1,000 years, the emperor and the entire seat of government relocated to Edo, now Tokyo. It's not a palace like a Cinderella's castle. Picture a meticulously groomed mini Central Park, a huge rectangular bastion of nature in the middle of the busy city. Wide gravel paths, arched bridges over coi ponds and shaded walkways connect small shrines to the preserved historic elegance of massive traditional structures that are still used for important state visits or as an abode when the Emperor or his family are in town. The atmosphere is cool, and oxygen charged, and that's because it is the actual domain of thousands upon thousands of trees. The real spirit of this safe enchanted forest can be felt when standing next to some of the old growth divine sculptures that have for several hundred years provided cool shade for generations of strolling members of the royal court and nobility.

A block away is my building. On the third floor is the Cat's Eye Neco (cat) Café where people come to spend money and "get their pet on." They play and cuddle with six or seven cats that make for delightful neighbors. Yuki chan, a rescued all-white charmer, is officially listed as the "Shop Manager" on the website. On the street level, Toriko, a tiny *oshare* (oh-shah-RAY= super cool designed), busy yakitori shop grills organic chicken and vegetable on skewers that include hearts, livers and anything else chicken, sending smoke into my school and everywhere else on warm summer nights. On the fourth floor is Honto (Really) Record Shop, a used LP and bookstore that sometimes has all night parties. The schools in the neighborhood are also top notch and, aside from the busy traffic, the streets are safe. The WAVE Center is the very definition of positive feng shui. It is a triangle pointing east towards the rising sun with the flow of air, light and positive energy through surrounding windows. On top of that it sits in the middle of a huge "power spot," as they say in Japan, and is a focused point of spiritual energy. In my first year of running the WAVE, I would look out the back window down onto an old, inactive elementary school. The three-story, L–shaped concrete building, unsophisticated and plain as could be, cast shadows on an unkempt, sandy sports field. I could have spit out my back window over a concrete wall into a stagnant, murky green concrete pond which back in the 1950s or 1960s was a pool frolicking with elementary school students. Until recently, the large courtyard/sports field was used often by local baseball teams for

The triangular Yoshinari Bldg.
Home to a grilled chicken yakitori shop,
a cat café, a used record and bookshop
and the WAVE Center, four completely
unrelated businesses.

practice, elderly adult Bocci ball clubs or an occasional community festival.

Three years ago, Kyoto City started demolishing the building for the construction of a brand-new school to accommodate the influx of young families moving into the area. However, construction stopped dead in its tracks as they began to uncover a slew of artifacts and ruins. What had been a busy, construction site, ground trembling with heavy machinery, turned into an all-out archaeological dig. Twenty to thirty people began spending the entire day on their hands and knees, carefully digging and chipping away at the ground, inch-by-inch, marking off the terrain with painted lines, measuring and taking pictures. White-haired scholarly men with glasses on the ends of their noses writing on clipboards replaced the burly construction workers and hardhats that had been there the year before. Every day I gazed out that window and saw them uncover old carved stone Buddhist statues or ceramic shards. They unearthed a large, ancient stone oven and meticulously arranged stone-lined wells along with several graves. It turned out there were two layers of history buried under the old school. The top level was the estate and grounds of the noble Takatsuji family. This property, being a mere five-minute walk to the palace and government buildings, indicates their once close association with the emperor. Underneath this, there were more ancient ruins from a temple from another era. Over the course of a year, there were often dignitaries touring the site and TV crews filming as they dug walking paths around old stone monuments jutting up from deep in the ground.

What's outside YOUR back window?
The construction of the new elementary
school was delayed due to the unearthing
of remnants of an old noble family estate
and an even older temple.

I entered the fenced off grounds for a one-day public information tour and was excited when I was told that there was a cluster of temples in this area. Ancient writings spoke of the one hundred temples near the palace that Hideyoshi Toyotomi, a general, samurai, and politician of the Sengoku period (1500's) had ordered erected. Old maps revealed that one of them, Sensho-ji temple, was directly under the Yoshinari building, under my school, at the very spot where I'm writing this book and all my songs. Directly beneath me lies the unexcavated remains of a temple, the bones and ashes and spirits of priests and scholars. I wonder if they could feel me as I'm screaming the lyrics of "NANANA" over- and-over again into a microphone at 1:00 am, trying to finish it so I can finally release the music video? In the Spring of 2018, after a year of being draped in concealing fencing and construction scaffolding, my backyard archaeological site is now the ultra-chic Gosho Higashi Elementary School.

Kyoto's history traces back over 1,200 years, which is partly why I find this place so fascinating. Established in 794, Kyoto was once Japan's capital, Heian-kyo. The preservation of ancient temples and shrines, as well as private houses and other public buildings, built in a style unique to Kyoto, show the depth of reverence the people have for their past. Countless festivals, ceremonies, and businesses also reflect Kyoto's desire to retain cultural traditions from its ancient past.

My neighborhood is lively, loaded with art galleries, boutiques, health clinics and hospitals, and two nearby universities. But mostly, it's full of restaurants. For a foodie from New York, there couldn't be a better neighborhood to spend most of my time in. Next to the casual Thai café is a Taiwanese noodle shop. There's Korean and Japanese Yakiniku BBQ shops, an Italian cafe where they grind their own homemade sausages, two Hawaiian burger shops, a gang of Izakayas, fine Japanese dining, Chinese, French, and German restaurants, an organic Farmers Market, and of course a Domino's Pizza and a 7-Eleven, all within a five-minute walk. And, thank the food gods for bringing us the Qué Pasa burrito shop a few years ago. It's a hot neighborhood that continues to attract many families and young professionals from Tokyo or elsewhere who can afford the booming real estate costs. You don't have to look too hard to find the scaffolding of old buildings under renovation or small, short-lived vacant lots where traditional Machiya-style houses recently stood, soon to be replaced by a luxury single-family home or small apartment building. Marutamachi Street is big enough to have a route number assigned to it on Google Maps. It's a loud wide road with four lanes, two in each direction. But the upside is that it gives me a front-row seat to watching some very cool national events, like the marathons, the Kyoto Men's Marathon, the Wheel Chair Marathon, and the Empress Cup Ekiden. The Ekiden is a female relay marathon with teams comprised of runners from Junior High School, High School, University and older runners that pass the baton, vying to bring the national trophy back to their home prefecture. Standing over the crowds of spectators and TV cameras from the 2nd floor windows in my school is like being in a climate-controlled VIP box with a fridge and a TV set, catching the closeups and highlights as they're broadcast in real time. There's also that life-changing Aoi-Matsuri cultural parade passing by my window on its way to Shimagamo and Kamigamo shrines that sparked this book.

I've come to realize that I can survive as a self-contented loner, or *ohitori sama*, and the fact I am a loner works both for and against me. On a weeknight, I can easily lose track of time and stay up way past what a normal working person should.

Without blinking, six hours may go by as I cut and paste and search for the perfect blend of beats to concoct a smooth dance feel for a new song,

The Procession of the Aoi Matsuri,
one of the three major festivals of Kyoto,
as seen from the front window of the WAVE

torturing myself over whether there should be a dash of rhythmic tension or a tablespoonful. I can wake up in the middle of the night and edit a music video on my iPhone or reformat a hard drive. I have no problems eating almost all meals by myself at home, school, restaurant or on a bench by the Kamogawa River a few minutes' walk away, so long as I have Wi-Fi and a charged battery. I've rediscovered the cultural benefits and the self-defined boundaries of living alone. For instance, laughing out loud at the top my lungs late at night until my stomach cramps as I watch late night talk show hosts "tear Trump to pieces" every night is permissible and unnoticed. After last New Year's, I spent three days in a row watching the entire 10-part Ken Burns Vietnam documentary series, frequently pausing and rewinding it to make sure I caught every word and image. I'm not sure if being an ohitori sama was always my true nature or if I just morphed into it by virtue of circumstance or by chasing my bliss. But, it works for me. If I wasn't living alone, I'd have never had the chance to watch that entire documentary series. Now I deeply understand that dark chapter in history and everything that led up to it. If I wasn't living alone, there is no way I could have pulled it all together to write a book.

I'm a teacher, which, by definition, means I'm in constant communication mode. Daily, I'm surrounded by people, engaging them, talking with them, or just listening to them. Sometimes I'm just coaching them in English, as in a student asking, "Jay Sensei, what do you say to someone who just told you their grandmother died? That's too bad?" But sometimes students just want to hear a non-Japanese perspective. And, sensing my genuine concern and interest in their lives, I have at times and when called for assumed the role of full-on life coach /spiritual advisor. During those times when there's no one in my classroom, there's still the sounds of footsteps and the talking moving shadows outside of my smoked glass door. The comings and goings of customers, employees and friends up and down the stairs to and from the businesses on the 3rd and 4th floors of my building. From my fishbowl glass classroom on the second floor, I look out the floor-to-ceiling windows with the same curiosity as those who look back at me. They may wonder what kind of crazy school I'm running when they see a foreigner in the afternoon keeping seven giggling kids in tow while they walk like robots to the beat of loud drum beats. Or, in the evening they hear the rhythmic drone of Buddhist chanting or even later, the rumbling reggae basslines and echoed live vocals.

My current theater of operations, my educational biosphere, at times seems like a clanging human pachinko machine with lights flashing and buzzers and bells sounding off constantly. I yearn for and treasure the sparse moments of solace. Through my headphones, through chanting, or maybe picking up a guitar and learning an old Rolling Stones song for a future solo performance, I can teleport myself away for short periods of time in between classes. A half-hour, semiconscious nap on the sofa in the afternoon is my sensory-deprivation tank therapy, my spirit soothed and floating in the warm, salt water and darkness. That is, until a screeching ambulance passes through the intersection outside my windows. Where is my Walden Pond?

Outside of a densely-packed checkerboard of one-hour to 90-minute lessons scribbled in coded blue, black, and red ink in my pocket planner, my schedule of free time bends and twists like smoke in the air, sometimes blown sideways by gusts of impulse. Hunger, the need for incense or a sudden onslaught of cabin fever may force me to grab my jacket, put my shoes on and go outside. It's a two-minute walk, traffic light permitting, to the convenience store around the corner. This trek alone entails a minimum of three hellos. As I walk past the window of my next-door neighbor, Takase the Barber Shop, there's a nod and smile to Hiro, the owner, and his 20- year-old-son Tsukasa, who used to be my student. Or, maybe I see their employee, the sharp and handsome Nakata-san, who, after three years of almost daily-eye contact still can barely find it in himself to smile back. Is it shyness or does he simply not like me? In the afternoon, there's a good chance I'll bump into one of my wild third or fourth grade students running down the sidewalk, my student and their friends clearly branded with their telltale blue Gosho Minami Elementary School hats and bright yellow, oversized school-commissioned backpacks. As I walk the fifty steps to the corner, I might have to dodge one of their moms zooming by on an electric motor assisted bike, or *Momma chari* (chariot). If I have the presence of mind and the physics are right, I might reach out and high-five the young toddler sibling who's strapped into the rear kid's seat as they pass by me. In this neighborhood everybody knows everybody, at least by face.

It's a universe away from the blissful anonymity of walking down a street in New York. But the good part is that it keeps me on my toes. As my wife, Misa, strictly told me when I first took over the school, "Don't do anything stupid! You'll ruin your reputation and lose all your students." I had a rough idea of what she meant by "stupid." She made me very aware that she knew some people in the area who didn't take the former owner/teacher of the school too seriously with his casual dress, reggae-decaled bike and loud manner. But I think "don't do anything stupid" more likely referred to public drunkenness, or worse. I have no problem on that end.

On the rare occasion of a contiguous morning and afternoon off, an early morning bike ride can turn into an all-day affair deep in the mountains around Kyoto. Abandoning my bike in the brush off the side of a narrow road I'll make my way through a tall, bamboo grove with solid, tubular shoots extending 70-feet into the sky, and too thick to wrap my hands around. Drawing in a breath of fresh air, I begin to follow the sound of a shallow fast-moving stream, the pristine upper reaches of the Kamogawa River near its spring source. Mysterious birds I can't see squawk from the brush and the summer scorch is cooled in the shaded canopy of old oak trees and cedars. A big, black hornet with a body the size of my thumb buzzes menacingly close to me. Sitting on a rock in the middle of the stream, I'll spend a few hours of solace swimming and communing with the Shinto gods that are present in all entities of nature. Breathing it all in, I chant a few minutes of appreciation at having found yet another precious chunk of paradise. I'm deep enough in the mountains that there's only one bar of intermittent cell phone signal at best. I've hiked way off the beaten track and if I fell and hit my head or drowned in the raging stream current caused by yesterday's downpour, I wouldn't be found for weeks, if at all. The practical engineer in me makes the decision to post a few pictures to Facebook with GPS on, just in case. I would want a proper funeral. Before it starts to get dark, I need to get back on my bike. I make one last sansho, or chant of *"Nam-myoho-renge-kyo"* three times, with hands clasped, and bow to the trees, rivers and birds. My reward is an effortless downslope glide along the twisting mountain roads, a full-hour ride back into Kyoto City.

It's nighttime now and I'm back in my fishbowl. Before I know it, it's 1:15 AM and I'm lying on the carpeted floor trying to sleep. Sometimes I need to stay here because I'm up late doing music and have early classes in the morning. The Yoshinari building doesn't lend itself to deep restful night sleeps. It's not supposed to. It's late and the yakitori chicken shop downstairs is having a typically booming Friday night. Coming up through the carpeted floor is the sound of a full house, and that means twelve people sitting in a line around the counter. I can picture Yosuke, the owner and chef, schmoozing the customers as he puts together amazing concoctions consisting of skewered cubes of chicken meat and organic Shishito peppers over the open charcoal fire. The sound of alternative rock 'n' roll blasting through suspended mini Bose speakers mixes with revelry and laughter. Yosuke is a charming man in his mid thirties with a two-year-old daughter. He's a little short and slight of build which aids him in moving about his low- ceiling, tiny cooking area. Plus, he's handsome, but even more so when he opens his mouth and smiles. He's livin' the life, having spent about ten years working as a cook in one of the many yakitori shops in the Pontocho section of Kyoto, which is basically, a long, narrow, cobblestoned, walking street with dozens of restaurants and little guest houses. It may very well be the best rendition of real Kyoto charm and allure. He spent ten years cooking there learning every culinary trick and then, three years ago, grabbed a lease on the first floor of the building.

Yosuke is busy all the time, or at least the times when he wants to keep the shop open. He's often fully booked for dinners and weekend lunches and can take days off and nights off as he wishes. The smoke of barbequed deliciousness billows out of an exhaust duct advertising the shop as it is blown around the neighborhood, clinging to the ground on rainy days. Like an olfactory bell it summons any noses within 100 feet to at least look in the windows to see what's going on in there. Some of that smoke idles its way up here. Aside from the noise and smoke, there couldn't be a better neighbor. And, although it tends to be expensive and eating chicken hearts, livers and other nondiscriminatory internal organs isn't really my thing, I've sat down there a few times. One time I was fortunate enough to meet an engineer who had become a student of mine for a few years until he was shipped off to his company's Shanghai branch. Yosuke's fortunes really changed about a year and a half ago when a famous Italian racehorse jockey, who now lives in Japan, had a TV crew follow him into the tiny restaurant to film him and his buddies celebrating his birthday. The jockey was from Tokyo and was being profiled on a segment of one of those ubiquitous television shows about food, dining, culture, and night life. After the 10-minute segment of these boys whooping it up aired nationally,

The windows of the WAVE school remain closed on a beautiful evening to keep out the lively sounds and enticing smoke from the grill of the busy restaurant below.

without a yen of advertising investment, this Toriko Yakitori shop became one of those places that when you're visiting Kyoto, you just need to experience.

Conversely, this late at night there's not a lot of noise coming out of the floor just above me where those seven cats are sleeping in the Cat's Eye Café. However, there's a good chance they're not sleeping very peacefully because on the fourth floor of this four-story building an all-night rave party is in full swing in the used LP and bookstore shop. Kazu and his buddies are at it again. The thud of a bass drum makes its way easily down to me on the second floor, the cats between us are getting a lot more decibels than I am. Maybe that's why they're so docile and just want to cuddle and purr in people's arms or lounge around all day. They're exhausted. The aggregation of sounds from the yakitori shop below combined with the pulsing low end sounds of dance music blasting from the fourth-floor party layer on top of the sounds coming from the busy road outside.

If the noise outside was continuous traffic, the miraculous nature of the human brain might somehow combine that noise to create white noise or gentle waves like the sounds that came out of those machines you could buy in the 1980s to help you sleep. But at 1:15 in the morning, it's more like one car every three or five seconds, followed by thirty-second red light reprieves. Lying here on this carpeted floor is tortuous. My brain is designed in such a way that it is constantly analyzing sound, tone, rhythm and the relationship between silence and sound. My neurons latch on to each vehicle and translates that audio into data, which is then analyzed into real, practical, useful conclusions. Like, "that's a small car coming from the west or there's two motorcycles coming from two different directions. One of them can't be more than a 250cc engine, the other one might be a hog and that truck is slowing down and likely making some kind of late-night delivery. Or, that sounds like a diesel, Benz, maybe a 2005 to 2010 SL 500 series." It's approaching two o'clock in the morning.

I remember reading in a Joseph Campbell book about the blue-light hour, that time in the middle of the night when the spirits are most active when the benevolent deities are embracing the land or comforting the sick in the depths of their sleep. Campbell took this notion originally from the French *l'heure bleue*, the blue hour, which is that very early morning hour when sky takes on a blue hue, considered a time of intrigue, confusion and mystery because it's neither day nor night. But for us sentient mortal beings, it's just too late. Four and a half hours of sleep just doesn't cut it. Maybe 20 years ago I'd have gotten away with it.

I don't necessarily have to wake up at 6:30 AM since I don't have to greet students here until nine o'clock. But when the morning traffic starts, things get very noisy outside. Even the early morning sun shines brightly into the fishbowl. Besides that, there's a lot to do. Cleaning up and turning the place from what appears to be a music studio crash pad into a school room takes time. There's YouTube videos to cue up and worksheets to be printed out in preparation for the kids' classes. On top of this, and for the sake of the kids as well as me, I need to squeeze in my morning ritual of chanting. On a good Saturday morning, I hope to get 30 to 45 minutes in, so I can greet the students not just with two darkened droopy bags under my eyes (a.k.a. in Japan, "Panda Face"), but with a bright shiny smile. And, that's just for Saturday morning classes. There are afternoon classes, too, as this is prime time for busy people who want to learn English. I lost my weekends when I moved to Japan. To me they're just another day that ends in y.

Life for me has now become a string of busy weeks that seem to flow into each other with ever-increasing, disorienting speed. There are the daily rituals of preparation and clean up, of frantically coming up with clever lesson plans and converting the room back and forth between "kids' mode" and "adult mode." Adult mode is when the couches are NOT tipped over on their sides (to prevent kids from jumping on them) and the plants and ceramics are NOT tucked safely away but are on full display on the tables. By now it has become an almost well-oiled chain of movement, a dance of motion and mental gymnastics to make every lesson count, or at least not fail.

But there are other rituals that precede these. One of these is carried out on a throne with one of my best buddies in life, my Washlet™. When I first came to Japan I spent two years teaching in schools in four different cities. Simultaneously I was working on a personal research project entitled, "The Quest for the Perfect Washlet™." A Washlet™ is an electronic bidet made by the Japanese toilet company, Toto, Ltd. But now the term is widely used when referring to any of the dozens of makes of these spritzy hygienic wonders.

After much bowl searching and deliberation I concluded the best one was in the men's room on the third floor of the Gran Via Hotel at Kyoto Station near the wedding salon. The epitome of luxury and comfort in an oversized dark wooden stall with a marble shelf and ample room for changing, this commode is pure elegance! As you enter the stall you are greeted by a perfectly timed slow opening of the lid triggered by motion sensor, backlit by a blue halo. Oversized and contoured, it's truly a one-size-fits-all. The array of buttons and fluid mechanics are the embodiment of high-end Japanese design and engineering. I am lucky to have my own washuretto at the WAVE. With a seat that warms up to perfect body temperature nanoseconds after butt contact and a wireless wall-mounted control panel, warm jets of water can be directed to wherever you need it most. It's pure refreshing morning glory. This treasure was gifted to me by a friend due to a minor factory defect that made it unsellable in the store. It's no Gran Via Hotel perch, or even a close second Maruzen Bookstore basement level commode, but I'm proud to say, I installed it myself. That engineering degree sure does come in handy sometimes. Plus, my tiny bathroom is at the point of the triangle in my room, so from that vortex with the door open, it's a straight shot from the throne to the huge flat screen TV on the other side of the school, a good 30-feet away. With an iPhone app that allows me to control my computer remotely, I can see "Morning Joe" or "The Late Show with Stephen Colbert" broadcasting on the Internet in high def perfect living-color booming over those studio monitors. All in all, I barely have a hint of homesickness. I am standing (well actually sitting) on the bow, and I'm the King of my World.

CHAPTER 9

DIVING
INTO THE FIRE

Ultimately, the decision to move to Japan was not born of a well-planned, meticulously executed project with a step-by-step timeline. It came on rather as a convergence of forces and subconscious prodding that were both sudden and long in the making. It was supposed to be a lengthy vacation, maybe five or six weeks, in the summer of 2010. My wife, Misa, and daughter, Mimi, were going to Japan for a long summer vacation so that my daughter could to get to know her Japanese grandparents who were failing in health. Both grandparents were in their mid-to-late-70s and hospitalized in Kyoto, Japan. This was considered a little early for this stage of decline since Japan is noted for its life-extending, healthy lifestyles and a great health care system. It was also a chance for Mimi to connect to her Japanese roots to get to know Obaachan and Ojiichan before they passed away, and for my wife to see her old friends.

I would stay in New York and hold down the fort. I was one of six national salesmen for M Management, which owned a group of companies that provided logistical services and owned warehouses all over the U.S. that were leased out for a variety of businesses. But, what was most promising, and exciting, was that I was now a key part of their latest venture, a fast-growing company called Mana Contemporary that had opened fine art management warehouses and provided art packing, transportation, and exhibition services. In other words, I had plenty to keep me busy, and besides, there were bills to pay. So, I stayed in our Jersey City penthouse with our fireplace, Manhattan skyline view, and our precious white Shih Tzu, Dépêche.

That summer, I did manage to escape to Japan for ten days to spend time with everybody. Although we were supposed to return together to New York, we decided it would be better for them to stay in Kyoto a little while longer since the clock was ticking on my in-law's health and it was important for them to be together. Back in New Jersey, my mother was also on her last legs. Well, she wasn't really on her last legs, as they didn't work anymore. She spent her last few years propped up all day in an elderly care home hospital bed watching TV, being spoon-fed.

Being an international couple and family, my wife and I had long discussed the possibility of eventually moving to Japan to take the next step toward further fulfillment of our mission. It was our true desire to be global citizens, although I wasn't sure exactly how or when this would happen. However, as summer turned into fall and my family was still in Japan, it soon became apparent that they weren't coming back. There I was, still slugging it out alone in New York City living alone with Dépêche. I skyped with Mimi and Misa a few times a week, and I could sense they were getting more comfortable with staying in Kyoto. Although there was one time when I got a surprise late night Skype call that caught a four-year-old Mimi at the tail end of a meltdown that had started minutes before. She was crying inconsolably to me and complaining, "Daddy, everybody's Japanese here!" I can only hope that it had something to do with her missing the daily presence of her daddy. Around Halloween, after a somewhat brief phone call with them, and without much afterthought but with complete confidence, I told my company that I would be leaving and moving to Japan the following year.

I wouldn't call the job I was leaving a dream job, but it was getting there. It defied all logic to leave a company growing as fast as this one was. I was deeply involved in art. I had clients I'd snagged through years of cold calls, such as the Guggenheim Museum and many important galleries and art collectors all over the U.S. But I trusted the universe and this innate feeling welling up inside that said, "it's time to grab life by the neck and make an important change." I know that sometimes you stick said neck out on the chopping board and risk getting your head cut off to break through the confines of mediocrity and accomplish something great. Throwing away a career, leaving my mother (who was to die later that year), and saying goodbye to my family and friends to go to Japan just seemed like the right thing to do. It would also be a good chance for me to try to rehab a difficult intercultural marriage. Also, aside from the new scenery and good food, I thought this would be the spark to reignite my dream. Maybe I could finally finish the songs I'd started years ago and write the music that needed to be written. Now, from a solid concrete launching pad reinforced with the steel bars of a deeply ingrained life mission and a confident singing voice, that rocket might just lift off and break orbit. This would be one, last ditch, serious effort to try and make it happen. An international band from Kyoto, Japan would be a new twist. What a plan! Kansai Rocks! I had two months to basically pack up everything, decide what to take to Japan and what to leave in my brother's garage in Mapleshade, New Jersey. I sold one car and gave the other one to my brother (it was my mom's anyway.) I gave away power tools to friends, went to goodbye parties, and obsessively chanted that all of this would work out. I held my breath, and on that January 26, 2011, boarded the plane for Tokyo, and "dove into the fire."

There's a Japanese phrase, *taiki-bansei*, which basically means "late blooming flowers are the most beautiful of all." When I first heard it, I believed it. Why shouldn't I? I had become a father in my 40s to a beautiful girl which seemed well-placed by my timeline standard. I sincerely believed that the dream of my music having a genuine impact on culture would blossom, not in the spring of my life, or in the summer, but in its fall. *Momoji*, or Japanese maple leaves, are every bit as iconic of Japan's beauty as *sakura*, or cherry blossoms. The almost mandatory ritual of *Koyo* or Autumn foliage watching is planned around the flows of dark green to red, orange, and yellow as they traverse the long, narrow country from northeast to southwest and from mountains to lower grades. The planning of these romantic hikes or family picnics is often aided by smartphone apps that track in real time the percentage of peak colors at a specific temple or famous park. When the sunlight catches even a single tree proudly presenting thousands of its tiny-fingered red and orange leaves in gradually iridescent gradience across the span of its canopy, you can't help but experience a series of audible "wows." It's nothing short of miraculous and is the horticultural payoff for having lived a good life. It's midlife divinity projecting wisdom and pride out into the universe as contrasted with the short-lived, fragile euphoria of a teenaged cherry blossom. The red momoji basking in its incredible, beauteous glory in the crisp autumn air surely does not think, "oh no, I'm gonna die soon'" or "it's all downhill from here" or "if only I was a young cherry blossom." I concur. Now is my time.

Mimi - "Where's that funny face, that makes me laugh and puts things into place..." "Sway" - Kansai Rocks! *Changing Poison into Medicine*

Now, I am here by myself in Kyoto. That's right. By myself in Kyoto. Misa and Mimi, who's now eleven, moved to Tokyo months ago. It was partly due to Mimi's pursuit of a modeling career. *Hafu* (half-Japanese) which, I believe, is a mildly derogatory term for culturally mixed children, is a hot item in modeling and entertainment agencies. There's genetic-based foreigner envy that many Japanese have, this being an almost completely homogeneous society. A little new spice in the stew makes you stand out. Anything different from the stereotypical Asian look works to one's advantage. It may take the form of natural, dirty-blonde hair from a German father or curly hair with a kink to it because one's parent is from Africa (usually Daddy). Maybe it's a darker complexion, muscular legs and a jutting butt like it is with my student Nobuko's grandsons who have a Dominican father. There's anything ranging from mild intrigue, to fascination, to snide envy for anyone who is not pure-bred Japanese. Combining this with a bit of New York hubris and rhythmic DNA from her father, my daughter, Mimichan, has all the ingredients required to make it as a successful soon-to-be-teenage "talent"- and little sister can dance!

So, day by day, and week by week I live a busy new life trying to clutch the still unfamiliar handle of complete freedom with my schedule, at least as far as the little margins of free time I have in between my work allow me. I'm running a business (i.e., the school that I bought) and work at a university which I love. I religiously watch Rachel Maddow, have binge watched six seasons of Breaking Bad in two months and try to make sense of America under Trump with eyes from abroad. I buffer loneliness with intense Buddhist practice, attend meetings to encourage others, give speeches, and drink Chu-hai to soften my solitary nights. Based on Shochu, which is made from fermented barley and with up to nine percent alcohol content, Chu-hai is carbonated and flavored with the fruit of your choice. Life in my seventh year has become more intensely colorful and deeply rooted than it was for the first few years when I was simply an employed teacher at a school. Now I work for myself and my fortune rises and falls by my own merit. I make proposals, hire people and even clean toilets regularly in my school.

Regarding Japanese culture, I now have a better grasp on its many appendages which, at first glance, seemed wildly flailing and at odds with each other. Now as I delve deeply into the old and new it's all starting to make perfect sense to me. I have come to know many Japanese bands, mostly by watching them on YouTube or on TV. I've gawked at videos by the E-girls and J Soul Brothers and other girl bands and boy bands, trying with limited success to extract and distill the hidden gems of talent and music or at least revel in and appreciate the projected images of beauty and sexy youth.

I've fallen in love with K-pop band 2NE1 (pronounced two en ee one) who took Japan and the world by storm a few years ago, and were even on commercials in the U.S. I've explored traditional Japanese arts and spent hours silently walking through gardens and temples. I've eaten sculpted specs of food off handmade earthen kiln-fired rectangles and drank exotic, rice-derived vintages from Tiffany-style glasses that overflow into wood boxes. My life perspective morphs like a cumulonimbus cloud, a thunderhead forming over the dangerous but heavenly sea of my horizon. Below the surface, the churning and shifting tides splash against my insides. I feel every drop as it seems to draw me deeper and deeper inside myself to a truth that is screaming to reveal itself. It is as painful as it is blissful. Somehow my Buddhist practice turns each difficulty into another log thrown on my fire, making my spirit burn brighter and hotter than ever before. It's a conflagration consuming the obstacles that try their best to block my path forward. I'm told you can hear that in my music.

Maybe it's the paradox of loneliness and freedom that helps me understand the contradictions and contrasts in Japanese society. Or perhaps it's the juxtaposition of being a language teacher and musician, or the anomaly of being a foreigner lost in an exotic land and a respected, important member of the local Japanese and international community. Maybe I feel the enigma of modern-day Kyoto because I'm a family man and single man at the same time, (although the jury's still out on whether that can co-exist). Or, maybe I see the quirky contrasts here because I have absolute confidence in what I'm doing and believe in its viability while questioning if it's a feasible path for me. Should I have tried to work full-time at a university? No effin' way! For whatever reason, these paradoxes stretch my heart like the skin over a drum to make that amazing resonant tone that only can come from a dead animal, howling and purring at the same time. Will this all work or will it come crashing down? Maybe, maybe not. [Watch at: https://bit.ly/lovesicinkyoto9]

MAYBE MAYBE NOT

By Jay Crystall © 2015 Jay Crystall

Wanna get it right...Wanna slow down time
Wanna drink some wine. Wanna pick your mind

Wanna drop a few (kg) Wanna be with you
Wanna find that groove...w'maybe someone new

Wanna sleep outside...Wanna come inside
Wanna see you cry (just once). Wanna live the life
Wanna shine some light. Wanna do what's right
And I feel just fine...Livin' in this mind...livin' in this time

So...Are you mad at me ...?
I'll give you everything...Maybe, Maybe Not

We got love...all we need and there's blood...we all must bleed
Maybe, Maybe. Maybe Not

CHAPTER 10

IT'S LIKE
PARIS IN THE 1920s

I was sitting in a café with my friend Atticus, originally from Texas, who runs his newly-born startup in Kyoto, *Kyoto VR* (Virtual Reality). We first met five years ago at a Starbucks where he interviewed me for a job that I saw posted online. Ten minutes after our first handshake, he hired me on the spot to join his teaching team at a soon-to-be-launched English immersion program for kids, held Saturdays at Seibo Elementary School, an expensive Catholic school in the Fushimi Ward of South Kyoto City.

I never got used to waking up at 5:30 AM to make it to the mandatory staff meeting before spending an entire day teaching English to kids. Truth be told, these kids weren't all that excited to be spending their entire Saturday at school in uniform either. Their fidgetiness also seemed to particularly erupt weekly in my class. It was my class that had a few of these hyperactive sugar-jacked ADHD devils buzzing around the hallways and classrooms after lunch, to the extent that they had to be physically restrained by an administrator or nun passing by in the hallway. This was the furthest thing from a dream job for me, as I'm sure it was for Atticus, who was Director of this budding and short-lived SEED Immersion program. But the pay was okay, and I learned a few things.

It was at Seibo that I was first exposed to using interactive games and physical movement in my instruction, including yoga and sports to make English more interesting and palatable for the kids – and, who was I kidding?! It was the first time I had ever stood in a classroom to teach kids, in any subject, in any country! Many of my fellow teachers had certifications in either teaching English as a Second Language (ESL) or children's education, or both, the acronyms of which escape me as they never played into my game plan. All except me had at least a modicum of a track record and some experience in teaching kids. I couldn't have been greener. I just needed to make some money and couldn't turn down a $200 Saturday daytime gig.

Did it help me change myself in ways previously unforeseen, develop new capabilities and force me to address things that I would have otherwise neglected? Hmm.... sort of, kind of, maybe. Was the experience priceless? Yes! Within the first four hours, I'd lost my pure-as-fresh-fallen-snow child educator's "virginity" in that I had my first dramatic and frustrating encounters with kids who were "on the Spectrum." Nobody ever mentioned these kids' conditions to me, not like I would have known what being "on" or "off it" meant. The strings of my karma had lowered me into this Twilight Zone shoebox diorama every Saturday morning at 6:45 AM. The sound of short, squeaky footsteps from feet squeezed into tiny plastic slippers echoed in the immaculate, marble hallways as I walked by statues of Mother Mary to teach under the watchful eyes of Jesus on the crucifix staring down on me. "What movie am I in?" I'd thought. Was I really in Japan? Had I truly come to Kyoto to experience this?"

I remember late on a Friday night searching for a glorious cloud image. It would be the background over which I would type the Lord's Prayer and make it build line by line, into the perfect PowerPoint animation for our morning kickoff prayer. I lasted about six months, which was one month longer than my boss, the director, Atticus, did.

Two or three years later, we were sitting in an ultrahip, high-end artisanal coffee shop, the kind of café I would never normally go to. To me, Starbucks Ethiopian Medium Roast or Guatemala Antigua (with notes of chocolate and spice) are about as far into the exotic coffee world as I need to delve. I'm too busy to devote time to sipping coffee. To me, life is everything that happens in between sipping cups of coffee. In the mornings I usually just drop a spoon and a half of instant coffee into a cup with one of those half pixie sticks of sugar and milk and I'm good to go. But there is a thriving "roasted on the premises" coffee scene in Kyoto. This specific coffee *labo* (lab) was tiny and resembled a concrete-walled-and-floored bunker with a few metallic and glass tube coffee percolating drippers (or whatever the %#$#^ they are called) placed along one wall. On the small counter there were four or five

Specials of the Day in large glass jars, elegantly spilled onto cloth around each jar for a closer bean inspection experience. As with most of these *Oshare* or completely hip, minimalist designed joints you get the feeling that you are paying for the atmosphere, and complete sensory experience, inasmuch as you are paying for the actual product. In the confines of these kinds of establishments which could be boutiques, gourmet incense shops, handbag stores, or more, you are immersed in the "better world" of refined modern Japanese cultural elegance that epitomizes their obsession with and pride in maintaining their pedigree amidst their Pacific rim neighbors. Soft spoken, super knowledgeable, almost bilingual baristas explain in poetic, lilting voices the characteristics of what you are about to pay 1,300 yen ($12) to drink. Your choice is served in a simple white runt of a coffee cup on a saucer that looks like it could have been an espresso demitasse, enlarged 110% and rounded in Photoshop.

As I opted out of the mouse-sized sliver of the cake selection of the day, I was all but nudged in the ribs by Atticus when I was about to ask for milk. Shame on me for even thinking about tainting this prized brew with milk! Asking for sugar would have surely been grounds for deportation. Atticus explained that drinking the sediment on the bottom of the cup is optional. I'll admit it was delicious. However, I'm a gulper and a quick $12 "coffeegasm" did not make or break my afternoon. But what did I know? I must be cut from a different cloth. I'm the same way with craft artisanal beers. It's not that I don't get it. I certainly do have a sensitive, discerning palate and enlightened nostrils appreciative of the finer things in life. I simply don't live or die on the merits of certain liquids. I'm much more attentive to food and even more so to the timbre and finer details of the human voices around me. My fine-tuned gaze and sensory analysis is much better at gauging the mood and motivation of people I'm listening and talking to and wondering if they are truly happy, or maybe gay. I ponder on what I can say to lift them up or make them laugh. But, sometimes I'm just feigning attentiveness when I'm, in truth, running a new melody I came up with by myself and wondering if I'd stolen any part of it from another song. I was never invited back to any of Atticus' craft beer parties.

So, there we were at this wonderful, culturally important bastion of caffeinated sophistication and culture, way outside my orbit, talking. (BTW, this coffee labo/museum was so "in" that it is now out of business. It's been replaced by a tiny, concrete-walled, concrete-floored vintage clothing store.) Animated, Atticus leaned toward me and exclaimed, "Kyoto is like Paris in the 1920s!"

For a year this profound insightful comparison continued to ring in me like a bell. His comment mirrored what I recently heard from a Frenchman named Yannick. He uttered it to me with that same glint in his eye, shortly after meeting him a few months ago. That was moments after he finished performing and conducting an amazing 10-person instrumental multiscreen video projected, poetry performance art piece that left all of us in the audience speechless. I wonder which one of them said it first. My guess is the French guy. They are both right. This is Kyoto, a petri-dish of international mixing with Japanese from all over Japan who scoff at and have opted out of the more economically sane opportunities in Osaka and Tokyo. These wayfarers "get" that there is something special happening in Kyoto. From roots that go back a thousand years, new buds of culture and technology are bursting out continuously, fertilized by a dozen or more universities, drenched in the sunny rays of worldwide tourist cash.

Jay and Atticus painting the town gray as they attend a musical arts performance piece.

There's quite a cool freak show in Kyoto. There are plenty of examples of foreigners who have "made it." When I slip into comparing myself with them and ponder why I work six or seven days and nights a week, I catch myself and remember it has been less than seven years since I uprooted myself from a good job in fine art management and came to Kyoto. I mean, fully uprooted myself. From a career perspective, I came here with a sack of complimentary but disjointed mini-careers tied together to the end of a stick with zero Japanese language skills. I'm not doing badly.

I'm both the slave and the slave master, running my own business. I'm able to support myself and my family of three in two separate cities in my new home country while impacting dozens if not hundreds of lives a year. And, my music? Well, it's where it's never been before in my life. There are people I have never met and will likely never meet sending me messages on Facebook and YouTube asking, "When are you coming to Brazil to perform?" or "Love it…AWESOME!!!!" But in terms of financial return on investment, I might make as much busking in the Union Square subway station in New York City as I do when I play solo live. However, just as the rocket ship must attain certain thrust after the countdown before the mechanical braces release it from the launching pad, just as David had to swing his sling several revolutions over his head before releasing that rock giving that fatal blow to Goliath's forehead, I have been building momentum and sheer thrust in preparation for this moment. I live and feel the exhilaration of this realization every day. Sometimes the pragmatic, engineering side of my mind pokes fun at the idealistic "yes, you certainly can chase and achieve your dreams" side. In moments of weakness words like "unrealistic" and "denial" flash in LED across my screen. On top of that, Misa's dissatisfaction that her soon-to-be ex-husband has not "made it" yet, something she had banked on, has all but frayed the strands on the knot we tied twenty years ago. But, I trust my own instincts above all and a slacker dreamer doesn't own a business, teach breast cancer researchers, work at a prestigious university, and speak in simple Japanese to encourage people at a Buddhist meeting on a Saturday night. I address reality millimeter by millimeter, 97.1% of the time like my life depended on it. I'm certain I'm not in denial of being in denial. So, despite the colossal forces weighing me down, trying their hardest to prevent me from "breaking orbit" of being an amateur, unpaid musician, I am stoked to the core and utterly convinced that millions of ears are waiting for me and that my mission of impacting people's lives with my music is within reach. As I mentioned, I'm a late bloomer. What I'm doing now seems to be the best script for the right movie I'm starring in, and I'm just getting to the good part. Besides, I feel I have achieved a much broader, clearer understanding of what it takes to penetrate ears and souls with sound and words. I was not born with the supernatural talent of Prince and I didn't have Joseph

Jackson screaming at and threatening me and my brothers to sing the right notes and dance in synch. But, at long last, I have developed something truly special in terms of ability. Plus, if I may be so bold, my songs sometimes make me cry they are so good. I'm finally a contender. I was reminded of that when I recently spent time with Robert Yellin at his ceramic gallery, which doubles as his home, in a gorgeous, old neighborhood near the Ginkaku-ji Zen temple. An American who's lived in Kyoto since 1984, Robert owns and runs Robert Yellin Yakimono Gallery and has been a contributing writer to several arts magazines and newspapers throughout Japan, as referenced in the introduction. His book, *Yakimono Sanka*, was published in English under the title, *Ode to Potter, Sake Cups and Flasks*. In 2012 he also hosted a television segment on Japanese artists for the Ministry of Foreign Affairs of Japan's series, *Japan: Fascinating Diversity.*

Riding my bike through the narrow streets, I got lost but felt embraced by and at ease with the relaxed, decidedly non-urban vibe of this modest but super-high-priced real estate neighborhood. It sits in the shadow of the Ginkaku-ji temple and the Atago Mountains (which are really foothills) that delineate the east border of Kyoto. From this neighborhood, there are narrow, winding, paved and unpaved footpaths that double as roads clawing their way treacherously up into a wooded hillside. Packed on the hillside are numerous temples, tiny, densely-packed monument graveyards, bamboo groves, and a few architecturally magnificent houses in an area most certainly shared by some *inoshishi* (wild boar) and monkeys. All this is located within the city limits. In a city of 1.5 million residents, this area isn't even considered the outskirts of Kyoto,

Robert's house is located down a hill near the poetically gorgeous Philosopher's Path, a shallow concrete-channeled stream bounded on both sides by unending lines of old cherry trees and walking paths with an occasional stone bench. The gentle gurgle of the stream is occasionally accompanied by the wispy, simple melody of a *shakuhachi*, or traditional Japanese bamboo flute player. There are cafés, ice cream and traditional sweets shops and trinket (in Yiddish "chachke") shops teaming with tourists during the daytime, especially in the spring Sakura season.

That day, realizing I was lost, I backtracked through the directions in my iPhone and wound up riding down a long dead-end street. Robert's house was at that dead end. Next to his stone wall, there were approximately 100 steps leading up and away from his property to the back entrance of the huge temple grounds of Ginkaku-ji Temple. This entrance was free and accessible until "some asshole bought the property and built a multi-million-dollar estate up there," blocking the steps at the top. There must have been some serious palm-greasing or connections to permit that lot to be developed. About a hundred yards away from me, I saw someone on his knees interacting with a cat that didn't fit the profile and aura of the typical old money Kyoto residents that live there. I approached this man with his long, grey hair and beige cat, and though I'd only seen him once before, this was unmistakably Robert Yellin. Before I could even stop and get off my bike to greet him, I didn't hear the anticipated "did you find me okay," "how's it going," or "*hisashiburi.*" (Japanese for "long time no see.") Instead, he was waving his hands in the air, calling out enthusiastically, "Hey, man, I really like what you're doing," referring to two or three songs I'd put on YouTube. "I can feel the passion and it's pure and rare these days," he raved.

Robert has the glow of someone who is living exactly how he was meant to live. There's a sense of "having arrived" that exudes from his smile and open attitude. Judging from his long, wavy, wiry gray hair he's also in the autumn of his life. I don't know much of his underlying story yet, but I do know he's one of the leading ceramics specialists in Japan, and he's a foreigner. I often see him on Facebook exploring long inactive earthen walk-in kilns in remote areas of Japan or consulted for a lecture or TV show on Japanese ceramics. It was very refreshing to hang with an American hippie, leave my "proper foreigner decorum in Japan" filter off and not be limited to simple words that are understandable to non-native English as a Second Language (ESL) - ers.

Robert invited me to his home a few months after we'd first met at that 10-piece performance, art event that I'd attended with Atticus. We'd kept in touch via Facebook. He'd posted a video of a floating, spiraling, dancing leaf pirouetting in his traditional Japanese garden, drifting on air currents and refusing to fall to the ground. When I first saw the 30 second thumbnailed Facebook video, it grabbed me and screamed for me to include it in a video for my song called SPIN, which was inspired by the spinning ceremonial dancing of Persian Whirling Dervishes. I thought it would be perfect. When I messaged the idea to him, he quickly replied, "what do you know about ceramics?" and "come on over."

At first, I simply felt privileged to be standing in his living room, or walk-through gallery in his low ceiling, wooden tatami mat, traditional *tsukiya-style house*, where tourists and collectors from all over the world came to purchase expensive ceramic pieces ranging from those crafted in ancient eras to modern sculptures. Robert's ceramics collection consisted of dozens of simple and oddly shaped pieces. Many of them were vases arranged on shelves or rectangular, color-streaked, flat pieces that hung on the walls. Some were functional, such as small tea cups, tea bowls or vases, but some were delicate, irregularly shaped sculptures. Everything was one-of-a-kind and perfectly imperfect; a universe away from the matching symmetry of mass production.

As I was standing there holding some of these finer pieces, I began to sense the depth and profundity of this juncture in space and time. I said to Robert that standing amidst those works, I could sense the spirit and feel the presence of the artists. These were crafted by artists from the Heian Period (794-1185AD) up to modern, living artists who put their souls and life's aesthetic into the pieces. His eyes lit up as he took this realization up to the higher ionosphere, above my stratosphere. He said, "Think about it, you can sense the flow of history, the sense of struggle and the human passion to create." He held a tea bowl into the air and explained with a voice of absolute and serious passion that the very clay from which this was made was formed millions of years ago and may have been harvested by the artists or their ancestors. The conditions under which some of these artists expressed themselves, he noted, are manifested in these truly original, enduring but fragile creations. When this wonder-struck 20-minute-old student pulled out my iPhone to ask him if he'd seen a recent BBC documentary entitled "The *Art of Japanese Living (2017)* he immediately recognized a black, irregularly shaped tea bowl that was used as a thumbnail for the YouTube video. "That's *Chōjirō!*" he exclaimed with the intensity of Dr. Frankenstein screaming, "It's alive! It's alive!" "That's punk rock, man! Fuckin' punk rock!" He explained that while other potters in Kyoto in the 1500s were designing tea bowls, cups and vases with delicate, muted and sensitive color combinations, this Raku pottery rebel had the audacity to mold his creations in bold, unrepentant black. Pure fucking punk rock!

Being a musician and audiophile to the core and obsessive dissector of all aspects and genres of music, I loved Robert's analogy. My wedding ceremony featured those previously mentioned bouncy bopping French horn lines of *Mozart's Horn Concerto No. 4 in E flat* which was played after I kissed my bride. It transitioned to "Olin Arageed," a 2,000-year-old Persian wedding song played on a tar, which is a guitar's great-great Middle Eastern granddaddy. The meditative 16-minute instrumental song was played entirely by the now-deceased Hamza El Din, who stomped his bare feet on the ground while playing the frame drum to form a rhythm track. Thank the gods I saw him live at Radio City before he died. My spirit, my personality and very outlook on life have been informed by music. So, there I was tripping out as Robert introduced me to the underlying, meaningful world of pottery. It broke new ground in my appreciation for aesthetics, and reinforced my deeply held belief that the past, present and future all meet in singular life moments. What a revelation that the complete, cyclical nature of time and the unity of all things and energy (cue Superstring Theory) could be expressed by human fingers, water and earth. That's Japanese ceramics. I've never again held a ceramic cup in the same way.

Japan has other influential art forms, including *shodo* (calligraphy). I am so fortunate to have a great friend, a spiritual sister, Ai Takaoka, as an English student. She takes her calligraphy art performances to New York and Europe, performing in full kimono to the beat of super cool music. Ai San is viscerally driven to express the power and passion of living and give her message of encouragement in dripping Kanji and English, with themes such as "Precious Now" and "Eternal Gratitude" (visit https://bit.ly/lovesicinkyoto10). There are several traditional Japanese art forms and practices that retain pure, unscathed orthodoxy. There are some that carefully and perfectly ingest the times and transform into new disciplines. Japan's architectural forms can often be precise and strictly minimalist, and oh so cool. From an ultramodern capsule hotel in Tokyo where you lie in a climate-controlled pod to an office reception area in a small Kyoto tech company, the spaces are awe-inspiring. The art of making kimonos and dyeing the finest, most amazing, vibrantly patterned high-end silks by hand is centuries old. Whenever I look at them, I'm reminded of a Buddhist saying that I first heard in New York City 25 years ago, "a blue deeper than the blue of the Indigo plant itself." It comes from the sixth-century Chinese Buddhist teacher, T'ien-t'ai and refers to how when you repeatedly dye something in the indigo dye, it becomes a richer color than the original color of the plant. This is likened to how a disciple (e.g. me) can study and reply to a mentor (e.g., Daisaku Ikeda) and, in ways specific to my life's mission, surpass him.

To me, these concepts seem a million miles away from Western cultural pathways and are truly and uniquely Japanese. Now I'm here. It's my home. I'm extending my upended Earthly roots into the soil of the land that, isolated by vast stretches of wild ocean currents and largely left to its own devices (with a nod to ancient Chinese heritage) has simultaneously intrigued and baffled the rest of the world with its success, beauty and prosperity. It is perfectly fitting that I devote the rest of my life to channeling this energy and draw the world's ears and eyes to Japan, not for profit, not to boost the tourism industry (they don't need me for that) but to inform and color western perceptions for their own sake. It's my best hope to help infuse the rest of the world with this sense, and at the same time to breathe a little American oomph and oxygen into the fiery Japanese spirit.

CHAPTER 11

SAKURA ONSEN
AND THE SNOW MONKEY

There's a famous Japanese haiku by Kobayahsi Issa, *"What a strange thing! To be alive under the cherry blossoms."* It's the peak of *sakura* season in Kyoto but it's still March. It seems to come earlier every year. Could this be a brighter side of Global Warming? Today is Wednesday March 28th, and the cherry blossoms are at 80% full bloom in Kyoto. This weekend, the season's beautiful pink and white cherry blossoms are predicted to be in 100% full bloom. How do I know? Because curiosity-driven Japanese scientists quantify nature's complex and unknowable mystical algorithms into a city-by-city report on the evening news. There must be ten different kinds of cherry trees or *sakura* in Kyoto and most Japanese seem able to distinguish between them. My favorite is the *yanagi*, or weeping willow blooms, that drape down and envelope anyone beneath them in pure, dark pink ecstasy. Cherry trees are everywhere, as ubiquitous as vending machines. But their presence goes more-or-less unnoticed except for the few highly anticipated weeks of breathtaking blossoming, the cherished sakura season in Japan. Planted along rivers and sidewalks, delineating paths in parks and in perfectly designed clusters on the grounds of shrines and temples, they are often illuminated at night. If you're one of those families who had parents or grandparents that were smart enough to plant sakura decades ago in your backyard, you may be privileged to have your own private *Hanami*, or cherry blossom picnic.

Everyone in every town and city in Japan has their favorite *Hanami* location where they perform this annual ritual of carefree delight. It may take the form of a leisurely stroll or a slow drive with the windows open. But it's also customary to move around year to year, checking out previously unvisited places and doing the circuit. ("Maybe this year in Kyoto it's Maruyama Park" or "How about we spend the day at a picnic table in the Asahi Beer tent at Hirano Shrine picking the fallen delicate petals out of plastic cups of *nama biru* (draft beer) and eating *yakisoba* noodles?") In the popular public areas of parks and riverbanks, a few scouting souls come out the night before to reserve space for their late-sleeping friends. The grounds are usually covered by blue, tear-proof plastic sheets, or what we call tarps in America. People put these shiny blue industrial grade sheets down solely to keep their butts off the ground and their food away from any foraging critters. They're not cozy and soft like a picnic blanket. They are employed for strict enforcement of a "no crawl zone" separating humans and their food from the wild realm of ants, bug turds and spiders. True to form, no human's

Hanami, or cherry blossom, picnic (Photos: C. Lenox)

shoes can tread onto the blue civilized domain. To many of us foreigners, these shiny blue sheets look like they belong on a construction site or in a toxic waste dump rather than littering the natural beauty of the shade of cherry trees with people sitting on them. The crinkly blue rectangles are folded into smaller squares for families to comfortably sit, eat and drink. Or, they can be spread out and joined to other blue tarps where 50 or more university students might be drinking white wine from plastic cups and eating sushi from little bento boxes bought from a convenience store. Or they may be passing around more traditional Japanese fare such as Doritos or buffalo wings. There is a twisted beauty in the irregular patchwork of blue sheets strewn across perfectly manicured landscapes to the soundtrack of laughter and *Kanpai* or toasting each other. The scenery transforms into a living, breathing sculpture as if contrived by environmental installation artist Christo, having designed it after coming off a bad hangover.

For the tens of thousands of European, Chinese and American tourists that paid high season plane fares and up to $1,500 a night for hotel rooms during peak season, Kyoto pays them back with the truest and purest cultural aesthetic experience that Japan can offer, one that will stay with them throughout their lives. If, God forbid, it rains, no worries. Under umbrellas, people can still enjoy the glistening pastel blankets of cherry blossom petals covering the ground under the trees and watch them collect and be channeled away into little pink and white rivers. The forces of nature, the Shinto gods, once again teach us the sublime majestic lesson of appreciating the transient, ever changing nature of life.

I didn't have a chance to go to any Hanamis this year. But I've been in good spirits just the same, as I got to spend ten or fifteen minutes under one of those blooming trees today. Gazing up through countless tiny white blossoms bursting out from thousands of buds on every centimeter of every tree branch toward the sunny sky, I felt what I could only describe as rapture, of celestial divinity. So, why would I ruin this moment by taking a picture? Why would I want to interrupt and distort my bliss through the lens of my iPhone camera, as good as it may be? What would be the point of preserving this unequalled moment of spectacular beauty in digital ones and zeros? So that I can look at it and check it for crisp accuracy and then later that day post it on Facebook? It's unremarkable how similar it is to all the others on my newsfeed and to the ones I took the previous year. Should we really care how many people push "like" or comment on our Facebook posts? What if I were to pull that smartphone out of my pocket, open the case, push the icon for the camera app and turn on auto exposure (or maybe leave it off), and frame it this way or that way? I would most certainly lose the stellar profundity of this moment, that never again juncture of past, present and future convergence. Oh, to just be alive under the cherry blossoms. Then, I'll continue my well-deserved "soul massage" tomorrow when I'll spend two hours of perfect downtime, middle of the afternoon solitude in an *onsen*, a hot spring.

One downside of living on an island that is smack in the middle of the Pacific Ring of Fire, the hyperactive hot zone of volcanic and seismic activity, is that the ground shakes a lot. A few times a decade or so a highway overpass may fall, or some buildings may collapse. The Japanese psyche does a good job of ignoring the imminent possibility of a volcano waking up near a major population area (cue Mount Fuji, which is, in fact, three volcanoes on top of each other). Seven years ago, a month after I moved here, the Great Eastern Japan Earthquake sent a fifteen-meter-high tsunami into the Fukushima Daiichi Nuclear Power Plant causing what they called a level seven core meltdown. Sixteen thousand people died from the earthquake, most by drowning. Two thousand five hundred are still unaccounted for today, which means they've either passed away or have ducked out of bad marriages or jobs that they'd hated. I remember my friends messaging me on Facebook saying I should immediately return to New York before the radiation made it to Kansai. But there was no way in hell I would have ever considered doing that. The force inside the atom had nothing on me and my resolve to make a new life for myself and my family. Par for the course in this land of countless contrasts, the upside of Japan's signature seismic tendencies is that everywhere magma contacts an aquifer, there's a hot spring. There are thousands of them in Japan. They inspire island crisscrossing domestic excursions and draw tourists from all over the world. Hot springs are the healthiest remedy and countermeasure to battle the crazy rhythm of daily life for Japanese from all walks of life. Some *onsens* are extravagant, even otherworldly. They can be jewels of landscape architecture, with natural fitted boulders and scalding waterfalls gurgling into irregularly-shaped pools surrounded by foliage. They may be perfect slate-lined rectangles with open bamboo channels gently spilling steamy water into the pool with splash-less, gold medal precision. Outside, they overlook deep valleys, cutting through snow-capped mountains or maybe look down upon crashing waves from the cliffs above. In Kyoto, which is somewhat off the beaten seismological path (through no fault of its own), they must drill down 1,500 meters to find that water and then heat it up before sending it into tubs and mini pools. A few even have daily tank truck deliveries of that prized natural Earth brew from the neighboring Shiga prefecture.

The water is pure, unfiltered groundwater. Most westerners don't think much about the makeup of the warm bath they take at home provided it's clear and odorless. Our minds don't obsess on the fact that most municipal water systems add trace amounts of chlorine to kill bacteria and viruses, and for the dental benefit, a little fluoride. But, what we're soaking in here in Japan is water that is chock-full of minerals, different salts and things that you've only seen in the periodic table of a chemistry class. The color and weight of the water varies from region to region and contains things like strontium, sulfur and rust-colored iron. Sometimes it's naturally carbonated or has high acidity or alkaline properties due to volcanic gases. Some even have trace amounts of radon. No lie, naturally occurring radiation. Every onsen posts the physical make-up of the water and the therapeutic beneficial effects, such as treatment for rheumatoid arthritis, or asthma, or an emollient for your skin that makes you feel years younger with each bath. Even though it's tapped directly from nature's belly, this is not water that's meant to be used to brush your teeth or make baby formula and should generally be washed off with pure water after bathing. The closely monitored temperature of the water in these onsens is often on the borderline of deep-tissue penetrating therapy and downright painful. In fact, in the famous Beppu resorts in Kyushu, they're proud to show that they can cook soft-boiled eggs in the same water where people soak. A big part of what makes the onsen experience so exquisite is that you are interacting with and immersing yourself butt naked in the natural water. You shed your high heels and stockings, your company's uniform, or your blue salaryman's business suit for your birthday suit. All hot springs share the same psychological benefit of providing isolation or at least temporary separation from the noise, busy schedules and hectic pace of life in Japan. By design, onsens reconnect you with nature, beauty, simplicity and silence. There's no bright neon *conbini* store signs, hum of motorcycles or clanging bells of a train crossing. Completely naked and thoroughly immersed in its warm embrace, you are, at least for a while, safe and comforted, back in the womb, nurtured in Mother Earth's uterus. In these shallow, stone-lined mini-pools there's no splashing or inflatable rafts. There's barely any talking. There are no clocks on the wall, and very few thoughts in your head. It's full nourishment for the mind, body and soul for as long as you can endure that scalding water, or for as long as the busy voices in your head allow you to stay there motionless. So, for an hour or so tomorrow, I'll get a little piece of that heavenly serenity soaking. But due to budget and time constraints, I'll be staying local and going to a *supersento*. You find these in cities, hybrids between the small public baths, or *sentos*, and the beautiful natural onsens.

The next morning, I took a 20-minute JR train ride into Shiga prefecture where I teach an hour-long English lesson at a Mister Donut café. After the lesson, fueled by the few doughnuts I shouldn't have eaten and a bottomless cup of coffee, I walked five minutes to the supersento. These places are all-in-one, perfectly laid out, efficiency designed buildings. The centerpieces of these large structures are the hot baths, indoor and outdoor. There are usually one or two little restaurants inside and a relaxation room with comfortable reclining chairs with swivel-mounted, personal TVs. There's also a must-have array of massage chairs that for one to 300 yen you can have everything from a foot, shin, and ankle massage to an all-out, fully automated, sequenced Shiatsu massage. Inflated leather pouches squeeze your arms, while heated rollers press into the back of your neck and slowly work their way down, realigning your spine. This is followed by other beaters rapidly punching your shoulder blades like a malfunctioning antique electric typewriter. All of this is explained and directed from touch-control panels that allow you to customize your 10-minute massage session, at least if you can read Japanese. Again, it can be borderline painful. I still imagine that one of those gears or levers could easily go one notch too far and cripple me for life. But ultimately, I trust the technology and know that that big red circle in the middle of the control panel must be a panic button. At these therapeutic complexes you can also get an above-board massage from a human being in a semi-private room or, if you want one, a haircut.

Upon arrival at a local onsen or supersento, the first thing you do is take off your shoes. A few steps away in your socks, you choose one small shoe locker out of hundreds and insert a ¥100 coin (*hyaku-en*) in a slot to release a numbered tagged key. You'd better not lose that key as you proceed to the next carefully sequenced preparatory procedure of public bathing. Making sure to walk through the blue *noren* door curtains if you're a man and the red curtains for women, you enter another locker room, the changing room.

You are now in the realm of yet another coin-activated, numbered key experience. This is where the rubber hits the road for the shy, inexperienced, not-yet-adjusted, non-public-nudity-inclined foreigner. Now you have two refundable coin keys you can't lose. It takes a few visits to get the hang of it. You put the shoe key inside your clothes locker, and after disrobing, slide the other key, attached with a coiled flexible arm band, around your arm or leg. It's easy to keep track of everything so long as the shoe key doesn't get lost in the clutter of your old clothes and clean clothes and other belongings crammed into an undersized locker. Or, so long as the arm band doesn't slip off in the powerful torrent of a jet bath. Then, with your little towel, you walk into the washing area, a huge room with stone floors and a ceiling that must be 40 feet high. Natural sunlight filters in through the glass roof. Along one side there are rows of little personal wash stations with shower heads hung in brackets on the wall. Small plastic stools are situated in front of each station which is also equipped with large plastic washing bowls and large Costco-size pump bottles of body soap, shampoo, and conditioner.

After washing, the fun begins. You can choose from an array of therapeutic jet baths. They are ganged up together in a long, narrow, rectangular, violently gurgling pool which is sectioned off by sudden, unmarked depth changes. Usually there are tubular metal safety bars to steady yourself as you make your way through the churning maze. You can stand, crouch down, sit, and even lay down on your back where those jets go to work on your lower back or shoulders. If you can stand it, there's high-speed jets of hot water shooting into the bottom of the soles of your feet, which personally turns me into a twitching, giggling junior high school girl. Then some sentos have another section that is almost never marked off clearly but really should be. Common sense dictates that there should be a warning, like a color change or big lightning bolt sticker. Most foreigners discover the *denki ofuro*, or electric bath by accident. I first lowered myself into one of these in an unfamiliar local city sento. I immediately felt something wasn't right as my mind raced to process this unfamiliar sensation. My lower back cramped, and my legs tingled. Was I experiencing a stroke or the beginning of some major cardiac event? It took several seconds and a glance down at some white plastic underwater plates to realize that my naked body was now a component plugged into this jacked up, live electrical water circuit. I avoid them at all costs and frankly think they are dangerous. In the middle of the room there's usually a large, square soaking bath. The aroma baths are filled with unnatural green, purple, yellow or blue water that carries the therapeutic flavor of the day. The orange pumpkin scented water on Halloween convinced me that these baths can be somewhat gimmicky and may provide little to no genuine therapeutic benefit. I realize now that they're colored and scented because many people enter them prior to washing up which goes against appropriate and expected decorum. Always included in these main bathing areas is the *mizuburo*, or ice-cold water dunking bath. This large, high-ceilinged echoey room looks like a cross between a hedonistic Roman-style water playground and a professional sports injury rehab center.

The nearby neighborhood sento, Sakura-Yu, complete with fish tank, steam sauna and aroma bath. The trick is to get there a half an hour before closing and have it all to yourself.

Off the main room shower area is a large sauna. You'd think the sauna would be a place of sensory refuge, but it's just the opposite. It's a small amphitheater-shaped room with a capacity of about 25 people sitting on pads. Everyone's staring at a large screen TV watching something fascinating like the host of a food show tearing open a chestnut-cream-filled doughnut with a camera closeup of the filling dripping out and the sound of excited "oos" and "ahs" of the people in the TV studio audience. Twenty naked guys are sitting in that hot sauna, not talking to each other, staring at that chestnut cream doughnut like it was crack. Relax our brains? Why? Who could relax their brain when they're in the tractor-beam of Japanese marketers? So, the refuge from this refuge is to go outside. Outside, there's a walled-in courtyard area with a *rotenburo* (outdoor bath) constructed of faux boulders that form an irregularly-shaped, natural-looking shallow pond, complete with an artificial waterfall or two. Foliage and stone paths flank the pool despite the fact it isn't pumped from an aquifer 12-hundred meters below ground. It's filtered city water. But it can almost do the trick. Almost, but not quite, because 10 meters away from this outdoor stone bath is a tatami area where you can lie down. There's an even larger flat screen TV, and at full-blasting volume. And as much as you're trying not to look at the TV, as much as you're trying not to hear the sound, there's that same infomercial about the chestnut cream doughnuts. So, if you are completely deaf, you can pull off some modicum of relaxation and not look in the general direction of that TV, maybe stare at the waterfall. But, as much as you try to filter out that doughnut infomercial, the news story about Kim Jong-un having his half-brother assassinated in the airport in Malaysia demands attention on the TV. Despite your best efforts, you realize you're just not in that zone. As I soaked in those waters, I started thinking about the beginning of the documentary, *Baraka*, directed by Ron Fricke (1992) and the snow monkey bathing in a natural mountain hot spring in the snowy mountains of Nagano. He's completely motionless. He's unquestionably standing in that hot water up to his neck as the camera close-up shows his completely trained, full-meditative state. Birds chirp in the background over a soundtrack of the mysterious entrancing tones of a traditional *shakuhachi* Japanese flute. My thoughts are pulling me slowly back into the "zone." Then, highlights of the Yomiuri Giants/Hiroshima Carp baseball game abruptly sound loudly over the TV and my reverie is broken.

So, this wannabe snow monkey from New York has only one place left to go and that's through a small wooden door with a rounded top. Crouching to get through the door, I'm led into the steam sauna, a low-ceiling, oval-shaped room with no corners or edges. It seems like it was formed out of adobe and resembles an oversized, dimly-lit kiln. Its only light comes from a recessed area at one end of the room where there's a large stone pedestal with a gurgling little pool on top and a bamboo ladle. You're supposed to fill that bamboo ladle with cold water and first splash it over whichever one of the ten ceramic cylindrical stools you decide to sit on. You also may choose to splash the cold water over your body as you try to endure the dense, stinging steam that penetrates your nostrils and lungs with every inhale. Every pore in your body is making you aware of just how uncomfortable you are and trying to convince you that five minutes is enough. It's dark and otherworldly inside. Aside from the recessed area with the stone pedestal, there is a dimly-lit panic button on the wall. As I sit on my ceramic stool, I squint and look around to see if anybody else is in its dark and hellish haze. There's no one else in there. I'm in this therapeutic torture chamber by myself, where I can chant for 10 or 15 minutes. So, with blazing nostrils scorched with every breath and super-sensitive skin now the consistency of over-boiled dumplings, I chant. I send out vibrations and connect my inner life to the farthest stars of the universe, turning that steamy, scorching devil's oven into the Buddha-land for 10 minutes, or at least until the door opens and some other naked man walks in.

CHAPTER 12

WHY ARE THEY ALWAYS RUNNING?

I had been in Japan for less than a year and was sitting in a city bus looking out over Kyoto's dark shingled roofs and busy streets pondering the difference between New York City and Kyoto. As I watched the day and mass of humanity moving through it unfold in front of me, a question popped to mind. Why are they always running? I'm not just talking about a group of school boys in uniform horsing around and running down the street. I mean everyone, everywhere. Out my bus window, I saw an old lady running to cross the street. The crosswalk signal was a flashing green pedestrian image with green dots counting down in synch with nervous signal chirps before it turned to red for three or four minutes. It was a Sunday morning. I'm not sure if she was rushing anywhere in particular. She was seventy years old, if she was a day, and with speed like that she probably wasn't going to an orthopedist appointment. But, she scurried quickly to catch the light anyway. Down in the subway station, I watched two people chasing forward. They also must have been around 70 and are also running to catch a train. Why were they rushing? Maybe they were running to get out of the city. But trains out of Kyoto leave every ten minutes. Yet, this couple wildly bounded ahead, and the expressions on their faces were exuberant! They were delighted to be running, grinning happily. The old man's cane bounced behind him as he ran with his wife, smiling. Why were they running? I guess it's for the same reason my 82-year-old student, Nobuko-san takes ballroom dancing lessons every Thursday: because she can. The subway runners have probably been riding bikes for most of their lives and likely walk to the store instead of driving. They probably also think about nutrition and calories more than their western counterparts might. In the broadest stroke, Japanese are more physically fit than Westerners. Being overweight is an anomaly as opposed to the norm. Gross obesity is almost non-existent.

In New York, people run if someone is chasing them or if they are the chaser. Or, we hustle to catch happy hour before it ends. Here, they run because it makes them feel alive and because time is so precious. Getting to that destination four minutes earlier than if they had waited for the next train translates into another successful accomplishment, a conquering of adversity, beating the flow of time. It means four more minutes to look at the clouds, or the mountains, or to squeeze in more conversation with friends or just to hang out next to a vending machine enjoying a cold drink.

In my first year here I thought to myself, I'll never be like this. I came from New York ostensibly to slow down my pace. I didn't need to run for trains. They ran so frequently. Besides, I'm always an early person. Two years later, I was running for every train if I thought I could make it. If I know it's leaving in one minute, I'll weigh my chances as I pick up the pace into a run. I'll need to go through the gates, navigate escalators, step through people, before getting onto the train. I make the effort because I know the doors are going to close in exactly one minute, to the second. I play the odds. If I know there's a 50/50 chance I'm going to make it, you can bet I'm gonna run for it like a maniac and might even crack a smile in the process.

It's old news that Japan, by nature, is punctual beyond comprehension to the rest of the world. Trains arrive to the second. If you watch the engineers at the helm of any train, you'll see them talking to themselves, counting the beat like a drum major as they approach a station, so they arrive there at the exact second the train is scheduled to arrive. It's unbelievable. People in all walks of life and all spheres, both social and business, from stadium concert producers, to store owners to school teachers, adhere to the strict, self-enforced protocols of punctuality. Now in the era of digital, calibrated precision I am aware of exactly what time it is by looking at my iPhone, at the clocks in every store I pass by, at my TV's bottom right corner, and at my laptop. I stopped wearing a watch years ago because as far as I'm concerned, they are an obsolete, unnecessary fashion statement serving no purpose. Time is serious business in Japan. I arrive at my school early to prepare and wait for the arrival of my students. With amazement, I watch a guy, who I know was out late the night before drinking, who runs a business and raises a family, walk in at precisely three o'clock on a Tuesday afternoon. I know he must leave his busy company, talk to his employees, drive a few minutes and park his bright red BMW a block away. But as soon as that second hand hits the 12 of three o'clock, his shadow appears behind the smoked-glass door of my school. Umm...like clockwork.

As far as the trains and transportation go, Japan Railway (JR) is the biggest with a network of lines connecting all parts of Japan with competing lines like the Hankyu, Keihan and Kintetsu in the mix. There's lots of local light rail electric lines in the "burbs" that might be as small as single cars coursing through small town streets and would be called trolley cars in some cities around the world. JR also runs the Shinkansen or bullet trains. They used to be government-owned (still are in some regions) and are iconic of Japan's mass transit infrastructure. In Kansai, there's the JR Biwako (or *Tozai*) line which courses through the wilderness connecting country towns of Shiga Prefecture tracing a route along Japan's biggest lake, Biwako, before connecting Kyoto to Osaka to Kobe and beyond. The line twists through mountains and valleys and gorgeous scenery. But, when there's a storm, it frequently runs late. By late, I mean by 3-minutes, 10-minutes, maybe longer, and rarely more than 15, although a typhoon or blizzard can knock it out for hours. But what's odd is that in the big transportation hubs like Kyoto station where most people get on and off, there's flashing red lights and public service announcements on scheduling boards overhanging the stops. These indicate how many minutes the trains are going to be late, in bold red. In English and Japanese, they say, "Two minutes behind schedule." These flashing apologies and the minute by minute updates on the PA indicate failure, breach of the promise to keep you on schedule, tacit dereliction of duty even though the forces of nature are the ones who dumped 10 cm of snow on the tracks in the mountains. To a former New Yorker, where the trains unapologetically never run on time, having a system-wide apology for being three minutes late is somewhere between delightfully cute and sincere to completely absurd!

Riding the trains in Japan is always an interesting experience in and of itself. It gives you a glimpse of the inner workings of Japanese culture and the Japanese mindset where you can see how the gears of engineering and design and social behavior mesh. It's a smooth, fast-moving metal petri dish where hard work intersects hard partying, and where leisure intersects with running errands and sightseeing sits next to the pursuit of education.

Six months after I arrived in Japan, I had one of those experiences. I was trying to get to Osaka from Kyoto to teach a special "Spartan" or intensive course in Business English at the Velco English School where I worked. It was a hot, rainy morning after a long, rainy night. It hadn't been a typhoon, but the storms and downpours had been heavy enough to close or delay most of the train lines. Of course, real time emergency announcements are never made in English, so I wasn't sure exactly what was happening. There were lots of red flashing displays, a lot of people on cell phones, and not enough station staff to address everybody's concerns, let alone the foreigners. None of the staff spoke a wisp of English. In that crowded, steamy train station, some people were panicking, and others were deliberating over what to do. Everybody was drenched in sweat and rain. The overriding question on most people's minds seemed to be, "should I stay here and hope the train service resumes in an hour or should I take a taxi to another train line and take my chances there?"

Of the three major train lines that go from Kyoto to Osaka, I prefer the Keihan Line. It's not as quick as the other two but it's a more enjoyable ride and has a slightly different route, planting me where I need to go. Consider yourself lucky if you find yourself seated on the top level of the double decker cars of the elegant 8,000 Saloon Series Limited Express train. That's what's proudly displayed in cursive decals on the side of each car. There are faux leather headrest liners draped over soft upholstered lumbar-perfect seats, and the window curtains and lighting are simple and almost elegant. There's even a single Premium car which costs extra and has wifi, even more comfortable seats and a roaming concierge. From the double-decker, you are elevated to a better view of the mountains and rivers, the cherry blossoms and farms and, of course, kilometers and kilometers of uninterrupted and sometimes ugly urban sprawl that lies between the big cities. But if you want speed and bathrooms, you take the JR. As I just mentioned before, the JR is susceptible to bad weather on the long countryside runs and is always the first and longest delayed, not just by torrential rains. Even light snow falls, or strong winds can ruin your day. The other reason for JR train delays is suicide. It is the train line of choice for suicides. In fact, in Osaka two years ago they changed the bright red lights at some of the major railroad crossing points to soft blue lights because they thought that might dissuade some people from committing suicide. I kid you not.

So, standing in the train station on that rainy Friday morning confused and panicked, I had a mission to get to Osaka come hell or high water or suicides. It was normally a one-hour ride, and in two hours I was supposed to be standing in front of this special Business English class for the first time. As I stood on the platform, I watched a few businessmen who were looking at their phones suddenly put them away and start walking quickly toward an exit. Scampering along, I followed them because they looked like they knew what they were doing, walking outside a few steps behind them. Truthfully, it was closer to a run in the rain with umbrellas. They made it to the Hankyu station ten minutes away which I know stops a lot more times between Kyoto and Osaka, but they seemed to know something I didn't. We weren't the only three or four people to have this idea because when we got into the Hankyu station we were packed onto a train, literally pushed by staff and crammed onto a train. I was holding on to my briefcase, but I didn't need to hold on to any straps if there were any because I was sandwiched between people, propped up by the four or five bodies surrounding me. Everybody was upset, wet, and on the verge of being late. For some inexplicable reason the air conditioner wasn't on and the windows were misty. Through that sweltering lack of air, I realized the back of my left hand was touching the hip of a business woman standing next to me. On other side of me there was the corner of a briefcase jutting into my gut. Behind me, a man with bad breath was panting.

As the train, which is generally a smooth ride, was rocking a little bit on the tracks, all I wanted to do was take my cell phone out of my left pocket and look at it to see what time it was and maybe get a message through to the manager of the school that I might be running a little bit late. But doing so would have entailed moving my left hand from my side which was pressed against the hip of the business woman. If I'd done that, I might have been called out for being a *hentai* (perverted) train groper. Japan is the only country that has ladies-only train cars during rush hour. Pressed in together like that, one can see why. Trains get very crowded during peak times and an inclination to not rock the boat and maintain harmony supersedes a willingness to ask for polite behavior or even speak up for justice. Add to that Japan's historical subservience of women to men, and you have all the ingredients for a decades-long epidemic of *chikan*, train-groping. Many people have told me stories about people being pressed up against them questionably, if not inappropriately, in the subway. So, Japan developed ladies-only cars, denoted by big pink squares on the train platforms, with no English translations, of course. Two or three cars are dedicated to female passengers during rush hour. I remember a few months after being in Kyoto standing in a train car and noticing that I was the only guy in the car and thought what a country, I could die here! After a few stops and noticing that maybe I was being looked at, I realized that I was, in fact, not where I was supposed to be and breaking the law, albeit ignorant of the fact. I quickly got off that car and went into a regular car,

Back to that sweaty train ride. When I wiggled and contorted as I tried to get my phone close to my face and eek out something resembling a text message, it warranted a dirty look from the business woman. Just then, the train turned, and I lost my balance. There was nowhere to fall other than into that chubby, middle-aged woman. She was a trooper and didn't budge or give me a second dirty look as I righted myself. I was thinking to myself, this is the worst train ride I've ever taken in my life.

The train made its way out of the center of Kyoto city and stopped at Katsura station in the outskirts where many people got off to transfer, including the middle-aged business woman who I swear I didn't grope. Thankfully, the man with the bad breath got off too, along with his briefcase which had been jutting into my gut. Before I knew it, the doors closed, and the train was full again. In fact, it was even more packed than it was before. But this time, I was surrounded by four or five young women. Everybody had the same desperate look on their faces as though they were going through this hell to get to their university or their job, and probably would get there late. We were all sweaty, our clothes were a little bit wet from the rain, and the windows were misty. We were all trying to keep our balance because, again there weren't enough straps to hold on to as the train bucked and swayed. But now, in place of the old man with the bad breath, there was a breeze of candied lip gloss coming into my nose, and that stagnant, humid air was a potpourri of perfumes and body sprays. Instead of a briefcase jutting into my stomach, there was a pocket book pushed against my crotch. I couldn't have moved my hands to text on my cell phone if I'd wanted to. But, who would have wanted to move when there were two pairs of twenty-something-year-old Japanese breasts pressed into my back and arms. I remembered thinking, "this is best train ride I've ever had."

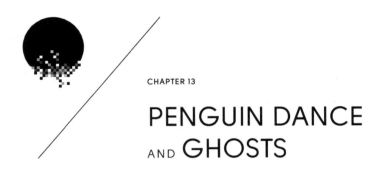

CHAPTER 13

PENGUIN DANCE
AND GHOSTS

Water assumes the shape of the vessel it's poured into or contained in. Like water, one innate capability of human beings is to adapt, change, and survive under any circumstances. I am convinced after watching a documentary on octopuses that they could in time evolve and develop to a point where if they had to, they could thrive and take over a world that had been laid to waste by the failures and misgivings of humans. These magnificent creatures have taken the back escalator up the DNA helix which has given them a "tentacle up" on humans in terms of adapting their behavior and learning how to survive. An octopus can contort its body shape and perfectly alter its colors to survive danger or to escape confinement. You may have seen video on YouTube of an octopus put in a small jar of water, entangled and squeezed into it with barely any space to move. In a quick minute, it had figured out it could use its suction cups and twist the lid in a counterclockwise direction, fling it off the jar and escape.

As I mentioned before, I came to Japan essentially winging it in terms of a career. I'm not a credentialed teacher nor have I had any formal training or, for that matter, taught anything in any kind of educational situation. It took a good two or three hours for me to start to get a handle on what it takes to be a good entry-level adult English teacher in Japan. It took a thousand more hours of experimentation, digesting feedback and self-reflection to get to the point where I am now solidly comfortable in the role of an English teacher. I may have achieved a level of competence, but I still feel as though I should be subsisting solely on writing and playing music. But, like the octopus, I'm contorting to fit my conditions.

Japan is still a ridiculously homogeneous society, with 98.5% of the country Japanese and less than 0.5% non-Asian. There are heated and ongoing debates about lessening immigration restrictions. Despite the fact I'm now a business owner, university teacher, a taxpayer in good standing with a family, and married to a Japanese woman, I've been turned down for permanent residency, though I am appealing this decision.

Facebook, Twitter and Instagram are huge here, and Japan voyeuristically looks at the entire world through smartphones and laptops. Young people are continuously extending their gaze beyond that of their parents, broadening their perspectives of what they could do with their lives. English is the only bridge by which to truly span the great distances that lie across the ocean, beyond the scope of mere sightseeing. Many or most Japanese of the last two generations realize that to survive and thrive in a changing world, they need to convert their basic tendency and attachment to self-fulfilled, self-reliant "islandism" to true globalism. Multiculturalism, from dribs and drabs to sold out Ariana Grande tours, has slowly been coming into Japan for decades sparking a lot of imagination. For decades, people have been listening to The Beatles and Oasis and watching subtitled *Mission Impossible* sequels. More recently, they've been singing Ed Sheeran, Bruno Mars and Beyoncé songs in karaoke rooms. There is and has been a real love and envy of foreign culture since the reconstruction after World Word II. In Japan, learning English gives you benefits that range from the epiphany of understanding the lyrics of your favorite song to confidently ordering from a menu in a restaurant in Berlin to a high-paying and fulfilling, country-hopping international career. It will make you many friends from other lands and perhaps increase your chances of snagging a great boyfriend or husband.

Some people need to learn English for survival. They're being transferred to an office in India or they're in the international marketing department of some tech company. Some want to make themselves more marketable when they graduate from their university or maybe they are a bored housewife that just wants to learn something new. Sometimes English study is pursued by elderly people to combat boredom and loneliness, or to keep their brains sharp. Then there's my mechanical engineering Masters students at Doshisha Unversity who use English to present their research at overseas conferences. They can speak adeptly in memorized English Powerpoint lingo from the podium, only to freeze like a deer in the headlights when a French accent is thrown their way during a Q&A. Many English learners are just as enthralled by meeting and interacting with foreigners (i.e., their teachers) and developing new friendships as they are with learning the language. Their motivation to learn English might be one segment of a weekly self-improvement regimen, along with yoga and a cooking class.

Leading up to my arrival in Japan on January 26, 2011, I knew I would have to adapt my somewhat well-honed business and life skills in all their divergent rays and focus them into making a living teaching English until, well, something else popped. I'd long since given up on the VH1 New Artist Music award of my twenties but how far away could financial success through music in Japan be? My music was on fire! So, I jumped into a real fire two months prior when I gave my notice of resignation to Mana Contemporary, the New York City company that had pulled me out of the musical tailspin of financial uncertainty. I pulled the plug on a nine-year career there. As the wheels of the plane touched the runway at Tokyo's Narita airport, I knew there was no turning back. I was now going to be a language teacher, like it or not. Goodbye cool Chelsea art galleries and collectors. Goodbye Guggenheim - we made a nice couple!

It wasn't until three years later, on January 2nd, 2014, a few days after I took over ownership of my school, The WAVE, that it all started to make sense to me. It was late at night and I was listening to a podcast on National Public Radio (NPR) while cleaning out drawers with papers and abandoned belongings of the former owner, Izah, who had moved back to Hawaii. The podcast spoke about how friendship, culture, and education are the only pathways that can lead countries away from tribalism to globalism. This jived completely with the basic credo of the SGI of which I had proudly been a member for decades. But then something else shot out of the speakers into my brain as they emphasized that "speaking and understanding English language is an essential component" to building those bridges. My jaw dropped as I found out that there are two billion people who are English as a Second Language (ESL) speakers. That's a lot more than native English speakers. I stopped sorting through drawers and stood motionless. I sensed that some master plan I had overlooked was in the works and it was quickly starting to congeal all around me. Tears of revelation and clarified life-purpose were running down my cheeks as I realized that I was standing on the cusp of everything I'd experienced along my twisted career path and philosophical journey that had led me to that moment. My new life's headquarters, this room, granted me true confirmation that I was on the right path. From this mystical vortex I would educate, help people communicate, write and record music, and promote international culture. I was finally the boss and it was smack dab in the middle of Kyoto. I'd only been in Japan for three years and now I realized that I was perfectly situated for what I wanted to do and exactly where I was supposed to be.

In my school, I have the liberty to design or purposefully NOT design a lesson. I must do whatever it takes to spark students' enthusiasm and get them talking. Tweaking the brain's left hemisphere language and speech centers can be as simple as sharing a story or a video. I might show a clip of *Meet the Parents* when Robert De Niro's mother's ashes urn is knocked off the fireplace mantle by Ben Stiller's champagne cork and then pissed on by the cat. For that, I would have made up a little worksheet. Follow that with adlibbing it into a role play and it becomes a fun and effective hour lesson. For the next class, we'll try Bob Marley's song "Three Little Birds" (a.k.a. Don't worry about a thing). It can easily become an inspiring lesson for children or adults, let alone an eye-opening experience in its positive vibration and simple English phrasing. With the new *Bohemian Rhapsody* movie out, I now have a chance to teach the true meaning of the lyrics. People learn how to pronounce and sing it right and get a little voice coaching in the process. They leave the lesson with one more "go-to" song in their pocket to be showed off to their friends at the next karaoke outing. A lesson with a cancer researcher might be comprised of watching and discussing a *Ted TV* lecture while following the script to teach more sophisticated English. But before I had the opportunity to do my own thing at the WAVE, I had to start from scratch.

In my first four years in Japan, I assembled a mixed bag of different types of teaching gigs based more on financial need than on any sort of cohesive career trajectory. I had to survive and support my family of three which doesn't come easy in this foreign land. A month after I came to Kyoto, I snagged a 20-hour-a-week teaching job at the Velco English conversation school, or *eikaiwa*. Eikaiwas are basically places where students could practice and develop the English they've learned in junior high school, high school, and college or from other schools. Generally, foreign teachers don't teach grammar in these schools. They just engage people in conversation. What a fun job it can be! If you take five people from all walks of life in Japan and put them around an oval conference room table with one foreigner and a white board with a map of the world behind them, it can go off in myriad directions. The "native speaking" teacher is at the helm and has the role of directing and provoking conversations between and amongst the students and with the teacher. The students are coached and infused with new phrases and vocabulary. They have the chance of taking their English out for a "test drive" while simultaneously being entertained, at least entertained enough to continue paying the next month's tuition. So, depending on the teacher and the chemistry of the students, those one-to three-hour conversation classes could be anything from congenial Q&A sessions on predetermined topics chosen by their teacher, lengthy over-spoken travel experiences, or outright sociopolitical debates on current events. In one of my first classes, I found myself talking to a biomedical researcher who focused on genetics, a brilliant woman in her early 30s. We forged an almost immediate connection through the fact that we were both big Keith Jarrett fans. It was thrilling to find out that each of our lives had been deeply impacted by repeatedly listening to his groundbreaking solo piano concert in Cologne, performed over 20 years ago. She then went on to talk about her experience climbing Machu Picchu. To be honest, it was a true awakening for me. I had never expected this level of sophistication and worldliness in a "typical" Japanese working wife. Sometimes it was just pure entertainment for me, the teacher.

Early in my Velco English private school teaching, I remember the delightful, sensory experience of giving a weekly lesson to one student every Wednesday afternoon. She worked at a famous, traditional and super expensive *Ryokan* (Japanese inn) in Kyoto. I had to pinch myself. I was getting paid to sit across the table for two hours alone with this smart, funny, 27-year-old genetic masterpiece, guiding her through her grammar as she tried to express the depth of hatred she held for her ex-fiancé, a lawyer who had dumped her suddenly the year before. In her little memo pad, she jotted down words like *disgust*, *retribution* and *trade up* as she spoke of going to an automated batting cage and smashing each baseball lobbed her way, imagining it was his head.

The irony and unexpected value-added benefit to this kind of job was that I often learned more from these lessons than the students did from me. During a "free talk" conversation class at Velco, a doctoral student from Kyoto University surprised me when he gave his response to whatever topic was being discussed as, "I'm a nationalist, and I'm proud of it!" Now, I had seen the movie, *The Last Emperor*, decades ago and was particularly taken aback by one scene that had stuck in my head. A Japanese government official lost his temper and crazily scolded the young Chinese boy, Puyi, who was now a political prisoner. He screamed in total anger something to the effect of, "Don't you know that Japanese is a superior culture?!" I remember thinking that was some crazy shit and clearly reflected the mindset that led to Japanese imperialism and expansionism, an attack on Pearl Harbor and the ultimate devastation of Japan. So, when this well-spoken, well-read student gave his unsolicited declaration of national pride my ears perked up. This soon-to-be Doctor of Philosophy in Management Science, a handsome strapping mesomorph who played baseball and was also a jazz bassist, seemed a perfect, well-rounded specimen of a human being. He was trilingual (Japanese, Chinese, and English) and proceeded to lay out a very convincing argument in his second language. After listening to him, I began to at least open to the notion that maybe if Japan had not been defeated in World War II, Japanese influence might have somehow benefitted and enhanced the development of economics and culture in the region. Maybe it would have helped unify and meld the volatile and complicated psychodynamics of East Asia. Is it not at least possible that with greater Japanese influence and less Chinese dominance many of the longstanding and ongoing problems that abound in the Southeastern Pacific Rim would have different outcomes? The more I get to know Japan and the more I interact with Japanese, the more I entertain somewhere in the depths of my mind that in many ways it IS a superior culture, but there's no point in ranking cultures. I am not justifying the invasion of Asia and the commitment of atrocities by any definition, I'm just sharing my observations. I was shocked to find myself a foreigner with hippie, libertarian tendencies thinking that way. Whatever the students' motivations were, the "free talk" conversation classes were a living, breathing, interactive experience for both them and me. We developed true friendships that allowed me to really dig in and explore the culture and attitudes that make Japan such a remarkable society. I learned about the depth and diversity of perspective and life experience of the Japanese. This in turn led me towards a greater appreciation of the solid underpinnings beneath the beautiful aesthetic veneer, which from the outside may sometimes appear shallow.

Not your typical English classroom and not your typical English class but teaching basic customer service English to these young women at a bridal, travel and hospitality career college was far from boring - and, they "spoke good!"

In tandem with being conversation class teacher, I had a few other gigs early on in my Japanese career. One of them was teaching at a trade college for people learning the bridal, travel, and hospitality industries. This school was a practical, skill-based alternative education to a standard university degree. I taught two back-to-back 90-minute lessons every Tuesday morning to classes of about twenty students. Except for one or two boys, they were all girls who had recently graduated high school, daughters from middle or working-class families that didn't have the ambition, means or desire to go to a good university. The classroom was a polished-wood-floored, chandeliered wedding salon with a teacher's lectern and four large tables surrounded by mirrors. Arranged around the room were wedding dresses on hangers and shelves of accessories, like glistening rhinestone tiaras and lots of lacey veils.

I would get there early to prepare for the class and always noticed the slightly "stanky" scent which was a combination of hard work, old perfume and poor ventilation. I was tasked to teach basic beginner English to young women who frankly did not want to learn it but had to as their curriculum required it.

It was my first day of class, and there I was, the foreigner standing at the lectern in this hormonal bastion of femininity with the lacey wedding dresses forming the back drop. After a brief introduction in slow, over-enunciated English, it was time for an icebreaker. The warmup was a little awkward as only a few of them spoke their names loud enough to be audible. After a few minutes, I asked for a volunteer to have a simple conversation with and got no reply. So, I looked at the attendance sheet and randomly chose a name. "Haruka, please stand up." I continued, "So what's your hobby?" Keeping a straight face and without hesitation she answered loudly and matter-of-factly, "sex." The room collectively giggled. All eyes were trained on the teacher to monitor his reaction as I tried to keep a professional demeanor and seamlessly launched into Plan B. I asked them in my rudimentary Japanese to ask me a simple question in English. One of the girls consulted her electronic dictionary, typing on the mini keyboard with her friend looking on, eyes widening in disbelief. As proper class decorum mandates, Ayano stood up to ask the question reading phonetically from the handheld screen. "Sensei - are you infidelity?" I had clearly said in my introduction that I was married and had a daughter. That was a trying start for a year gig teaching these girls.

I realized over the next few weeks that this teaching job was going to be a battle on many different levels. One, I had to get them motivated to learn English as this was a required class for them that they needed to pass however marginally that might be. Two, I had to continuously wrestle control of the class because they all knew each other, putting me at a considerable disadvantage. Three, half of them were sleepy because they were admittedly out partying the night before and frankly, English was boring. Four, because Tuesdays, the one day a week that I came to their school to teach, had become "short skirt day."

I'm happy to say that teaching in "Candyland" was overall a successful experience. All of them passed and most of them improved their English, which they may very well use in their future careers. They even developed a liking for simple conversation. On their handwritten, anonymous teacher evaluation questionnaires which were translated and emailed to me, the comments ranged from "uses the iPad well to make lesson interesting" to "he has a great smile." While staying comported and maintaining a professional demeanor I gained a little perspective on the abundant two billion dollar a year Japanese porn industry which draws from a culture of formality and suppressed naughtiness. I was asked to teach the following year at a slight increase. I declined.

A few months after that, Solomon, who had in short time become my newest and coolest best friend in addition to Kansai Rocks! bandmate told me about a part time job opening. Kyoto International School (KIS), where he and his wife were both teaching, was looking for a music teacher. KIS was an International Baccalaureate accredited (IB) school which meant that it had to meet certain academic standards. They were looking for a music teacher. Naturally, it appealed to me because I live and breathe for music. But, I couldn't read a note of music if you held a gun to my head. I've had no formal music training and I can't even properly tune a guitar. But somehow my life was channeled and squeezed through some narrow mystical plumbing of the universe and I was deposited in a chair for a 20-minute interview, which I passed. They were desperate for a music teacher.

The job would involve one full day a week teaching music classes from pre-K through to middle school students. The kids there were mostly children of mixed parentage or families that were willing to pay close to $7,000 a year for the kids to get a special education based on English. Some were financially comfortable returnees, Japanese families that moved out of Japan due to overseas work, and then moved back. The dozen or so teachers at the school were well-trained, experienced and certified internationals or English-fluent Japanese. Kyoto International School was bound by its IB certification to staff a music program. And that was to be me. I taught six different classes in a row with a 45-minute lunch break every Thursday. The school was built after World War II. It was a concrete, boxy, institutional-looking building situated in the middle of a densely-packed but quiet residential neighborhood. It sported the typical features of these old school buildings that you see throughout Japan. There were the long, creaky, wooden planked floors, a big sandy sports field and the signature, fenced-off, decades-long-neglected algae-ridden science experiment which used to be a pool. Large concrete walls separated the school domain from the rest of the world. Essentially, it looked like a prison camp, complete with light towers, resembling the courtyard where the prisoners in *The Bridge Over the River Kwai* exercised, but it was far from it. The school was a wonderful, friendly international environment that was buzzing with laughter and children's artwork hanging in the hallways and taped to the windows.

One of the reasons I took the job is because the money was good. It was a full eight-hour work day. But the clincher was that the music room in this World War II, boxy, concrete building with creaky wood floors was in the aptly-designed bomb shelter of the school, in the basement. Inside a large, vault-style door was a concrete, carpeted room that was maybe 20 by 20 meters (that's huge), filled with xylophones, marimbas, drum sets, electric guitars, acoustic guitars, percussion instruments, and other miscellaneous instruments that had been donated over the years to the school or that previous music teachers had purchased. There were microphones, mic stands and colored plastic tubes that when swung in the air in circles made different tones.

Neighborhoods in Japan are generally quiet places, especially in the evenings. I lived in a small apartment in Kyoto where even playing the acoustic guitar in my bathroom in the late afternoon was loud enough outside to warrant a knock on the door from my next-door neighbors who had an infant. I was sold on the job the moment I walked into this room like a soon-to-be-unsupervised kid let loose inside the FAO Schwartz toy store on Fifth Avenue in New York City.

I made it through my first year there, which was way beyond challenging for a good-natured uncertified octopus. These kids didn't learn chromatic scales and musical theory as I sure as hell couldn't teach them something I didn't know. Even better, it was an opportunity to expose them to culture and nurture their natural, creative spirit. I had complete leeway to do pretty much anything I wanted to do, under the observing eyes of those accredited teachers.

For example, in a darkened room with the kids sitting cross-legged on the floor, I would project a two-minute movie clip, an aerial view of someone jogging along a snowy deserted street deep in the countryside. I would show them how when juxtaposed with Dixieland New Orleans jazz playing in the background there would be nothing to worry about. It might be the opening sequence of a lighthearted comedy. But then I would change the music to a dark, slow, ominous experimental piece setting the mood of impending danger, suggesting that someone on the screen was surely about to be murdered. How fun it was to learn together about the power of music to evoke emotion and define context! I had the responsibility and opportunity to involve and inform these students musically in a way that a piano teacher never could have.

For the four and five-year-old's classes, I would sit them in a big circle and give them percussion instruments. We did a massive call and response percussion routine while counting out the beats. They loved it because they could be unrestrained and loud. One of my main responsibilities was to prepare the kids for their Christmas concert. Talk about a crowd pleaser! You can't go wrong with 20 four-year-old kids dressed as penguins, doing the Romanian penguin line dance with the sound effect of a blizzard over a loud, bopping accordion track. Cute doesn't get any cuter. With the older kids, I might teach them a traditional Korean folk song with lyrics written phonetically on the blackboard. The nine-and ten-year-old students loved the musical *Grease*, which they had learned and performed the year before I met them. In my classroom, they created a ten to fifteen-minute musical of their own. The concept of nerdy, geeky boys being bullied and then embraced by cool, popular girls was their creation, I just guided them and helped with melodies.

The older kids, however, were more challenging to teach. Aside from the normal naughtiness and mob mentality in classes, I would find out later that a few kids were "off the spectrum." As mentioned before, I had zero training in education. I knew nothing about the normal boundaries and classifications of child behavior, let alone classroom management. When I first heard the words "Asperger's Syndrome" it sounded like something that you might get on the Coney Island boardwalk after eating one too many chilidogs, to be resolved in a dirty bathroom. I had ongoing problems with one kid in a class.

Once when the principal dropped in to observe my class she whispered to me in wide-eyed, clinical disbelief, "he is oral stimming all over the place." Oral stimming? What the hell is that? I just knew that this boy was licking the tambourine, the wood blocks, the electric piano and basically anything he touched. Later that night, Google helped me to understand that oral stimulation is a common symptom of Asperger's.

There was another boy, cute as can be, in another class. I'm not sure if he was on or off the spectrum or struggling with something else. During one class when I wasn't looking, he meticulously disassembled an expensive marimba, lining the fifty or sixty rectangular wooden blocks in size order on the floor. When confronted by the angry, untrained teacher, me, he simply smiled back with a look of true accomplishment. The same guy did an impromptu performance with those colored plastic wind tubes at one of our class talent shows. He basically just sat cross legged on the floor and methodically picked up the flexible tubes, swung them in the air over his head, dropped them, and threw them up again, all the while laughing. The other students and I were riveted, we were witnessing one of the most brilliant performance-art pieces I have ever seen!

Instead of teaching music theory, I was guiding students from a purely experiential sensory perspective. This experience stretched me in all directions. It forced me to not only further develop and express my love and affinity for music, but it also expanded me in many interesting ways, not the least of which was personal endurance and tolerance. Although I had my moments of doubt, it was a successful enough experiment that I was asked to come back for a second year, which I did.

When it came time for end-of-term student assessments, although I was warned during my initial twenty-minute interview, I was a little unprepared for filling out the forms per the guidelines of an IB accredited school. I couldn't candidly express what I had truly experienced and felt as there was a certain lexicon that had to be used. We had to be diplomatic and cop an internationally accredited academic tone. For example, "Sara would benefit from developing better self-management, and when collaborating with her classmates she should focus on improving listening and communication skills." What I really wanted to report was, "Sara rarely pays attention to anything going on and habitually disrupts her classmates. In fact, she is often totally out of control and for a ten-year-old is turning into quite a little bitch. God help her future coworkers, let alone her husband or anybody who will have to deal with this evil little psycho."

I know the "certified" teachers felt the same way, but we had to be professional and conform to accredited international standards. "It was a pleasure teaching her. I'm looking forward to helping her develop her skills next term." And, if you're gullible enough to believe this, I've got a bridge in Brooklyn to sell you!

This kind of teaching wasn't exactly on my bucket list, but I had a colorful and life-altering two-year stint there. And that was just one day of my seven-day work week. But, the big payoff from this school was that I had a music room at my disposal, one that was almost completely soundproof. Kansai Rocks rehearsed there many a late night. I would also spend hours alone in this big, cavernous room, perfect for recording with no neighbors within earshot. I'm pretty sure there was a ghost or two in this old building. Being there alone at midnight, far from my apartment in this big, World War II prison of a building with the creaky wood floors, was spooky. I'd be there in the basement bomb shelter music room with headphones on belting it out into a microphone, recording vocals. By my second or third beer I'd need to go upstairs to the bathroom. I would walk quickly past darkened doorways to the john at the end of the hallway, slightly trembling in fear. If I were to be killed by someone or something lurking in the musty-smelling blackness no one would find me until the next day. My practical, engineering side struggled to convince me that there was no such thing as ghosts. Then, I'd go back down to the music room, finish my vocals, make sure I took the empty beer cans out, and lock the door on the way out. That's where I recorded a good part of my "Kansai Rocks!" CD.

I climbed that mountain because it was there, and it led me closer to the sky. At the time I didn't know that in a year I would have my own school, an unsupervised laboratory from which to continue the experiment of opening doors of cultural appreciation for myself and others. But this time it would be with my very own guinea pigs, I mean students, and it would be combined with teaching the English language.

CHAPTER 14

PERFECTLY NAUGHTY LITTLE PERVS

Let me start by saying living in New York City and my Taiwan Bar Mitzvah could have never prepared me for anything quite like teaching kids, aged four to thirteen, in Japan. So, when I had the chance to buy the school from Izah, it was part trepidation and part intrigue, to discover that buying the business meant that I was buying the students with it. Blithely, I accepted the responsibility. But nothing could have prepared me for what I had jumped into, and I mean nothing. I had barely any experience teaching English to kids and it was something I'd have to learn very quickly.

These little people in Japan are scary smart and highly independent. They've been taking trains by themselves since they were five and six years old because this isn't the kind of society where somebody is likely to rob them or snatch them off the sidewalk and into a car – this is Kyoto, Japan, a very safe place. And I happen to be in a particularly nice neighborhood here. Some of my kid students have parents that are both doctors. Although not specific to Japan, many kids that come from advantaged, highly educated families don't get the parental attention and time that other kids might get, or that I got in my upbringing. Japanese elementary school kids have developed wildly independent spirits, sometimes acting out in ways that could not be naughtier or more rebellious.

In Japan, schools including the weekend cram schools, or *jukus*, are zones of proper and respectful codes of behavior, an extension of disciplined conformity. Add to that the fact that there is most certainly a Tiger-Mom culture in Japan. Moms can be strict and demanding, pushing their children to excel academically and to be the best in their piano school's annual recital. There are even lengthy summer break homework assignments given out to keep young brains focused and in tune for the short six-week break. Many attend special Summer juku courses. Is it possible that all of this takes a toll on their psychological and emotional well-being? Could it be to the detriment of developing social skills needed later in life for things like conflict resolution? Time will tell.

My school is not a Japanese-run cram school. It's a completely different platform where they can loosen up, unfurl and spread their little wild wings. Unfortunately, in the beginning I had no training in teaching kids, and sometimes things got out of control. My bad. I didn't know that the smart thing to do would have been to draw boundaries from the get-go, things like "no go" zones, "don't touch this" zones and lines of bad behavior that couldn't be crossed. I also soon realized their previous teacher, Izah, the guy I bought the school from, hadn't been much of a boundary drawer either. A few of these kids are prematurely developed, professional button pushers and "limits of tolerance testers" who sometimes literally bounce off the walls. My only intensive face to face experience with children up until that time was with my daughter, Mimi, and she was an angel and not prone to that kind of misbehavior (except for the time that I pulled some anime character cards from her jacket pocket that she almost shoplifted from a convenience store.) I was neither warned about nor psychologically prepared to be the 60-minute steward of these amped up and wired kids! To give you an idea of what I mean, the very first day I took over the school, I set up my $400 studio monitor speakers on chest-level shelves. These would support my audio-visually-rich lesson plans which would include music and dancing, chanting, YouTube videos and more. I'd carefully packed them up and brought them with me from New York. I was proud of my high-end, compact Rokit brand studio monitors, they'd been an integral part of my music production life. I thought they'd be perfect for teaching in my new "language and culture center." But the cool, shiny black encased yellow woofer circles, round rubber bubble tweeters and LED light proved utterly enticing for kids. To a young child's untrained curious eye, they looked like some sort of interactive robot toy. After my first class of six-year-olds on a Saturday morning, I noticed while cleaning up that the round silver centers of the meticulously designed yellow woofer cones were now pushed in on both speakers. They were no longer shiny reflecting circles but were now little finger-dented honeycombs that don't quite woof like they used to. I thought, OMG, this was the first class! All my fragile shit is history! They're going to destroy all my cool stuff! God help my guitar and plants!

To my students, the WAVE represents a fun oasis away from responsibility. Here, they can pound on drums and climb on sofas with abandon. There's games and books and even a mini basketball hoop here. They see this place as a hiatus from boring textbooks and regimented exam-driven curriculums. I'm delighted when I stick my head out of the window and see them enthusiastically running down the street on their way here.

Part of the challenge of teaching children English is their short attention spans. It's said that kids have the attention span equal in minutes to their age in years. Although the original Aiza Aloha English was a tried and true kids' school, the WAVE has morphed into a cross between that and an English immersion fun center; a refuge from their ridiculous schedules of ballet classes, violin lessons and jukus. They get to spend an hour with a foreigner who is a little bit off and a lot different from their fathers. Or anyone they've ever met, for that matter. So, I use a lot of music and games in my teaching and completely let myself off the hook with acting and role-playing, doing funny impressions, and making impromptu games. But, what really intrigues me and sometimes shocks me is how extreme some of the kids' behavior can be.

Westerners so often associate disciplined civil behavior with the Japanese mindset. They envision obedient, uniformed well-behaved rugrats doing what they're supposed to do, especially in front of adults. This little story contrasts that and perhaps shows a shift away from it. Or maybe it's just my karma. These kids are likely much more measured at home and in school, so when they get away from the structure, the pendulum swings wildly in the other direction.

For example, Nanami and Yuki are sisters. They're part of my extra wild Friday night crowd. I have three after-school classes in a row that seamlessly overlap a little bit as sometimes kids arrive early and there's no reception area outside of my triangular fishbowl classroom. As I mentioned before: some of these kids particularly struggle with boundaries, especially when there's none drawn for them. Imagine this, if you will. There I was in one of my very first classes, focused on doing a successful job and making a good impression on the kids. I was committed to teaching them English. Building a good reputation for my school depended on it. Their new English teacher, Jay Sensei was attentively standing ready.

Then, I met Nanami and Yuki for the first time. Yuki is six and Nanami is nearly eight. I was trying to control the five or six kids present and develop some semblance of an educational lesson flow rather than just hanging out with them playing games. There are soft comfortable inviting sofas in my school. As I walked by one, six-year-old Yuki was sitting there with her dress hiked up. She flashed me more than a mischievous smile as she pulled her panties aside, showing me her vagina, testing me to see what kind of reaction I'd give. I was shocked but didn't lose stride as I walked by calling out to the kids to sit at the desks for worksheet time. All I could think was, "well this is going to be an interesting gig, teaching kids at this school."

Then there's Cocolo who was also six years old. With a voice that booms like truck driver, she has the cheeky personality of a schmaltzy Japanese comedian. With her dark complexion and a cute, short-haired, page-boy haircut she looks like a little Mexican kid. Pound for pound she has more punch in her than any kid I've ever met her age. One day, she picked up my school's phone, yelling into it in some sort of improv role play all by herself. She was completely off what I was trying to teach the other kids and suddenly

PERFECTLY NAUGHTY LITTLE PERVS

A future comedian? Can you tell from the look on one of my favorite student's face that she once picked up the school phone and yelled "Emergency, come quickly! Jay Sensei is a pervert!?" These kids are too much.

started yelling into the phone *"Hayaku hayaku! Kinkyu desu! Jay-sensei wa hentaidesu*! (Teacher Jay is a pervert, come quickly! It's an emergency!)"

She yelled it three or four times, and each time the grin on her round face widened more until she was laughing hysterically. All the other kids were also boisterously laughing. It was summer and the windows to the street and sidewalk were wide open, so people walking by would look up to hear laughter and a kid's voice yelling, "Jay-sensei is a pervert, come quickly, it's an emergency!"

On another day, a little boy had found pieces of original artwork I was gifted by my former roommate in New York, Takeshi Ishikawa, a talented artist. They're bright swirling oil and sand textured surrealistic symbols of culture that I prize. Painted on unframed stretched canvass, these one foot square cubes of a toothy fish, a high-heeled shoe and a house catch the eye of anyone who sees them. Whatever possessed this little boy to climb up the back of the couch and remove them from where they were hanging on the wall? I have no idea, but I should have noticed it sooner. It was almost too late when I realized that he was systematically taking them off the walls as if he was some sort of curator in a gallery, carefully placing them on the floor. His plan was to apparently embellish this original artwork. I caught his hand a moment before the sharpie marker reached the canvass.

A big part of teaching in my school involves vigilant observation. These kids are way too wired from so much schooling and pressure from their parents. Often, with sarcastic, perverted humor, they completely entertain each other. In doing so, they can completely challenge every nerve and fiber in my body. Sometimes it's completely manageable and I can corral that energy into

132 / LOVESIC in KYOTO

constructive learning again with some semblance of lesson or education. But, occasionally the kite string breaks and the class flies up and away and who knows where it will land. It is my intent to always come up with something completely different, to feed them an educational meal that they would never be served in another one of their schools. Could I successfully harness these young broncos? Sometimes I succeed. Other times, I am amazed by how their behavior thwarts my best laid plans. If I took myself too seriously and didn't have a good sense of humor, I'd be swimming upstream daily toward certain mental collapse. Here's some examples: I do an energetic call and response chant to get them to memorize natural phrases in English. It's the polar-opposite of a text book. As I sit on a cajón box drum, I play a loud hip-hop or dance beat and yell out Japanese and then the English meaning in rhythm to the beat.

Me: "KUrikae su" (i.e., repeat) Them: "KUrikae su"

Me: "Repeat" Them: "Repeat"

Me: "Metcha kuCHA!" Them: "Metcha kuCHA!"

Me: "What a mess!" Them: "What a mess!"

Me: "HOttoite!" Them: "HOttoite"

Me: "Leave me alone"

Them: "Leave me alone!" (and so on).

They love it. At least they did for a year or two. Today's brilliant culturally hip idea was, "Why not teach them 'We are the Champions' by Queen?" In theory, it seemed like a perfect thing to do. Put on a karaoke version with lyrics on a big TV screen. I prepared them by translating and drilling them on the chorus. "We are the champions, my friend! We'll keep on fighting 'til the end." They would learn the three or four lines, and I would sing the verses all fully amplified with lots of reverb through my dented studio monitors. I must admit, the idea was inventive, but the execution very quickly went south into questionable. Three of them had the mic and began to sing loudly and surprisingly in pitch. The first time they sang the lyrics perfectly, "We are the champions, my friend." But I noticed that while I was singing the second verse, they were whispering to each other. The second chorus came out as, "We are *unchi*, my friend (we are shit), We keep on fighting 'til the end. We are *oppai* (tits), *Sensei wa hentai* (teacher is a pervert)," yelling on a microphone at full volume as people walked by outside. They were laughing hysterically, having the time of their lives as I dove for the volume knob on the mixing board. Yes, it was just another typical day at The WAVE. That's what I get paid to do.

So maybe, just maybe the joke is on me. By necessity I have taken on a new career, but I'd like to not think of teaching English as a career. It's an expedient means toward a glorious end. Remember, I'm a songwriter. I'm a producer. I'm a singer. I'm that white percussionist in the reggae calypso rock band. I was a contorting industrial alternative rock singer in New York who used to jam with my friend Jim, with an old Indian tabla player sitting on the mat next to me, on a stage obscured in lights and strawberry flavored-fog. I'm the culture-fusion chef that cooks Middle Eastern melodies over three chord rock songs with hip hop beats. I am the chosen one! I think so, therefore I must be so. Right, Rene Descartes? The familiar adage, "you have to suffer if you want to sing the blues" worked for me in justifying almost two decades of the self-inflicted hardships I've endured. But is there an expiration date for this dream? Absolutely not! Dreams don't have expiration dates. I've learned and continue to relearn a few times a week that when push comes to shove you have to be able to inspire yourself. When laid out in a pile on a table in front of you the broken, colorful disparate little pieces of your life experience may seem unrelated and unexceptional. The varied colors may seem plain in juxtaposition or even clash, as do the jagged textures to the rounded beads. But take that seemingly random collection of particles and confine them in a small chamber at the end of an opaque tube. Now shake it, twist it and hold it up to light. Through a simple mathematical, optical arrangement of lenses, you can experience the swirling multi-dimensioned beauty, a kaleidoscope that is alive and radiant. Disorganized randomness becomes delightfully symmetrical and chaos becomes purposeful and gorgeous mystical alignment. That's how I perceive the swings of my life as they now go back and forth from teaching kids to teaching adults, from writing music to navigating the labyrinth of Japanese government bureaucracy (just so I can live here), from watching the collapsing Trump debacle on TV to the "Ten Deadliest Animal Attacks" on YouTube. There is humor and wisdom to be mined out of anything. The joke is on me, and thank the gods, the punch lines seem to write themselves.

One of my adult students is a gynecologist in his early thirties. He's charming and handsome, maybe too handsome for a gynecologist, and happily married with a young son. He's also a great guitar player, an active, published researcher and a fertility specialist. I learned more about endometriosis and the causes of irregular menstruation from him than I probably will ever need to know. One night after his lesson, I was so tired at 10:30 PM on a Friday night that I didn't erase the whiteboard. In fact, I didn't go home at all that night as I had early kids' classes on Saturday morning and there was a sofa in the classroom calling my name. There were unerased hand-drawn diagrams in black and blue markers of a woman's reproductive organ on the board when a few minutes before 10:00 AM the first few kids walked into my class. They looked up at the white board with the outline of the human uterus and dangling fallopian tubes drawn on it and screamed with delight, "I know, Sensei. It's a horse! It's horse's head, right?!"

CHAPTER 15

HEY, MR. BALDY!

Though it takes years of study and diligence, many Japanese do eventually develop admirable English language skills. They can read, write and understand enough to communicate clearly and effectively. Perhaps they are confident and look forward to successfully haggling in the markets over the price of a tapestry on their upcoming trip to Turkey. But it's possible it won't go as smoothly as expected, and that's due to subpar pronunciation. Understandable pronunciation is a whole other mountain to climb, and many Japanese English speakers have great difficulty mastering this feat. It's a slow, steep trek up the learning curve and it's not as interesting as developing the skills needed to speak and understand English. Pronunciation is simply not a priority. In spoken Japanese, most sounds are formed deep in the chest. They are then deftly routed through specific mouth and tongue movements to formulate the unique symphony that brings a smile to any foreigner observing an animated conversation between two or more Japanese. Even if you don't understand, it is still entertaining to watch as whatever it is being communicated comes out forcefully and melodically. In contrast, English has a lot more linguistic nuance than Japanese. The English-speaking tongue must have a wider range of motion and is more agile and flexible. (But that doesn't mean Japanese aren't great kissers!) Formulating natural and accurate English sounds is seemingly built in to most western and native English speakers and hardly given a second thought. But, it's very difficult for Japanese students. However, to my Japanese friends, I can't overstate the importance of at least semi-accurate pronunciation. The impact and effectiveness of well-formed arguments and carefully structured sentences can be obliterated by poor pronunciation, and even more so when ESL speakers are speaking to other ESL speakers. Many have bad habits that have never been addressed and corrected or they "oo" and "ah" and "hmm" in between phrases making their conversation difficult to follow. At my university, I can barely understand some of the great technical speakers I'm training. They speak too fast, or in sleep-inducing, robot-like monotone. Perhaps there's no supporting hand movements or body language, or they have the slow meter of a drum machine on quaaludes that slurs and bores the listener into drooping eyelid detachment.

I met a guy for a "trial lesson" at my beloved first teaching stint at Velco English School in Osaka. The trial lesson was his free-of-charge opportunity to decide if this was the right school for him to join. Sometimes people attend trial lessons just to exploit an advertised free hour to practice English with a foreigner. He was a refined, debonair, and obviously successful man with a corporate demeanor about him. I remember he seemed a little too well-dressed for this Sunday afternoon group class of five or six students. In a booming baritone voice, the kind you would hear in a radio voice-over, he confidently said upon meeting, "Hey, how are you? I'm Izuki. It's a pleasure to meet you." Coupled with a smile and a firm handshake he sat down at the oval conference table next to the other students. He was ready to show off his stuff to all the female students and the other businessman in the class. To start off the conversation class, I had the students introduce themselves to each other. When he spoke, he said, "I'm Jun Izuki and I work for a pharmaceutical company," in perfect inflection with girded confidence. After all the students introduced themselves, I asked him a simple question, "How did you develop such incredible English skills?" His answer, "Movies, watching movies," echoed off the walls and ceiling with the acoustic cojones of a late night talk show announcer. My follow-up question was, "Can you explain to us exactly what your role is at the pharmaceutical company? What do you do there?"

He never broke his smile for a good ten-seconds of silence, which was a dead giveaway. I have come to realize that an extended silent smile from someone you are talking to in English usually means "*no comprende*." This guy had no idea what I was talking about, clueless as to what was being asked of him. Apparently, it had never come up in any of the several movies in which he had painstakingly paused and repeated to memorize the dialogues in English. The people around the table were as shocked as I was since he first came across as a self-assured, confident English speaker. He was somewhere between what we call a super-beginner and a beginner. So, that was another culture in the petri dish, this social experiment known as an English conversation lesson. It was always an experiment because I never knew who was going to show up each day, what mood they'd be in, or if there'd be new students. I loved and thrived in it. It wasn't so much teaching as taking people spelunking through the dark caves of English grammar. Sometimes the students just wanted to hear a foreigner's perspective on life. I was sincerely being interrogated about such topics as, "Do you have any friends that are gay, or why aren't you Christian? I thought all Americans were Christians. Why does everybody in America have guns?" Or, "Have you ever shot somebody?" So, sitting in that teacher's chair was in a sense like standing on stage doing some educational performance art or hosting a talk show. It was a never boring combination of teaching, prodding people to speak or stimulate conversation, deflecting or inviting flirtation, while always steering away from potentially deadly cliffs. I was Oprah Winfrey, Deepak Chopra and Stephen Colbert, wrapped up in one Sensei.

At Velco, in addition to several group adult conversation classes, I was tasked to teach a pronunciation course on Sunday mornings. Since we native speakers take articulation for granted, I felt it important to research the subject and how to teach it. There are names for sounds and entire chapters of books written about forming different sounds. I learned that a diphthong is a sound that can only be made by moving your mouth, lips and tongue in a certain way to say to get out an "oy," or an "aw." There's an entire science to teaching pronunciation and, naturally, I wanted to put my own flair to it. I have come to realize that many Japanese are not biologically equipped to pronouncing certain sounds, especially when it comes to the R and the L sounds. So, to solve the conundrum of mixed up L and R sounds that taunts pretty much all Japanese ESL speakers, I Googled and found a four second video on YouTube. It was a disgusting illustrated cross-section of the human mouth with a tongue formulating the "R" sound. I thought this would be a great way to teach "R." I did verbally explain that the tongue stays flat and doesn't move from the bottom of the mouth but simply changes its shape. I reminded them that in the L sound, the tongue becomes thin and pointy and gently kicks off the two front teeth on top like a swimmer making a kick turn. But discussion could only go so far. We needed visuals and drilling. The video was interesting but a little gross and too short. I had to keep rewinding it.

I don't know if you've ever seen a cross-section of a tongue, from front to back let alone drawn one on a whiteboard with a black marker. The shape of a human tongue doesn't look like the cow's tongue that you see sliced in a kosher deli. It's fat and cylindrical. So, when you're drawing the tongue in a relaxed "pre-R sound" position on a white board in front of a class of five female students from 18 to 50-years-old, basically what you're drawing looks like the outline of a horizontal flaccid penis. Then, when you show them how the tongue changes shape to make the "R" sound and how the tip points slightly upward so that the air can flow over it, you're basically drawing what appears to be an erect penis. The rounded back or base of the tongue morphs into the attached balls. No matter how professional I tried to come across, I was still a foreign man who'd been up late the night before drawing a dick on the board. Everybody was doing their best to restrain themselves and be respectful, not acknowledging out loud that the foreign man had just drawn a flaccid penis on the whiteboard with arrows to show how it becomes an erect penis. It was now time to put this mouth-opening knowledge into practice and do some pronunciation drilling. One by one the women around the oval-shaped table touched their tongues to the back of their upper front teeth for the L or bent their tongues to catch the R. My job naturally was to coach them from my chair at the head of the table. I would have to zoom in on their faces, one by one, to properly evaluate their technique. Analyzing tongue and mouth movement against the sounds coming out seemed the quickest way to help them improve. They tittered in self-conscious giggles and beamed proudly when realizing they'd done it, and slayed the grinning L vs. R dragon, at least for the moment. I was also giggling inside, because truthfully, if there was no talking and some funky, cheesy disco soundtrack to what was happening in the room, those close-ups sure looked like the beginning of a porn movie.

Tongue twisters can also come in handy when training the mouth and brain to pronounce English properly. Go ahead native English speakers. Try to say, "Rupert is very rarely late" three times in a row fast, or "Recently Larry really, really likes Lorraine." They're fun – and, they can turn into good songs! "Really, Really Risa" came out of a funny conversation from one of those lessons and turned into one of my favorite songs, hopefully to be included in my next CD.

For foreigners trying to speak Japanese, the same is true of the Japanese language. What are deeply ingrained, clear distinctions in phonetics taught and solidified in Japanese kindergartens can be slippery slopes of confusion to foreigners. *Kawaii* (kah WAH EE) means cute and *kowai* (ko WAI) means scary. To untrained foreign ears they sound the same, especially in a speedy conversation when the brain is trying to distill context. It's akin to how trouble and travel sound the same to Japanese ears. Foreigners should not wimp out on copping a Y sound when it should be the common RY sound in Japanese (Your friend's name is not Yo, it's more like Urrrryyyyo). Note to beginner Japanese learners: Before attempting this, make sure there is no food in your mouth and avoid chewing gum because it can become a dangerous projectile. Don't ask me how I know this is true. I am still seriously Japanese-challenged although I am improving by osmosis and a twice a month "language exchange" lesson. The quest for survival, constant exposure and contact has manifested in my skewed, almost viable Japanese language skills. I can rattle off a clever phrase or sharp, well-timed remark when called for. But that can get me deeper in trouble than if I just pleaded guilty to monolingualism, much like that movies-taught trial student. I live to communicate and be communicated to, so I have made a point to amass a wealth of great phrases and impressive words. Some of them draw from old traditional concepts and phrases and are expressed only in kanji. Like the previously mentioned *taiki bansei*, late blooming flowers are the most beautiful. They always elicit a smile and a "how do you know that? You speak great Japanese." Other phrases in my arsenal are business related and some are simply wise-cracks. I've put together a patchwork that combines useful phrases with expressive intonation that can make almost anyone smile, laugh, or assist me despite any semblance of proper grammatical underpinning.

But that still leaves me stranded in the middle of the beginner Japanese-speaker category. In addition to my lightweight grammar skills, for the time being, I still can't read beyond kindergarten level. I'm like a wise-worded six-year-old kid reading from a dictionary, and my listening skills are pre-teen on a good day. It has been enough to survive but has caused me some unexpected embarrassment as well.

There's a fine Italian restaurant, Il Piano, which is near the WAVE. I went there three years ago with my wife and daughter shortly after I took over the school. We had a wonderful Sunday brunch in the shadow of the grounds of Gosho, the former Imperial Palace. The owner, a jolly and pudgy but serious Japanese guy in his 50s, was nearly completely bald, if it weren't for a few combed over cartoon-like strands. I didn't get a chance to talk to him that day, but we exchanged smiles and nonverbal niceties. A week or so later, I was giving a lesson in my school to a young man of great upbringing and stature who owns a nearby French restaurant. He's a good-natured guy and a great English speaker. I said to him, "I went to Il Piano last week, are you familiar with it?" He said, "Oh, yes. It's great restaurant. Did you meet Hage san (HAH gay san)?" and I said, "Oh, yeah. The owner. He seems like a nice guy. The food is really good, a little too expensive, though." After talking with the French restaurant owner, I was under the impression that the Italian restaurant owner's name was Mr. Hage, as it seemed a given that restaurant owners in the same neighborhood would be acquainted.

A few weeks later, I was riding my bike in the neighborhood. I was new to the area and was starting to be recognized by my neighbors as the teacher of the English school around the corner. That afternoon, I saw "Mr. Hage" outside his restaurant. As I rode my bicycle by, in a friendly animated voice, I called out, *"kon' nichiwa, Hage san,"* (good afternoon) and waved to him. I noticed he didn't wave back. He just looked at me. I peddled down the street a bit and turned around. He'd walked inside. I thought it was odd that he didn't say hi back to me. At our next English lesson, I mentioned this to the French restaurant owner. I said, "I saw the owner of Il Piano and waved at him, but he didn't wave back." The French restaurant owner was a little puzzled and replied, "Oh, but he's a nice guy." I replied, "Yeah, I saw him and yelled '*Hage-san*,' but he ignored me," to which my student fell off the couch laughing. The word *hage* (HAH gay) apparently means bald in Japanese. Essentially what I'd done was ride my bicycle down the street in my new neighborhood where there were maybe four or five people within earshot and yelled to the owner of an exclusive Italian restaurant, "Hey, Baldy! Good afternoon!" I haven't been back there since.

Another language-challenged moment was during a Monopoly game which is another name for what I thought would be a clever kids' lesson at the WAVE. There were six kids. My idea was to introduce them to Monopoly and teach them phrases like "build a house," "save money," "expensive," "change please," "bad neighborhood," and other useful life concepts. I was fully prepared for a lesson but not prepared for the kids' behavior. There were three teams and they were all enjoying the hell out of themselves until one of the kids, Shinichi, was caught cheating. He was passing Indiana Avenue behind his back to Ayano, his second-grade girlfriend of sorts. Yuki and his brother, Daiki, saw it and a huge fight ensued. It quickly escalated to an all-out free-for-all with tears, two brothers screaming at the cheaters and even some hair pulling as a shamed Shinichi ran out of the school crying. I couldn't get him to come back in. He ran upstairs to the Cat Café and cried in the vestibule.

Again, I mention that I have never had training in classroom management and have a relatively low tolerance for rude behavior or what I deem unacceptable behavior. It took about ten or fifteen minutes for me to get the whole thing back together and get everybody sitting down. There were a few red faces and some bruised egos as basically two kids had been busted in the act! What else could I do but try to salvage a lesson from the excitement and continue with the game? Checking the Google translator app on my iPhone, which I affectionately call "Google Sensei," I looked up the word "cheating." Cheating came out in Japanese as something like "*uwaki*." So naturally, I did what I thought I should do and put the negation suffix nai on it and said strictly to everyone three or four times, "*uwaki nai!...OK!*" By this time, they were all getting along. At the end of the class when the parents came to pick them up. I thought it would be above and beyond to explain to them that we were playing Monopoly and that there was an incident and some of the kids might still be a little upset. So, in my broken Japanese, I explained that the school had a strict rule, *uwaki nai*, there is no cheating. I noticed a strange expression from the parents. A few days later I had another group kids' class and I did the same thing. I'd firmly stated to the baffled expressions of the kids, "*uwaki nai...OK*" and repeated it to their parents who barely spoke any English. My intention was to have the parents reinforce to their kids my newly proclaimed policy of no cheating in any class games or contests.

At my next language exchange lesson, I proudly conveyed my experience to my Japanese teacher. She informed me that my new phrase *uwaki nai*, the sword of justice and fair play that I had held high in the air over two-dozen elementary school kids and their mothers, translated as "no seducing, no sexual affairs allowed." Thanks again, "Google Sensei." I'm glad I could "trust" you!

CHAPTER 16

%#@! MY RED CAT PLEASE

Some people have spent years studying Japanese before moving to Japan. Some go to formal Japanese language schools while living in Japan or they study or work in universities and have access to intensive language programs. But I haven't had the time to commit myself to serious Japanese language learning. I often work late into the evening supporting a family and two homes in two cities. I run a business by myself, soup to nuts, and teach at a university. I write, perform and produce original music and make my own videos. I've had a difficult time trying to find time to write and edit this book. As mentioned before, I can get by on what I have learned in a few years of English - Japanese lessons along with body language, intuition guided reactions and responses, and gestures. It's a wonder how far you can get with smiling, nodding, laughing and high fiving. I also benefit from the fact that Japanese has borrowed lots of words from English and other languages, especially since World War II. These words or *gairaigo* did not exist in ancient times so they weren't carried forward into modern Japanese.

Many describe western concepts and things that have been imported into Japanese culture. Sometimes they also express an attachment to the fashionability of English. Simply "over-pronouncing" some of these words in English will get a point across. If you look at a guard in a department store and in an inquisitive tone say *esukarētā*, you'll be pointed towards the escalator. As you get more accustomed to this, you can even predict what many words would sound like after being fed through the Japanese pronunciation meat grinder. You learn that a *chiketto* is a ticket. That you want *miruku* (milk) when you order your *kōhī* (coffee) at *Sutabakkusu* (Starbucks). You can order a *biru* (beer) with your *hanbāgu* (hamburger) or have a *soseji sand* (McSausage sandwich) while working on your *pasokon* (personal computer, laptop) at *Makudonarudo* (McDonald's). Don't forget to hit the *toiletto* (bathroom) before you take a *takushi* (taxi) back to the *hoteru*. If you're lost, just check *guguru*! Then there are words derived from English that have a less direct connection to the original English meanings. These *wasei eigo* or Japanese-made English can be downright delightful and show the playfulness that Japanese have with language. *Bebī-kā* (beh BEE kah) is a stroller. A baby car! A *gasutando* (gas stand) is where you fill up your car or *motobaiku*. If you have a license but don't own a car you are a *PAYpa doRAIba* (paper driver.) *FurEE saizu* (free size) is one-size-fits-all. So, day by day, week by week I hear something and inscribe it on my spinning wobbly mental "rosetta stone," and that gets me through ordering food, finding places, buying things and communicating with severely English-challenged Japanese. Even if I'm not able to communicate accurately or in detail, at least everybody in the bar has a good laugh!

Regarding that translating technology, the Google Translator app is free, and thankfully its features, capability and language databases are continually being updated. What's great about it is that it has voice recognition and character recognition. You can go seamlessly from German to traditional Mandarin Chinese to Spanish and back and forth, all in real time. You can walk with your smartphone in hand and point it at a sign in a Thai vegetable market and know exactly what you're buying. You can be that Global Citizen, communicating clearly and effortlessly no matter what corner of the universe you happen to be in...NOT! As good as digital nonhuman translation is, there are severe deficiencies. The complexity of linguistics between different languages can cause a lot of confusion that even these algorithms and databases can't manage, at least not accurately. There are also local dialects to contend with, speech impediments, those "oohs" and "aahs" fillers that come out of us as we're thinking of what to say, not to mention dead batteries and bad reception. If you do use it, be aware that it may completely miss the mark and cause more confusion than those simple hand gestures, and absolutely pay attention to the settings. In a culturally sensitive environment like, oh, say an English class, make sure it's set to filter out dirty words.

At the WAVE, there are times when you just need to ditch the lesson plan and just let them go.

Generally, English slang is known by Japanese, at least the big, dirty words and phrases. If you let your proper decorum guard down and shouted "asshole!" at a cyclist who almost ran you off the sidewalk into the street, he would get it. However, it's highly unlikely a Japanese cyclist would do the same. I was at my school teaching children ranging from six to eight-years-old. Kids get a kick out of speaking into the cellphone translator because the app replies in English to their fast-spoken Japanese in a female voice that is somewhere in between robotic and sultry.

On that memorable day, I don't know what was being discussed or taught. But I do remember we had a make-a-sentence game where English words and pictures on puzzle pieces were connected to form sentences. While proudly looking down at his creation in the sentence-making game, one kid yelled something into my iPhone. It came blurting back as a polite and robotic "Fuck my red cat, please." I had to fight to pry their little fingers off my phone as they just had to hear it again and see if the Japanese text matched what they think they heard. I had alarming visions of disgruntled parents scolding me about the colorful language I was teaching to their children. So, be forewarned and check your settings! Despite this noticeable faux pas, it's getting better year by year as Google is constantly updating databases and adjusting those algorithms.

All in all, for seven years and through a variety of gigs, I am hopeful that I have instilled something different and useful in the myriad people I have engaged. Frankly, I'm not just opening their eyes to English language but to another cultural perspective. The dynamic is fun, unpredictable and eye opening at times, for both sides. Often, I feel as though I'm sitting in the front row of a movie theater watching an incredible drama that's feeding my creativity and getting paid for it!

Foreigners have been coming to Japan to teach English for decades. There are native speaking English teachers everywhere now. I have seen that many Japanese have developed a palpable distrust and a smidgeon of contempt for them. This is because a fair amount of resident *gaijin* (foreigners) tend to not aim so high and fall into low-ceiling lifestyles of daily drinking and excessive dating, often exploiting the fact that they're an exotic foreigner in this homogeneous society.

In addition to improving English literacy in Japan there is such a need for people to have a fresh source of inspiration, to broaden their perspective and to raise their periscope up further than before. It is not just my opinion that there is a real lack of spirituality across much of Japan. This positions me in an ideal situation to really impact people's lives, which is unbelievably gratifying. Somehow it justifies my being a teacher and sparks a lot of fire into wanting to further impact people's lives through culture, especially music. I'm also humbled every day by how much I still have left to learn.

So, having the chance to buy a school, teach with my own style and be an upstanding member of this community has been a great opportunity for me. It ties very neatly into my Buddhist practice and mission to be socially engaged and to somehow help educate and lift people up, or at least help them connect to their greater selves. I know that may sound lofty and heavy-handed, but when it comes from face-to-face, life-to-life connections, it's what I'm about. At this stage of my life, I feel like I'm accomplishing it almost every day.

CHAPTER 17

POWER
OF THE WORD

"Words have the power to both destroy and heal. When words are both true and kind, they can change our world."

- Gautama Buddha

"**D**on't worry," I told my students for over a year. "Don't worry, he won't be president. I know what you see on TV is scary. But, don't worry." After taking my foot out of my mouth, I found myself trying to explain the unexplainable, how what Donald Trump says may not actually be true, in fact or to his real intent.

In Japan, spoken and written words, and communication are usually taken literally. When Japanese people speak, generally they think over the intended consequence and what the reaction of the listener will be. They pay just as much attention to the tone of their words. After spoken words exit a human's mouth, it's almost as if they take on a life of their own. What was once a thought has now been converted into moving waves of air capable of being heard. The words and their weight live long after they're spoken, hanging on the air with full intent. Words uttered in everyday conversations in America and many other countries tend be focused more acutely toward having intended short-lived impact. Donald Trump's words are downright weightless.

Let's say someone has bumped into you accidentally on a sidewalk of New York or you have an argument about who's next in line at a supermarket. If bad moods overrule common sense and it seems a reckless enough act on someone's behalf, there is the chance of a brief ugly exchange of expletives to follow. The result is that steam is blown off and people then go on their way and forget about it. That is likely the end of it, unless it isn't (i.e., there is always the possibility of someone walking around with an exposed fuse just waiting for someone to light it.) In Japan, though, words have more impact on and deeper penetration into people's lives. Cultural mores also seem to cause people to keep more of their frustrations inside. True opinions are often trumped by decorum or the intrinsic culturally identified desire to maintain harmony and keep everything cool. Keep a smile and don't stir things up unnecessarily. It's simply not worth the trouble it may cause. The default tendency for most Japanese is toward politeness, and it's endearing. Foreigners come to Japan and notice there's an abundance of respectful civility here, which may be lacking in a large part of the world. But sometimes I think that politeness masks insecurity and often quells an important impulse to speak out for justice. Perhaps it's a way to deal with that internalization. Generally, it's a good thing. However, it can lead to a lot of miscommunication and misunderstanding. Add to that the fact that the complexity of the Japanese language, with its gradations of formality and various dialects, plus the fact that there are three different written languages wrapped into one, and you have all the ingredients for awkward or worse miscommunication.

Japanese challenged foreigners panic even more than Japanese when these alerts blare up on their phones. "Osaka, prepare yourselves, a strong earthquake is about to happen." Why can't they also be in English?

For example, I remember someone sweating for hours over an email they were helping me write. I was attempting to follow up on a meeting I had with an executive at AVEX, perhaps the largest entertainment company in Japan based in Tokyo. He had initially requested this meeting and, upon finding out I was a songwriter/musician, had also asked me to send him my music. Two days after our meeting, I'd sent a detailed proposal for a teaching program along with a half dozen or so of my songs. The guy never took the time to get back to me. After two weeks of radio silence, I was now tasked with writing a somewhat sensitive email to get an answer or elicit a response. If I wrote it in English, it would be, "Dear such and such, I am confirming that you received my letter and proposal of two weeks ago. I ask that you kindly get back to me with feedback, or with any questions you may have." I might include an addendum, "and, by the way I'm curious as to whether you listened to the music I sent you, per your request."

But there's so much to consider and grapple with here in Japanese. Balancing the complexities of formal Japanese written from a near stranger who wants to sound polite to a big wig, while at the same time getting the point across and maybe showing a little bit of annoyance that no time was taken to reply, was no easy task. It's easy to do this in English. I just did it in thirty seconds. But it can and did take hours for somebody to put that same message together in Japanese. You want to strike the right tone, but you don't want to push it too far. Should I use this word or that one for feedback? Or, this word or that one for urgency? How do I get my point across without offending the receiver? The entire experience is just so fucking cerebral and over-adjudicated! I just needed to say what was on my mind. As it turned out, the executive V.P. or Assistant Director, whatever his title, of the largest entertainment company in Japan never got back to me, which in any business culture would be considered outright rude and unacceptable.

Regarding direct communication, typically most New Yorkers are raised with it. It's a way of life. I remember being in New York around Union Square near the SGI-USA Buddhist culture center. I had a meeting to attend, and that area is a busy neighborhood. In New York, people drive around the surrounding blocks for a long time waiting for a parking spot to open, a free parking spot, that is. A full day parking in this neighborhood on a Sunday costs $21. Miraculously, I saw a car pull out of a spot which I then quickly pulled into. At the same time, a working-class guy in a big station wagon had been in the street a few yards in front of me. I didn't notice his backup lights which he claimed were on. As I got out of my fortuitously parked car in victory, he got out of his car and yelled, "Hey, that's my spot!" I replied,

"It's MY spot. I'm in it. What are YOU doing? You've been sitting in your car." So, he said to me with a slow, menacing smile on his face, "I wouldn't leave my car there if I was you." This was about as clear and direct a threat as anyone could express. I didn't think twice. I quickly got back in the car and pulled out, leaving the spot for him to take. I really did appreciate the directness of communication. That would have never happened quite that way in Japan. In Japan you'll never hear anything like, "That dress makes you look fat" or "Are you crazy? I'm not going to eat that shit!" Gene, the Israeli president of my former company, Mana Contemporary, once scolded me in a manner that would have surely driven a mid-level Japanese manager to take a dive in front of a rush hour train and end it all. Imagine in full view and earshot of an office of 25, being scolded and insulted by, "What the fuck are you doing here in the office?! You should be out in the streets launching this new division!" When I tried to calmly explain that I was waiting for a delivery of brochures from the printers it was just "gasoline being poured onto his fire." "Bullshit! You're just masturbating! You're just MASTURBATING!" as he marched into his office and slammed the door. Although flabbergasted, I soon came to realize that it was nothing but tough Israeli love - a little motivation, if you will. When my coworker, Wendy, in our Chicago office encouraged me to lowball a client to get them to sign with my company instead of tiptoeing around my bosses she lovingly said, "Don't be such a cunt! Just get them in the building and deal with Micha (my boss) tomorrow." Every man should be called a cunt by a woman at least once in their lives. Part of me misses those days.

But it's not just the "world's apart" manner of communication that, as a foreigner, I find confusing in Japan. There are also bold-lined boundaries drawn between what's appropriate to talk about and what's not. I once asked a student at a group lesson, "So, who did you vote for?" It was the day after a regional election and it seemed like a good conversation starter. A few sideways glances between students preceded a very polite explanation from one of them that it's a little rude to ask and they'd rather not reveal their selections. On Japanese TV you'll rarely see fiery pundits from opposing parties battling it out which is the staple of many a Westerner's TV diet.

Backing up the power of words in Japan, how and whence they're spoken, is also the sanctity of the promise. "I'll get back to you soon" or "let's get the families together" may have been said as a cordial nicety, but it is expected to happen. That invitation will never be forgotten, and that person will eventually invite you and your family to dinner at their house. Even if it's two years later, they will live up to their promise. Their word, even said casually, is their bond. It is rare that was has been said out loud is just discarded. There is no such thing as "fleeting words" in this land of honor.

CHAPTER 18

FOOD
ALCOHOL
IZAKAYA

What the hell did I just eat? I thought it was your basic *onigiri*, or rice ball, from the convenience store but it was clearly something more exotic. About 20 different kinds of rice balls are sitting on the shelves, all wrapped in cleverly packaged cellophane that sections the dried seaweed away from the rice to keep it dry and crispy. You can't see what's inside the hand-pressed, molded rice triangle or flattened ball and the labels are all written in Japanese. Most foreigners don't understand the labels and the tiny printed images are small and indiscernible. If the store staff is too busy, you just try to recall the *kanji* characters for what you're looking at as best as you can. Let's see, the kanji for salmon (SHA-kay) is a big tree next to a fish skeleton standing on its tail. 鮭 But, unless you've studied written Japanese, you've no choice but to just pull the lever on the slot machine and hope for the best.

I often grab this cheap, quick fix between classes. As I walk down the sidewalk from the *conbini* (convenience store), I perform a ten-second sequence of unwrapping, sliding the dried seaweed out of a plastic sleeve, unfolding more cellophane, and then folding the whole kit together. One must precisely follow this well-designed origami ritual to get a perfectly triangular, crispy seaweed wrapped onigiri. I don't think the samurai had to go through this to eat their onigiri before going into battle. If you fuck it up, you'll wind up shoving a sticky amorphous mess, piece by piece in your mouth, followed by picking sticky grains of rice off your fingers.

This time, the assembly was a complete success, the seaweed didn't tear! But as I bit into it, my taste buds went haywire, pushing the emergency eject button on my tongue. Inspecting the exposed interior of the mystery rice ball

I could tell that it certainly wasn't salmon or a vegetable. I knew it wasn't kelp or some type of bulbous seaweed. It was fibrous, tasted unfamiliar and had a rubbery texture. The more I looked at it, the more it didn't look like any meat I've ever seen on a plate or even on Japanese TV. It certainly wasn't a fish. In fact, it looked a bit like something ripped off Shrek's face, little suction cup-like structures attached to a tough meat-like shaft. I didn't take a second bite. I'm a firm believer that humans should not eat something that their brains don't understand, so I spit the piece out into a napkin and dropped the entire thing into a garbage can outside of the conbini. I have no idea what it was and figure it must have been some nondescript organ from something that flies, swims or walks God's earth. In retrospect, I realize it may have been *tako*, or octopus, which generally doesn't belong in onigiri anyway.

For the untrained foreign eye, trying to figure out a menu in full frontal Japanese, void of any English or photos, can be daunting. For non-Japanese readers, buying food and ingredients in a supermarket can be a crapshoot. Now and then if you can find any uniformed employees bold enough to connect with you, there's a good chance you may have your question answered. But much of the time, it's luck-of-the-draw. The staff are usually very busy and "*gaijin-shy*," making them reluctant to reach out and help a confused foreigner.

After three years, I thought I had a pretty good handle on how to solve the daily continuous string of cryptic brainteasers that had become my new life in Japan. I could now pick up on little line drawings and recognize colors and themes on the containers in supermarkets and conbinis. If there was no image, I could at least make a high probability, educated guess. A few years ago, I had prided myself in the belief that I had finally arrived in Japan until I brushed my teeth with a tasteless toothpaste that turned out to be vaginal yeast infection cream. Even though I had the receipt, they wouldn't refund its cost.

Regarding food, I was excited initially at the prospect, "I'm moving to Japan. I'm going to completely change my diet and get healthy." Japan's fish and vegetable based diet puts Japan firmly in the category of a "blue-zone" which are areas where people live to comparatively older ages. Among other factors this is partly attributable to all the wonderful fatty oils that are consumed in a fish heavy diet. There is plenty of fresh fish in every corner of Japan and it comes in all shapes, sizes, colors, and textures. These range from bags of tiny little dried fish called *jako* to larger specimens. Back home I would have bought jako in a PETCO and given it to my cat as a reward for keeping everything cool in the litter box. There's also the finest sushi and sashimi in the world. But it didn't take long before I realized that half of the country now lives off food from those conbinis or what's been prepared and sold for take-out in supermarkets. The same factory-farmed chicken nuggets and other fast food you find in convenience stores in the West are everywhere in Japan. Ham, bacon and pork line the shelves and coolers in the ubiquitous 7-11's, Lawsons and Family Marts that are a short walk from anywhere. In addition to western standards like hot dogs, sausage, ham sandwiches and cheeseburgers, there are experimental hybridizations of cuisine that defy Western sensibilities. Who gave that baker the right to drape a strip of bacon over a crusty boat-shaped, open croissant that holds tuna salad in its cargo hold? I would say that about half of Japan eats a severely Westernized diet every day. What happened to all the fish I was supposed to be eating?

Co-opting cuisine, or rather cherry-picking dishes from other cultures and "Japanifying" them, has infiltrated the collective Japanese palate and worked its way into the national menu. To be fair, the bacon draped, tuna-filled croissant that would likely give conniptions to a French chef really works! I'm serious - it's killer! Now enter Domino's Pizza and Pizza Hut of Japan. The jury is still out on whether the "grilled beef tongue and asparagus" or the "juicy shrimp with sweet corn and melted mayonnaise and cheese" pizzas are guilty pleasures or well-marketed science projects. But one thing is for certain. Most of us foreigners agree that Japan doesn't do sandwiches right. Ramen yes, sandwiches no! It is true that a 700-yen ($6.38) bowl of ramen is usually packed to the gills with noodles and ingredients ranging from pork to scallions to ginger, garlic, bean sprouts, and Korean kimchee; a zillion plus calories at a reasonable price. It's filling as hell and contains most basic food groups, as well as high cholesterol and fat. It's good *cost performance* as they say (in what they think is normal English). But when it comes to sandwiches? Fail! The infatuation with bread and baking came to Japan with the Portuguese in the late 1500's. In modern times it has become an obsession in this bafflingly skinny, carb-obsessed rice-and-noodle-based society. And nowhere more so than here in Kyoto where bakeries are found on every block and have avid local followings, making them fixtures in their neighborhoods. Bread is practically worshipped here where loaves are sliced thicker than in the West. I grew up in a society that focused on the actual filling of the sandwich with the bread playing an important yet secondary role. Naturally the layered and sometimes folded array of meats and salads with well-paired cheese, lettuce, onions and dressings define the character of what we know of as the "sandwich experience." To most humans the bold presentation of the guts is the sandwich's appeal! In true-to-form attentiveness and sensitivity to detail, sandwiches in Japan are meticulously designed, delicious immersive experiences. But the emphasis is on aesthetics, with a limited offering of the themed, prized ingredients in the middle (which reason dictates is supposed to be the sandwich's appeal!). The innards of sandwiches here are often scant samplings of savouriness, proportioned and treated as if to embody the Japanese notion of *Wabisabi* (i.e. imperfect, impermanent, and incomplete). On this I call bullshit! Honestly, it's a frickin' sandwich and from a stomach's point of view it doesn't do the trick. A typical sandwich bought in a bakery or conbini is packaged so that there is an alluring layered cross section showing the meat or egg salad or tuna (i.e., *sea chicken*) smushed between two slices of bread. Ok, it's certainly fresh and seems worth the price. But upon tearing off the cellophane packaging you are confronted with a stingy arrangement of meats or whatever, ganged up in the center of the sandwich which tapers off into nothingness, well before it reaches the corners of the triangular cut half-sandwiches. Add to that the fact that the crust of the bread is trimmed off, and you have essentially a four or five bite mini "flavorgasm," leaving you wondering why you didn't buy two or three. Wake up Japan! A sandwich is supposed to be a meal all by itself, not unfulfilling, nibbling foreplay. An "overstuffed" sandwich in Japan would be laughed at by the Italian owners of Carmine's Deli in Jersey City. Oh God, please let me eat one more double cheesesteak special with "the works" before I die!

But, naturally, there's a different side to this premade convenience store life-on-the-run consumption. Japanese culture proudly and rightfully claims the title as the most food-centric society in the world. Every detail matters.

Each ingredient is acknowledged, brought to attention, and talked about down to its finest detail. Their food history spans centuries, and I wonder if this obsession has always been the case.

There's a vegetable called *nano-hana* which means yellow flower. It's a spring flower that grows in this region and Kyoto is famous for it. I remember sitting in an *izakaya* tavern as the *master* (i.e., owner chef) explained each dish served to me in his carefully rehearsed, beginner English. I was instructed that the nano-hana greens served that night at his restaurant were particularly extra green and crispy because they were harvested under a sudden late spring snow in the mountains around Kyoto. Maybe they were, in fact, a deeper green and a smidgeon crunchier than nano-hana harvested elsewhere, but really, when it came right down to it, who gives a bite? There are people starving all over the world that would kill for a single spoonful of the normal run-of-the-mill, less crunchy *nano-hana* that the rest of Japan was eating on that early spring evening. But subtlety, gradation and flavor pairing are taught and passed on from parent to child, from friend to friend, and from TV to living room. Understanding and mastering this vast body of information defines being Japanese. *This food gets dipped into that sauce, but don't dip that food into this sauce.* In fact, if you do make one of these culinary gaffs, glances exchanged between nearby diners seem to say "What's wrong with that foreigner? Doesn't he know better?" But, you know what? They are generally spot on when it comes to food! The Japanese have made it a point of pride to have figured all of this out, and it does work better that way. You don't even have to be French to realize that the deep-fried skewers of mushrooms taste better when dipped simply in the small pile of salt on your plate as opposed to the *yuzu* soy sauce in the tiny little three-sectioned rectangular, individual sauce tray. After seven years of scientific observation and testing I now realize that mayonnaise has never reached its full potential in America.

To a Western mind, even one born and bred in New York City, this food centricity can be one thinly deli-sliced strip of pastrami away from being over the top. It's not just the food, but the whole culture of food, including eating technique and etiquette that can seem ridiculously obsessive to non-Japanese. How meticulously the food is prepared, where it is arranged on its special dish and how it is placed on the table is a beautiful expression of Japanese pride. They take it to an entirely different level. This is a country where watermelons are not only seedless, but many are raised confined in boxes so that in midsummer you'll get a cube-shaped watermelon that will run you the equivalent of seventy dollars. Snacks and sweets in infinite varieties are found on shelves in conbinis where new flavors are debuted every few months. The same cookie, the same chip, and the same ice cream bar will appear but with a new flavor. Old favorites are also rereleased for a few months at a time. If you keep your eyes open, you can catch the famed *Gari Gari Kun* ice bar in "spaghetti" and "rare cheese" flavors for about ¥120. The marketing geniuses in Japan have a keen and direct understanding of the Japanese palate, leading consumers of all ages by the short hairs from one profitable season into the next.

In the cities and downtown areas of suburbs, food is present everywhere. You can't turn your head without seeing restaurants, *cafés*, fast food *donburi* (i.e., meat over rice bowl) shops, ramen shops, tiny bakeries and sweets shops. Supermarkets are also everywhere with many located underground in the basement sublevels of large department stores. In a certain way it doesn't make sense or seem compatible to put food and fashion in the same building. Imagine walking through Macy's or Nordstrom and, going down the escalator, being surrounded by the smell of fried *takoyaki* (Octopus balls). It defies logic. But in Japan's swirl of humanity, somehow it does seem to make sense. I'm always amazed to see the endless array of food counters and mini preparation areas with hundreds of different kinds of food for sale. There are vast selections of salads, fried foods, meats and fish, and god-knows-what else. So much stuff that it's baffling. As I walk by, aproned staff yell at me in Japanese about their wares, "try this, you gotta try this!" Throngs of people walk in different directions and wait patiently in lines. It's a veritable feeding frenzy of humanity in a prosperous land surrounded by oceans. When you realize that the store you're standing in is just one of the dozens of mega feeding centers in your city, it's mind-blowing. Where does it all come from? How can it all be eaten? It's a half hour from closing time and there's so much unsold food. What happens to it? How much of it is just thrown out? Incidentally, it's seen as a sign of success and prosperity to have too much food. To serve more food than can possibly be eaten at a dinner party and have lots of leftovers is not outright gluttony, it's just Japan. It's fascinating to witness this celebration of comfort and now fun to be a part of it. One takeaway is that nobody starves in Japan. Food is so deeply integrated into Japanese life and culture it's hard to imagine any setting without tea, snacks or a meal. Life for most here is the extreme antithesis of a simple wandering monk begging for alms or just enough food to sustain another day of prayer. This results in a society grappling daily to not just supply it all but to manage the waste that comes from it.

No one goes hungry! The variety and abundance of freshly prepared foods is mind blowing as these daily feeding frenzies are played out in thousands of basement level supermarkets in department stores across Japan.

In my first few months in Japan, I wandered into the Hanshin Department store in Osaka's Umeda train station, underground of course. There, I saw the most amazing, tantalizing sweets I'd seen in years. In white, crispy beige or matcha green, these little oval-shaped cake tarts were stuffed with *anko*, sweet red bean paste. I'd never seen anything like them before and from the small line at the counter, I knew I had to taste one. Everyone was buying boxes of these delectable gifts to bring to their families or coworkers. But I just wanted to buy one and eat it while walking the last fifteen minutes on my way to a five-hour stint at work. So, I chose one of the crispy beige variety.

A quiet, delicate woman gracefully handed me a beautiful paper bag with a small store logo on it, with foil taped over it so it wouldn't fall out. As I walked through the underground maze of the train station, I was consumed by the fire of immediate gratification. I tore open that foil-taped, quite elegant paper bag, keeping one eye up to avoid any head on collisions. It was wrapped beautifully in a cardboard box that had a golden, embossed, foiled seal attached to it. Inside the box, there was another bag, more like a folded smoky white fabric paper with the sweet inside. I was there, or so I thought. But then, I had to tear open that bag to take out the sweet, which was wrapped in cellophane with a gold twist tie around it. Opening that, I had to peel off the telltale little package of desiccant under it. I ate the prized sweet in three or four bites and yes, it was one minute of ecstasy in my 15-minute walk to work.

Now I was walking through the train station, (which by the way has no garbage cans because again I must remind you this is a carry in/carry out society) holding a handful of cellophane, paper bags, cardboard with a rope handle on it, and tape. I had just consumed a three-dollar snack which had a carbon footprint on the order of driving my beloved Honda CRV fifty times up and down the West Side Highway of Manhattan.

Food porn. That's what it is. Every day there's TV shows about how to cook it, and where to harvest it or catch it. Television talk show hosts interview the farmers, the restaurants, or the owners of a new shop in the city. The entire country watches the same shows on the few nationwide TV channels. After filming the above-the-pan view of someone's perfect technique of frying those things in a skillet, the producers show a close-up of chopsticks holding the food. I can almost hear the collective orgasm of everyone watching this unbelievable piece of *Unagi*, eel from a certain river that's served in a certain restaurant in the summer in a special locally seasoned sauce. Then as the cameras zoom in for an even closer close-up, the chopsticks are gently shaken, vibrating the steaming morsel of eel. In corners of the TV screen the faces of the celebrity hosts of the show smile and comment in onscreen PIP (small boxed "picture in picture") so that the entire country can see their reaction to what they're seeing. Japanese people love to see the reactions of the "talent" on the TV. That emotional, experiential bond provides a feeling of nationwide unity as all gawk in unison at the same thing. As someone in the main frame puts that eel in their mouth you can hear the collective "oohs" and "aahs" of the TV audience. It builds such a sense of community. We are many in body but certainly one in palate.

Speaking of that poor eel, for some reason the deep respect for harmony with nature that people perceive as a constant in Japan is misinformed when it comes to food preparation. In real life, the show flashes back to an eel that was grabbed by hand from between the rocks in a shallow river. In living color, it wriggles as it is pulled out of a bucket and laid on a wooden plank or chopping board. Alive and fully conscious, a large push pin is stuck into its head. It is then stretched out and another pin is pushed into the meaty area just above where it tapers into a tail. So, I guess you can imagine what happens next. It's cut open, right there, alive. It is forced to suffer an extra ten seconds with a needle stuck in its head and tail out of the water with people and TV cameras around because, somehow, it's fresher that way. Of course, the whole process could have been more humane by simply cleavering its head off first, which is not eaten. But by putting pins in it, stretching it out, and cutting it open alive, it somehow adds to the whole experience of preparing it. I can't say that this inhumane attitude towards animals in food is an anomaly in our industrialized world of animal agriculture. Factory farms are the worst offenders, trampling animal rights on a much huger scale. I am as "McGuilty" as anyone, killing cows, pigs and chickens with every bite. But when it comes to a simple revision of technique that doesn't affect output, I don't get the lack of reflection and detachment from causing unnecessary suffering. In Japan, it co-exists alongside Buddhist temples and harmonious, polite mindsets with seemingly no conflict at all. In some parts of Japan, people even gulp down tiny swimming fish live from a bowl, festively celebrating it as a delicacy in the springtime. I imagine those minnows don't suffer too much in the stomach.

Last year, I watched a TV crew filming a man pull an octopus out of the water with a net and place it in a bucket. I've shared my intrigue earlier that they are in a sense possibly the most intelligent creatures on earth. But on the docks, they are only fodder for a hot griddle. The live octopus is taken out of a bucket, and that drooping, self-aware creature is thrown on to a gas heated, smooth-surfaced grille. As it tries to scamper off in its suffering, they throw a big pot over it to confine it for probably 30 seconds more suffering. Basically, it's cooked alive. Then they take the lid of the pot off and serve the steaming octopus. Why not kill it first? Freshness! It's just better that way.

There's a real sense of comfort in this indisputably prosperous society where nobody goes hungry unless they're on a diet. There will always be enough food for everyone, and despite the general homogeneity of the island, there are so many regional dishes and "sub-cuisines" that bolster that sense of "living the good life." Domestic tourism flourishes as families, old couples or bussed elderly group outings seek out the lobster-size *Ise Ebi* shrimp in the Mie region or make a pilgrimage to Kobe for the world-renowned Kobe beef. Some are drawn to Fukuoka for the signature *Hakata Ramen* with its savory, but gritty, milky soup made from boiled pork bones. For a taste of China without going through customs, they'll go to Yokohama's huge Chinatown. There's longer trips up north to Aomori where the water's cool and the scallops are off-the-charts. Nagoya has the best fried chicken wings that would give any of the original buffalo wings shop in Upstate New York a run for their money, and don't get me started on the unique cuisine of the tropical islands of Okinawa. The menus in paradise include everything you would expect from the tropics, with the addition of a lot of pork, the cure-all *goya* (a.k.a. bitter melon) and the perhaps all too powerful Awamori spirits distilled from long grain Indica rice. You can spend a lifetime in Japan trying new food and sampling drinks, whether it's on a short trip or even in your local food store.

When it comes to alcohol consumption, I'm willing to bet that, per capita, Japan drinks more alcohol than any other country including Russia, and Korea as well. You need to see it to believe it. I first saw it in my own neighborhood on the day of recycling for cans, glass and plastic bottles. Kyoto really has it together when it comes to recycling. The city issues clear plastic certified bags (at a small charge) for recyclables. In the morning, I would walk by single-family homes with large plastic bags bursting with beer cans, bottles, a few single drink coffee cans, and kids' drinks. Sometimes two or three overstuffed bags will line the streets outside of homes that contain no more drinkers than a father, a mother, and maybe a grandparent. When you do the math, you can figure out how much alcohol is consumed at home. On the weekly recycling day, two-story apartment buildings have multicolored bagged mounds that you'd expect to see outside a fraternity house after an all-weekend party. These numbers don't even count what people drink after work in restaurants. A long work day typically ends at around nine or ten o'clock at night because often the last two or three hours of work are spent at a bar or *izakaya* with coworkers complaining about the boss. Entertainment budgets encourage *settai*, or wining and dining customers. Or perhaps you're just meeting a group of friends or have more insidious, darker reasons for being out drinking on a weeknight.

Almost everybody drinks, and a lot! What's more remarkable is the way that people mix alcohol. That pushes many over the edge and I think is downright dangerous on many levels. Typically, one starts off with a beer or two. Then works it into something else, say the almost dietetic, low-calorie highball. I find it amazingly cute that most Japanese believe the highball (HAI-boh-oo-roo) is a Japanese invention. Whenever I'm challenged with this notion, I show them on my iPhone that people were drinking highballs two-hundred years ago in England. The Japanese tend to co-opt and "own" many imported things. The newer the generation, the less aware people are that all things delicious or refreshing were NOT originally "made in Japan." The highball session might morph into a celebratory bottle of wine, followed by sake tasting in glasses or small pitchers. Every sip of each newly served drink is commented on and melded into the conversation.

On almost any given night out in the establishments, the alcohol flows and flows. The clanging glasses of *kanpai* and good time banter get louder and louder and the patrons get drunker and drunker. Public drunkenness is under the norms of acceptable behavior. It is a way of life that if exhibited to this level in New York would warrant an arrest, a robbery or a good ass-kicking. I remember visiting Japan before I moved here and seeing a menu option called *nomihodai*. These "all you can drink" deals are exploited to the hilt. They usually run from 90-minutes to two hours and cost maybe 3,000 yen or about 27 bucks. Near my mother-in-law's house, I saw two college-aged kids lying outside of a bar puking into the street like some sort of Lower East Side New York performance art thing: two friends on their bellies on the pavement on a Summer night, puking in tandem. Passersby didn't even blink an eye. Nobody stopped to help them. From out of the windows of the bar, the boisterous sounds of the wild party survivors could be heard. I watched in disbelief as a police car drove slowly by them. It paused for a moment, but never stopped, only to drive away. It was just another Wednesday night in Kyoto.

I remember the first time that I saw an inebriated salary-man standing up, sleeping on a train. Despite basic physics and physiological principles, it IS possible to stand up stoned drunk, and sleep vertically on an hour train ride in a suit with a briefcase. With the dominant hand placed through the train strap with a half twist and briefcase secured on the floor between legs this lifesaving, marriage-saving technique is pulled off every night in every late train in Japan. My guess is it that it can be traced back to the strict, disciplined training regimen of the *ninja*. Alcohol is also readily available to anybody and everybody. It's promoted on TV, on posters and kiosks in train stations and bus stops. It's stacked in the easiest-to-grab locations in coolers in 24-hour convenience stores. The variety is astounding, starting with cheap, low-malt beers called *happoshu*, which are made mostly from fermented rice. You can drink milder alcohol in canned, fruit-flavored cocktails or you could drink beverages that have the words "strong" in boldface written across the labels. These 8-9% alcohol content, 500 milliliter cans of carbonated *chuhai* feature *shochu* infused with a variety of fruits like bitter lime or pink grapefruit, or whatever fruit happens to be in season. Somewhere in a distillery tasting lab they figured out that *umeboshi*, or pickled salt plum, mixed with this high alcohol, poisonous concoction might become a big hit, and they were right. There is huge fondness for whiskey throughout Japan. When the Suntory company bought the iconic American Jim Beam whiskey brand in 2014, giggling pride could be heard as livers twitched throughout the island. As for wine, I had never heard of a Bordeaux season before, rife with tasting parties and specials on cases lugged out of liquor stores. But I've now been invited to a few. The drinking age is twenty in Japan and it's not strictly enforced. If someone looks young, convenience store staff will surely check ID, but usually the customer is just asked to push a button on a touchscreen to self-confirm they are of age. I don't think anybody's ever been flagged from buying alcohol because they've been too drunk. And praise the Lord! Out on the sidewalks, if you know where to look, there's beer and sake vending machines. Do you know how many high school kids in the U.S. would be lining up if there were beer-stocked vending machines lit up at night in their neighborhoods?

As abundant, aesthetically pleasing, and scrumptious as food gets in Japan, it's easy for your stomach to forget about how life tasted back at home. There are foods I and many New Yorkers grew up on that simply defy Japanese sensibilities and could never have been born here. My student, Chihiro, reminded me of how much I miss one of them. Last year I spent two or three months preparing her for her lifetime dream trip to New York during Christmas and New Year's. Chihiro is a thirty-year-old swim instructor and Junior High School water polo coach, and not the kind of young woman that studies *Ikebana* flower arrangements or has spent years perfecting her piano skills. She'd rather go out drinking and dining with her friends. I can't even picture her in a kimono because she rocks the hell out of jeans and a sweatshirt. At her first English lesson, I asked her, "What's your goal? What do you want to do in the future? She said, "I want to go to New York." Two years later, she and three of her Junior High school buddies had already booked tickets and hotel reservations. She and I spent a few weeks in class going over the streets of New York on Google Maps on my large screen TV, swooping down like a drone on sites like MOMA (the Museum of Modern Art), carefully selecting the best entrances to Central Park and marking where they shouldn't go at night. We talked about how she should shop for clothes in the East Village and stroll through Williamsburg, Brooklyn for a day. But the major focus, of course, was a crash course on dining in the Big Apple. How can a group of four young ladies on a hard-earned budget squeeze the most out of three days in New York City?

I'll never forget that afternoon in late December when a chime on my iPhone revealed a photo she had sent me via Facebook from New York. Oh, what a joy to realize that I'd successfully instilled in my student one of the most important aspects of New York culture. It wasn't simply that she was able to say things like "Thanks, anyway," to the guy outside the Empire State Building that tried to flag down a taxi for her and her friends, or "Leave us alone" to the sidewalk peddlers trying to sell them bootleg watches.

It wasn't even the fact that she told me proudly how she studied a check from a restaurant to see if it included gratuity (there's no tipping in Japan), instructing her friends to multiply the tax by two and then add a little bit for the tip. Those alone could have been testimonials to the quality of education students get at the WAVE Center. No, it was much bigger than that. She had led her friends to Mecca! The picture she sent me was a closeup of an overstuffed, encrusted pastrami sandwich from Katz's Deli, a world-famous landmark on Houston Street. I immediately recognized the signature brined, partially dried, herb-seasoned, perfectly maroon-colored, thick-sliced meat bulging out of New York rye bread with a hint of mustard dripping out of the crust. There was a clear plastic cup of beer next to it. *Oy vey* is me! I was crying for it. At the time, I was teaching a doctors' class and it was a challenge to maintain composure for another 30 minutes while the quintessential New York bite was staring me in the face. This was the same pastrami sandwich that my father ate back in the 1960s, that I've eaten five or six times in my life. Its status as a sandwich is nothing short of legendary. I would think nothing of paying a big 10,000 Japanese bill (*ichi-man yen* or about $91) to eat it right here in Kyoto, and my student and friend Chihiro, was in New York City experiencing it. Gold stars for my student! We both had succeeded. Once again, I stood proudly at the intersection of culture; Japan, New York, food, teaching English, attractive women, Google maps, and more as they all converged in that grisly, hard-crusted sandwich on rye. Who would have thought that I'd need to leave civil engineering to find out how to truly build bridges?

CHAPTER 19

LOUIS VUITTON
AND ENLIGHTENMENT

Exquisite Buddhist temples, Zen gardens, and Shinto shrines are everywhere in Kyoto, with architecture dating back a thousand years that has been perfectly restored. Fifty-one million visitors come here each year to experience the serenity and selfie themselves amidst the beauty and majesty. There are dozens of sects of Buddhism throughout Japan. But, ironically, there's very little religion. If you ask Japanese what religion they are, although you might get an occasional Christian, you'll mostly hear, "no religion" or "I'm a Buddhist." When pressed for what sect their family practices, it is surprising how many people don't even know. But, when Grandpa dies and there's a funeral to be planned and conducted, you'll need the services of a professional Buddhist priest – and, that's a big expenditure made in addition to funeral home and cremation costs. Families pay a small fortune for the priests to lead a service which consists of him chanting unrecognizable ancient sutra verses alone while participants sit quietly and one by one stand up to offer incense. There is virtually no effort by the priest to address and encourage the bereaved, let alone memorialize the deceased. In fact, there is barely eye contact made between him and the attendees during the solemn ritual. But to family and friends it feels like the right thing to do and somehow ensures Grandpa will live eternally in the land of tranquil light or something like it. It's more like an obligatory formality providing closure than true acknowledgement and celebration of the life of the deceased. And, that closure is paid for again and again after the passing in a series of memorial services usually held at 7 days, 49 days, 1 year, 3 years, 7 years, 13 years, 17 years and so on. Religion is present but, in a philosophical sense, more-or-less non-existent in Japan.

The transformational journey of Buddhism from India to Japan has pretty much manifested here as the esoteric domain and culture of those who protect the temples and perform the rituals. They make a comfortable living off the tax-free donations of their followers and that of tourists who pay admission fees to walk these hallowed grounds. It's interesting to see them conducting their lives outside the temples, dressed in robes with shaven heads as they blend right in riding motorbikes and standing in line at supermarkets.

The function and signature theme of Buddhist temples and shrines varies from location to location. One shrine, Jishu-jinja, located atop Mount Kiyomizu in Kyoto, manages love. If you haven't found a boyfriend, go to this temple, pay a little money and get a little fortune piece of paper. After which, you'll greatly improve your chances of finding that special boy. Another one, Fushimi Inari shrine, decrees success in your business. International tourists love visiting this shrine and walk through its thousands of iconic, bright reddish orange *torii* gates. Kitano Tenmangu Shrine in Kyoto, built over 1,000 years ago to honor Sugawara no Michizane who in addition to representing honesty, sincerity, performing arts, and agriculture, is the "god of academics," is a good place to go before finals or mid-terms, or if you're about to take any kind of important test. Once there, offer some incense and a few coins and maybe pay a little extra money to get that tiny, fortuitous piece of paper.

Japanese society is comforted by and culturally attached to a mishmash of Buddhist and Shinto rituals and services. The ancient folk religion of Shinto is not based on dogma, it's practice generally takes the form of making offerings to the gods. But these cultural traditions are like taut strings of morality that serve to tether the upward pull of a big prosperous balloon of a society that is drunk on rampant consumerism. In truth, worldwide iconic fashion brands seem to have more importance and connection to divinity than self-reformation, contributing to world peace or trying to disentangle and address the suffering of a complicated dysfunctional family. I'm not saying that Japanese lack social responsibility and engagement. It's just that by and large they really don't endeavor to reach up to the heavens or deep inside for answers or inspiration. Although yoga is big in Japan I don't see all that much determination or concerted effort to unlock and unleash capability, or to make that connection to something greater than the Coach handbag. Nothing is as big or important here as eating food, drinking, enjoying times with friends, going shopping, visiting museums, taking trips to Europe, or going to beaches on weekends.

This disconnect between spirituality or religion and Japanese daily life really hit home for me about three years ago. I was teaching an adult conversation class at Velco English school in Otsu, a suburb of Kyoto, where I met Saemon. We connected immediately. He said he was a big reggae fan, at least as much as he could eagerly express in his beginner English. He dressed cool, sporting an orange leather jacket which I found out was worth $700 dollars. He wore it proudly to class, even on hot summer days. I remember when he told us he was wallet shopping and his budget was $500 dollars. Saemon was an interesting student. In fact, Saemon wasn't even his real name, it was his "priest" name. He was a 28-year-old, tall, lanky, bucktooth boy with a shaved head whose father was the chief priest of a famous temple of the Tendai sect. By birthright, Saemon was a high-ranking junior priest, and had the responsibility of training acolytes every day at this temple. I'm not sure exactly how his formal doctrinal Buddhist training informed or influenced his life but one of the basic precepts he followed was drinking as much alcohol as he could in public situations. This led to a few instances where he embarrassed himself to the point where he was no longer invited to group student social outings because the girls felt uncomfortable. In fact, during my lessons, the young women in my classroom felt very uncomfortable with the way he carried himself. He wasn't rude or overtly hitting on them, but he had a mousey laugh and a twisted look in his face and a kind of smirking, loose demeanor. In general, he created a weird energy in my class. Eventually I had to speak with him about not talking so much in this class.

I've been a practicing Buddhist for over twenty years. Upon meeting him I thought, "What a great opportunity to engage with a real, live Buddhist monk. I knew that I wouldn't have a theological debate with him because of our language barrier, but I thought I could do a little exploration of what it's like from behind the robes and inside Buddhism in Japan. I had access to a Buddhist priest in charge of training young wannabe priests of the Tendai school. But, he regularly drank too much and shared lots of stories about drinking. He prided himself on the fact that he had something of a *donburi* addiction, eating pork over rice bowls almost daily. I think eating of pork by monks is banned by a lot of Buddhist sects. Due to his knack for wearing highly expensive clothing, and the fact that he was horny as hell and couldn't conceal his desire to hook up with a woman, Saemon certainly didn't fit the model I'd imagined of a young Buddhist monk. His stories included getting pulled over by police for going 40 kilometers over the speed limit. The status of his license was blue, which I think is one parking ticket away from losing your license. But, all the tales were conveyed with unrepentant delight because he and his family received lots of money tax free from their devoted parishioners, thousands of them. What a life he led!

One day Saemon came to class and he had a few bee stings on his head. He said he'd been clearing the grounds of the temple and, in raking some overgrown area, had disturbed a bees' nest. The bees had started to swarm and attacked him. But, because a true Buddhist must respect life, he couldn't kill the bees. In his view, even the bees that landed on his forehead had such precious lives that it was better to let them sting him than to swat them away or smash the crap out of them. So, in some way he did follow an underlying precept of Buddhism of respecting the viability and dignity of life. But by not killing those damn bees that were attacking him, I think he lost context and threw common sense and reason out of the window. Eventually, he was asked to leave the school because the girls just couldn't take his behavior anymore.

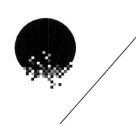

CHAPTER 20

WHO'S EXCEPTIONAL? JUST US?

"And the rockets' red glare, the bombs bursting in air, gave proof through the night..."

The U.S. national anthem is a real piece of work. Singing the lyrics to 'The Star Spangled Banner" which extolls the glory and pride of victory in the heat of the battle for freedom brings tears to any patriotic eye. And, my president has not in seventy-two years of American life memorized those lyrics. Not standing in reverence to its solemnity at the beginning of a sports event is seen as an outright rude and divisive act that sparks an emotional charge of treason and further drives wedges of misunderstanding between already conflicting sides. Also, I am certain that most people on either side of the political spectrum do not know what a rampart is. Putting aside the words, it's a workout for the human diaphragm to force that much wind up through the vocal chords to power and channel one's "inner baritone" and maintain it until the climactic end. The melody splays out in an unpredictable arrangement that rises and falls in a way that is, frankly not intuitive. It's like weird math that it is far removed from any kind of ABACAB arrangement (A being verse, B being chorus, C being bridge) which is the typical structure of most Western Euro-American songs. Ironically enough, "The Star Spangled Banner" melody is derived from an old English drinking song which has a completely lewd and sexual tone. It's been the downfall of many a singer. I think it was Christina Aguilera who once forgot the lyrics at a Super Bowl in front of over a hundred million live viewers from around the world. It can be a minefield even for trained singers. One must carefully stay in tune for the climb to the false climax, while pacing his or herself, so as to nail the pay off. If you can hit that rockets' red glare piercingly high F note, then you have that singer's gene or maybe just buy your pants two sizes too tight. It's most certainly a memorable melody that imprints itself in your psyche.

I was surprised when five years ago during an adult English conversation class at Velco three of my students, hip successful people between 28 and 35 years old who by that time I'd considered friends, broke out into a "Oh, say can you see." I don't remember what provoked it, but I do remember it was perfectly timed as it spun out of our conversation. They didn't know many words beyond that first two lines, but they sang it in unison with smiles on their faces in a very innocent mocking of the song before we all broke out into laughter. It's the embodiment of bravado, the machismo of conquering, the triumphant spirit behind the song, that gets the blood pumping.

If you were to compare the U.S. national anthem to the Japanese national anthem, "Kimigayo" (a.k.a. His Imperial Majesty's Reign) you'd find the Japanese one very simple and understated. I couldn't hum a few bars of the Japanese national anthem if you offered me a million yen ($8,944). In fact, I don't think anybody outside of Japan would know any part of the song or its melody. It's a very reverent, respectful, slow, solemn, sweet anthem that conveys loyalty and admiration for Japan and its heritage. It's based on an ancient Waka poem written between 794-1185 and is a diminutive 19-word sentence in English: "May your reign continue for a thousand, eight-thousand generations until the pebbles grow into boulders lush with moss." It is not meant to uplift and energize the spirit and bolster courage. It is a quiet, polite reverence that would not be played over loudspeakers on ships going into battle or in the cockpits of zero fighter planes as they were closing in on Pearl Harbor. But it, as well, brings tears to patriotic eyes.

When you live away from home and outside of your native country for an extended length of time, you get a different sense of what national pride really is and what it really means to be an American. American Exceptionalism is a somewhat loaded term and I happen to subscribe to it, to a point. How could I not? The United States is a country that for 240 years has tried, at least in theory, to express the Magna Cartan ideals of freedom and equality through its Constitution and Bill of Rights. I said tried! It has tried and, in many ways succeeded, to instill principles of democracy and social justice around the world, and before you interrupt me or throw this book on the floor, hear me out. No country has come close to contributing more money or people power towards infrastructure development, disaster relief, agricultural development, immunization programs and toward countless other efforts in abating human suffering. Period! Check your almanac or Google it. It is indisputable. Give credit where it is due.

But, I acknowledge that America's history is far from stellar. Thomas Jefferson was a slave owner and a sexual molester. Perhaps millions of Native Americans were slaughtered (by settling Europeans and then frontier Americans) and the surviving 10% of the population have been exploited and marginalized. America has stuck its military nose in many corners of the world with sometimes questionable intentions resulting in some obvious failures and much-debated successes. Again, I am not a historian. I am a simplistic-reasoning observer, and proudly so. The Vietnam War? We'll put that in the failure column. Korean War? I think if you took a random survey of residents of Seoul or Busan, you'd get a thumbs-up. World War II? You're welcome, Europe. Our stakes in the Middle East and elsewhere are often a mix of a well-intended civilization-promoting "make the world safe for democracy" impulse and outright economic opportunism and exploitation. Overall, I think we Yanks have gleaned a lot less bad than good when we've left our shores. Speaking of leaving our shores, compare the above to the profound history-defining results of centuries of European colonization. Look at a map of Africa and notice all the straight lines that help delineate national borders, logically carved out by the invaders from abroad. To say that the natural progression of the mosaic of African tribal culture and social structure was disrupted would be a ridiculous understatement. The map of India and Pakistan was drawn by a British lawyer, Sir Cyril Radcliffe, shortly after arriving on his first trip to India. I submit that the spilt blood and festering ongoing legacy conflicts caused by British, French, Spanish,

Portuguese and Dutch imperialism far outweigh the negative consequences of American exploits, some of which have backfired, to say the least. As we collectively dig our heels deeper into the 21st Century, I don't think anyone would argue that China and Russia aren't exactly altruistic in their dealings with their neighbors and other countries. There's a lot that makes me proud to be an American. At our core, there is goodness, benevolence, industriousness and a persevering spirit. Besides, we have Hollywood, McDonald's, Disney and American football to our credit.

Living by the calendar of another country can be a little disorienting. Firstly, Japan has its own designation for the current year. To the rest of the world, it's 2019. But on almost all official forms, from taxes to job applications, it's the year 31. *Heisei* 31. The *Heisei* period started on 8 January 1989, the day after the death of the Emperor Hirohito. His son, the 125th Emperor Akihito, acceded to the throne. Some forms require both years, 2019 and 31. Is that completely confusing, if not unnecessary?

As an American in Japan, my life is undeniably out of synch with holidays back home as they fall on the calendar. The anticipation of Thanksgiving, the fourth Thursday in November, that I used to time my whole life around now goes by silently as I scroll through dozens of posts of warm family reunions on Facebook. A few calls a year to my brother, Gregg, or my cousins in the states takes away some of the sting. New Year's Eve in New York is baked into the crust of the American psyche. We spend every year of our lives counting down to the last hour before the ball drops in Times Square. As the last few minutes approach the energy surges in the party, the living room, the bar and the noise gets louder and louder. The thumping in your chest gets stronger as something explosive is about to happen at the exact stroke of midnight. It's New Year's Eve! But in Japan, New Year's Eve is solemn and spiritual. Although it is celebratory, it's entirely subdued in every sense of the word. Many people go to shrines and temples on New Year's Eve, usually standing in long lines or slowly walking with the crowds to listen to monks ringing a huge bell. Or, they stay at home and watch a few New Year's television variety shows with singers and celebrities. There's eating soba noodles at or after midnight but there's no confetti. There are no fireworks! No drunken debauchery! No kissing and hugging and dancing! Shortly after the stroke of midnight, we newly landed Martian foreigners walk to the windows and look outside or step outside our front doors and listen for the clanging of glasses or drunken hoots and hollers or a lone firework in the sky. But there's nothing but silence. The cacophony in my mind reaches out in desperation to connect with some indicator that it's New Year's Eve. But it's the same as any other night, utter silence, spare the sound of a taxi dropping someone off who's coming back from a temple. But, in the past decade, the westernization of Japan is creeping its way into New Year's Eve, too. You can find noise and revelry in some confined areas of the big cities, especially Tokyo. The Americamura (American Village) retail and entertainment area of Osaka gets riled up, spurred on by lots of foreign residents and tourists. Traditional Kyoto is deafeningly silent except for a speckle of New Year's festivities on Kiyamachi Street with bar specials. Outside the clubs you might even hear something resembling hooting and hollering. But it's restrained, so as not to draw the attention of the police.

Perhaps most sentimental for me is July 4th. There's no backyard barbecues or neighborhood fireworks displays. No beaches to frolic on. Nobody here is even aware that the annual July 4th Coney Island hot dog eating competition was dominated for a decade by the legendary competitive eater Takeru Kobayashi (until Joey Chestnuts stole his technique and title). The closest I've come to a real Independence Day celebration was two July 4ths ago with my friend Atticus. We were standing in the pouring rain early on July 4th evening on concrete steps that led down to the mighty Kamogawa River, which, by the way, is only mighty after a heavy rain. It was gushing dangerously that evening as we gave up trying to light perfectly legal fireworks in the downpour. We stood 10 feet away from raging, manmade waterfalls, hoisting our 500-milliliter premium malts up in the air, pouring rain dripping into the beer. There was only one single obvious and appropriate action to take! Spontaneously we broke into a rendition of "The Star Spangled Banner" at the top of our voices charged with the passion that can only come from drinking three or four of those oversized cans of beer. We commemorated Independence Day in booming baritone that even the pouring rain couldn't mute from echoing in the mountains a few kilometers away. I wonder if the deities that dwell there enjoyed our performance as we laughed hysterically and held onto each other, so we wouldn't go tumbling into that raging river. As two loud, rowdy Americans drenched in patriotism, we must have been quite a sight for the few locals riding by us on their bikes.

CHAPTER 21

WORK LIKE
A SAMURAI

The Japanese work ethic is well known throughout the world, and maybe unsurpassed. It's based on an almost genetically engrained behavioral instinct, a sense of duty to fulfill one's obligations to the best of one's ability. Privilege and entitlement rarely well up in the minds of overworked Japanese. By overworked, I'm referring to half of all full-time employees. The "give me a break" or "throw me a bone" mentality is simply not in the toolbox of an exhausted, disgruntled worker sitting at their desk on a Saturday afternoon on his or her "one Saturday a month" rotation. In fact, in Japan "overworked to complete exhaustion and fatigue" is officially classified as an actual cause of death that can be checked off on a death certificate. That work ethic, that unchallenged and unquestioned determination to devote your life to the "cause" and get everything done on time, with satisfactory or better quality, permeates every aspect of Japanese life. That attitude, in fact, is rooted in loyalty that can be traced back to the Samurai serving his lord.

How else could a society that was devastated economically and emotionally rise from the radioactive ashes and leveled cities of World War II to become the economic powerhouse it is today? It certainly took something special. Add to that the fact that, unlike Saudi Arabia and other successful economies, there are no vast reserves of oil or natural gas to boost it up. In fact, besides timber and a plethora of hot springs, there really aren't any "built-in" resources to exploit and enrich the country. The answer is clear. It is the invincible Japanese spirit, the will to survive and the resourcefulness that lives on in the culture of the workforce that causes it to thrive.

When most people graduate from their university in Japan and successfully land a job, they generally stay with that company for the duration of their lives. The typical salaryman, tech specialist, medical professional, or corporate employee signs on to a life-long commitment to their chosen company. As years turn into decades, they scale or rather incrementally crawl up that ladder of successive raises and promotions in their company, usually impeded by their seniors who block the path ahead of them. There isn't a way to even politely maneuver around them because seniority tends to trump capability and talent.

Workers may feel incredible frustration and pressure in their roles, and there stands a good chance that they may be suddenly transferred to another prefecture or an overseas office. Being uprooted and living apart from your family is part and parcel of a secure, allegiance to a one company career in Japan. And that loyalty goes both ways and pays off in the dividends of completely stable income and an enduring predictable career. There will most certainly be projectable salary increases and bonuses for the next thirty or forty years into retirement.

Teams of engineers and technicians, in their uniforms of coveralls with their company names embroidered over their chests put their noses to the grindstone and do whatever it takes to get the job done. Those office dwelling salarymen are dispatched to their respective regions, working hours-upon-hours taking their customers or prospects out to dinner on company expense accounts after meetings. It's an intense rhythm with the three big holiday weeks of Golden Week (May), Obon (August) and New Years that almost the entire working force and all schools takes off in tandem. This naturally leads to overinflated peak season travel pricing and long lines. It's not begrudged, it's just the way things are and have always been - another expression of national unity. You can take solace in the fact that your job provides you and your family with great, low cost health insurance and a pension. You simply must uphold your end of the bargain, even if it kills you. That means performing up to par, staying late when called for, working inhuman amounts of overtime (usually uncompensated) and sometimes eating a fair share of crow. You must endure the obligatory company outings or perhaps the mandatory company golf tournament on a Sunday. But, the up side of that is, the company will stick with you and "has your back" through thick and thin. Severe recession – no problem. The company's bottom line plunging due to

China and Korea grabbing more market share by underpricing products - no problem. Or perhaps you're going through a difficult time because your undiagnosed bipolar disorder is flaring up, disrupting and burdening your team – no problem. Not to worry, you will not be laid off or fired. You'll be reassigned at worst. The companies benefit from this relationship greatly. Employee turnover rates are next to nil for large companies.

Compare that to the typical American career trajectory which is based on elevating income, hedging skill and talent and maybe stepping on the shoulders of senior staff who are one rung up the ladder in front of you. In the U.S. it's a cinch to be stepped on or even "let go," especially if some hot new talent is coming up through the ranks and can out-perform you in your position. And there is greater possibility of dramatic, unpredictable, limitless potential for growth for both people and small businesses. This model, incidentally, has made the United States the world's number one economy since its inception 242 years ago. However, it would be close to unthinkable in Japan.

CHAPTER 22

A DANGEROUS NEIGHBORHOOD?

Anyone who's lived or spent enough time in any big Western city, knows it is wise to keep your guard up all the time. Even wise travelers going to Toronto, São Paolo, Madrid or Nairobi will heed advisories printed in italics in guidebooks or have read online Trip Advisor reviews about what not to do and where not to go at certain times. You don't have to be well-traveled or particularly savvy to know that in cities you must exercise common sense. When standing on the platform of any New York subway station you make it a point to know who's standing behind you. You don't stand anywhere near the tracks, either, not for fear of falling, but because you've seen shocking news stories every few years about some psycho shoving someone onto the tracks to a certain death just as the train pulls into the station. Vigilance and reflexive survival instincts become second nature. They're just a part of growing up in the West. But when standing on a Japanese train platform, you don't think twice about who's behind you or how close to the tracks you're standing. You're too busy checking Facebook, texting friends or playing a smartphone game to notice. The comforting safety and civility of their society is perceived as the norm, and Japanese tend to take it for granted. That can have adverse side effects. Two of my former students and a co-worker have told me stories of their wallets being deftly slipped out of a purse or backpack in Paris. One was standing in front of the Mona Lisa at the Louvre, and the two others were in the train station. Taketo, my old friend and the bass player for Kansai Rocks!, proudly conveyed at an English conversation class how he was lured into a back alley at the market in Fes, Morocco while traveling alone. He found himself surrounded by a group of young men intent on robbing or at least extorting something or other from him. Luckily, he used his sharp

English skills and street smarts and got away with just a good tale to tell.

For foreigners who have moved to Japan this sense of security and not having to constantly think about self-preservation when out in public, becomes nothing short of delightful. I remember one warm summer night walking on a quiet street in Kyoto. It was after midnight and there were three young men in jeans and t-shirts walking in the opposite direction. Laughing a little too loud they were obviously a few sheets to the wind. They were walking three-file, side by side towards me on the narrow sidewalk. As we were about to cross paths, my decades old gut reaction was to divert my path a few feet to the left and tighten my grip on my computer bag. But just as they bore down on me, realizing they were hogging the sidewalk and maybe a little too boisterous, I was politely "mugged" with a sincere "*sumimasen, gomenasai*" (i.e., excuse us, we're sorry) as none of us broke stride. I could only smile to myself as I realized that I could finally let go of some of that deeply entrenched survival mode mindset bordering on paranoia that is part and parcel of growing up and living in New York and New Jersey. And, the longer you stay in Japan the more endearing this sense of safety and civility gets. Where else in the world can you save a seat in a crowded university cafeteria or a McDonald's by simply placing your bag or iPhone on the table while you go to order food or use the impeccably clean bathroom?

Violent crime? *Nani kore*? (What's this?) The concerns that keep Japanese school children up at night are having too much homework or anxiety about upcoming tests. Although there is a fair share of bullying in the schools, it would never result in crazed killers stalking schoolmates through hallways and shooting into classrooms. Mass shootings, the likes of which have started to become an almost accepted fact of life in America not only do not exist in Japan, they are not possible. In this industrialized country of more than 120-million people where gun control measures are taken very seriously there is under ten gun-related deaths a year. Police used guns in five incidents last year. Interestingly, they are required to master martial arts. Even traditional katana swords, those long curved shiny steel razor sharp blades that were used by Samurai to sever an enemy's head with one swing, must be registered and permitted by the local government. The real danger in modern-day Japan does not come from those who inhabit the island, it comes from nature and from neighbors across the ocean.

Like many Americans, I spent most of my adult life watching the evening news at night, usually when I was at home eating dinner. To ensure that there was nothing to upset tomorrow's plan and, with an eye on choosing the right clothes, we'd watch as charming meteorologists pointed to colorful, symbol-rich graphics depicting swirling weather patterns and temperatures across the country. The huge projected maps of the U.S. show an enormous contiguous landmass stretching from sea to shining sea. Our borders are bold and well-defined. There is nothing but huge expanses of oceans to the east and to the west. Hawaii's somewhere way out there and from the East coast, Europe is a 7-hour flight away. To the north, we Americans take solace in the fact that our friendly, more balanced brother, Canada sits calmly above us, and the sometimes feisty but generally stable, civilized Mexico lies to the south. There is a palpable sense of safety within the borders of the huge stretch of American soil. If anything is coming at us from far away, say a missile, there's plenty of ocean that it can be detected over, and hopefully shot down. At the very least, we'd probably have enough time to make it to a shelter or fill our bathtubs with nonradioactive water. If there was an invading zombie apocalypse approaching from the north or south, a panicked call from Canada or Mexico would buy us a few days to prepare for it or allow us to kiss our loved ones, and our asses, goodbye. On the whole America doesn't fear physical danger from beyond her borders. With a few exceptions, particularly the 9/11 attack, the lion's share of terrorism happens overseas. Secure and buffered by thousands of miles, we watch the wars and strife throughout Africa, Asia and the Middle East, relieved by the fact that they are half a world away.

But when you see those weather maps on the nightly news in Japan, you get a sense of the vulnerability of the nation. The Japanese islands are essentially a long, skinny archipelago of islands that stretch far from northeast to southwest but are not all that wide from shore to shore. From the Pacific Ocean to the Sea of Japan it's maybe a four-or five-hour drive at its widest girth (the Shinkansen bullet train can do it in two hours).

Most of the natural landscape of Japan is comprised of small to medium-sized mountains and forests. If you look at it from a satellite image, you'll notice that the bulk of the entire land mass is green, almost wholly intact, untouched nature. The 120 million people on this relatively small island only occupy 31% of the land. Naturally, there are geological and situational reasons for this, such as access to ports and fertile river plains and natural barriers from harsh weather. For the most part, the old historic centers of trade and feudal governing have developed into huge modern cities and megalopolises clustering the population together. A few months before moving to Kyoto, I used Google Earth to get an idea of where I would be living in relation to Tokyo and the rest of the island. It was a little confusing to me because I expected to see the distinct, well-defined city of Kyoto built in the interior of the country. But instead there was a long contiguous white mass denoting dense urban sprawl that stretched for what appeared to be a hundred miles. It was labeled with three cities' names in bold type. If you take an express train from Kobe, through Osaka to Kyoto, it is an hour-plus ride with sparsely a speck of nature in between, sparing the green forest-covered mountains in the distance. In truth, it's only about fifty miles or so. Japanese society is community-based. People love to live next to each other.

If you zoom out on Google Earth from Japan, you see China nearby and the entire South Eastern Pacific Rim, most of it within a four-hour plane ride. The Koreas are even closer. China and Russia are huge and loom menacingly over this skinny archipelago of kimonos and killer toilets. One would think that ocean-defined borders would be distinct, but they're not. The unstable geologic history in this area of the volcanic "ring of fire" has sprouted several specks of intermediate islands that lay between the countries of Japan, China, Taiwan, and the Philippines, to name a few. Wars and invasions have crisscrossed the seas since ancient times. But it's the not-so-ancient wars of the last century that have most notably blurred the lines. There are outlying Russian territories that form a border with Japan. I use the word border loosely because these are the disputed Kuril Islands north of Hokkaido which are causing tensions to flare up even today. In fact, there are a lot of disputed islands out there in the oceans separating the countries of Asia. There's a hundred-plus-year-old tug of war with China in an area known as the Senkaku Islands, which have an abundance of rare earth minerals. The occasional flag planting and circling of Navy ships by both China and

Japan lead to no clear resolution and are simply tit-for-tat unsettling rattling of sabers. As well, there are islands between South Korea and Japan to which both countries lay claim.

Tensions flare and distrust taints the pristine fish-rich waters as ongoing disputes over fishing rights and territorial boundaries never seem to approach settlement. Chinese fishing vessels come too close to Japan and are stealing Japan's precious lifeblood and means of sustenance while at the same time diminishing the ocean's yield and upsetting the ecology of the waters. In the past few years Chinese ships have been removing red coral from the Sea of Japan by the boatload. The coral is regarded as a precious jewel throughout Asia. My student Hisayo, who works at a traditional Kyoto prayer bead company, told me that the polished red coral *juzu* beads can cost the equivalent of a Hermes handbag, tens of thousands of US dollars. The darker the red coral, the more expensive it is, but its power promises to bring unsurpassed fortune to those who hold them in prayer. China has also laid claim to the "territorial" waters and islands of the Philippines and Vietnam.

Add to this the vexing, unresolved grudges that stem from Japan's militaristic expansion leading up to World War II. There are still tender scars of Japanese aggression throughout Asia. Truthfully, these are not mere scars. They are occasionally festering sores that still twinge as "friends" try to manage and reconcile their entangled, complicated relationships in a changing world under the shadow of a growing China.

There is also the ongoing issue of "comfort women" with South Korea. Should more reparations be made for these women who were kidnapped from their homes and exploited seventy years ago? If so, how much should the reparations be? What should a formal Japanese government apology and admission of wrongdoing look alike? During World War II, women were taken from their homes by the Japanese military under the promise they would be given work in factories or restaurants. They were then imprisoned and forced to prostitute themselves in the most brutal and degrading manner as sex slaves for up to seventy soldiers a day in "comfort stations." These "comfort women" may have numbered up to two-hundred-thousand and were mostly seized from Korea and China although this happened throughout Southeast Asia, wherever the Japanese army exerted itself. One must consider: was it just the Japanese army that incorporated this practice into their wartime tactics?

It's been seventy years since this happened, yet it continues to be a source of distrust and smoldering anger held onto by many South Koreans and Japanese. It still makes the news as it is as sensitive as a topic can get between these two friends. In South Korea, a statue of a comfort woman was built across the street from the Japanese embassy in Seoul. As recently as last year there were statues temporarily placed on city buses in Seoul. Does this represent a true unsettled score that gnaws at the hearts of most Koreans or is it opportunistic exploiting of a regrettable chapter in South Asia's history? In Japan, a visit from a Prime Minister or Cabinet member to the Yasukuni Shrine in Tokyo will make it to the nightly news both in Japan and South Korea. The shrine pays homage to millions of Japanese war dead including fourteen Class A war criminals who led atrocities in the war. An official state visit there appears to many as Japan's acceptance and justification of what it did during World War II.

Now add to this boiling *nabe* (hot pot) the highly volatile situation between North Korea and it's democratic Siamese twin connected by a narrow and symbolic DMZ. Then throw in a fair amount of the severe tension between North Korea and Japan. The pot seems like it could easily boil over with the slightest provocation. Anger and distrust abound in the region. But despite that, very few incidents of outright fighting and killing have occurred (excepting a few skirmishes between the Koreas) since World War II. The psychodynamics of the Southeast Pacific Rim are complicated, continually changing and potentially explosive. There is an understanding by all that if one country fails or acquiesces to China's pressure or something upsets this delicate interrelationship they all may suffer. For the survival of all, there must be at least a continuance of status quo. Like many a complicated marriage, there is the hope and chance for a sustainable balance between dysfunction and lasting mutually beneficial co-dependence. For the sake of hundreds of millions of lives, for God's sake, there needs to be.

There are strategic business alliances that bond many Pacific-rimmers as the more developed and economically powerful neighbors (i.e., Japan, South Korea, Taiwan and China) help less developed countries like Indonesia and

Malaysia build high-speed train systems and solar parks. Panasonic and other giants are making huge investments in Cambodia and other countries with city-changing infrastructure projects, kick-starting industrial growth in these countries and cultivating customers for decades to come. This symbiotic and tangled co-dependence flows in all directions. Conversely, it is a fact that Japan is not self-reliant and cannot sustain its population through domestic agriculture. It imports much of its food from China and elsewhere.

The long-rooted ties between the three big players China, Japan and South Korea run deep. Ramen, Japan's signature staple food and *Kanji*, the expressive characters of Japanese communication both came from China. Although Japan has changed and added many of their own characters to *kanji*, a Japanese tourist can almost make sense out of a menu in a restaurant in Shanghai. In addition to the rivalry between South Korea and Japan, there is a deep camaraderie. They're both successful industrial democracies with a high standard of living. Japan and South Korea both take pride in their respective cultures. The Japanese love the K-pop boy bands and girl bands of South Korea. The seven-member boy band, BTS, sells out the largest venues in Japan hours after a tweet announcing a tour. Many Japanese are addicted to subtitled Korean TV soap dramas, and for both countries, fashion and dining are a way of life.

Japan and South Korea are both super-friendly with and supported and protected by America. They're like the two cute Asian girlfriends of America that are true "frenemies" in that they are not sure if they love each other or are rivals to the core. One student told me that Japan is more like America's lapdog than girlfriend. But one thing is for sure, they both exist in the shadow of China and wouldn't stand a chance if left to fend for themselves, if they had to. Taiwan, which Japan and South Korea both love is also an industrialized, successful democracy in the hood with its own international draw of great cuisine and thriving culture. It's on the top of the hit list of tourist destinations for both Japanese and South Koreans.

An increasingly booming tourism industry tightens and complicates the relationships between Japan, South Korea and China, in particular. Japanese tourists love to go to South Korea. A short 90-minute plane ride to Seoul or Busan can serve as a weekend jaunt where they can immerse their taste buds in authentic "non-Japanified" Korean cuisine. Korean barbecued beef ribs, tofu soups and gooey concoctions of noodles and just about anything else you can imagine are enjoyed even though they can very easily pin the needle in the red-hot, spicy danger zone by any international standard. Self-immolating Japanese palates can be extinguished with a cool Makori, a traditional drink that is milky and tangy and often served in a small metal pan.

Korean and Chinese tourists also love to come to Japan, and they do, in droves. Busloads of tourists, many Chinese, are ubiquitous throughout Japan's major cities. Historical and natural attractions draw them to Kyoto year-round but especially during the peak seasons of spring *sakura*, cherry blossom season and *koyo*, the fall autumn leaves season. In Kyoto, the sound of suitcases being wheeled down sidewalks and Chinese, Korean or Malay banter on trains and buses has melded into the background music (*BGM* in Japanese) of everyday life. Families or organized group tours of Chinese and European tourists are fueling the economy to an extent that could never have been imagined by city planners, and the momentum seems to build year to year. More accommodations are popping up all over Kyoto, from cheap guest houses that were converted from family homes to the new Ritz Carlton and Four Seasons. Even the announcements on city buses and in big electronics retail stores are in Japanese, English and Chinese now. As with all foreigners that visit Japan, the Chinese tourists are enthralled with Japanese culture. Exploring Kyoto's cultural treasures, visiting its shrines and temples is, to many, a yearly excursion. The beauty and dignified atmosphere of the city provides a refreshing reprieve from a hectic life back in the busy cities of China. Many rent kimonos and spend the day walking around "playing Japanese," sitting down for a meal at a café or attending a tea ceremony in full traditional garb.

But it's not only the richness of Japanese culture and the gentle atmosphere that draw millions of tourists from other Asian countries. It's the goods. Souvenirs are purchased in bulk as the uniqueness and quality of Japanese crafts and snacks are not only of a different fare, but maybe a notch above the things that are made back home in China or Korea. If you're looking for the finest silk kimonos, gorgeously dyed and patterned, that can cost upwards of $10,000 you'll find them in 300-year-old family-owned shops in the back streets of downtown Kyoto. There is a kind of quiet acknowledgement that many Japanese products, from clothing to cosmetics, are of better quality than those made in China. And it's not just the Chinese that spend their cash shopping for themselves and for those back home. Shopping, eating, and seeing the sights of Japan, and Kyoto in particular, is like a dive into another dimension of Asia for visitors from all over the world. You can feel, see, and taste the difference. (Note to Japan Tourist Bureau: please send all checks to WAVE Center)

The influx of millions of tourists has raised a lot of concern for Kyoto residents and awakened a need for self-reflection as they look toward what the city will be like in the future. The traditional small-city atmosphere of Kyoto is in a sense becoming overwhelmed by tourism, and that is beginning to challenge its very mission as the keeper and protector of the Japanese culture pedigree. Government officials, business leaders and neighborhood groups debate building codes including Airbnb standards, and things like the painting of cycling lanes as they weigh how wide to open the flood gates to travelers. I urge them to carefully strike the right balance and not give in to the temptation of enriching the city recklessly. Preservation is more

important than the almighty yen.

Sadly, in a way it may be a losing battle as I am starting to see what I call the "Disneylandification" of Kyoto. It will never become a tourist trap, per se, but it may lose some of what makes it so special. For example, it was reported in the news this year that, for the first time, graffiti was scratched into several stalks of bamboo in the treasured Sagano Bamboo Forest of Arashiyama in Kyoto. This is the same forest from which Thomas Edison sent an envoy to government officials in 1883 to carefully collect slivers of the prized bamboo to make filaments for the first generation of incandescent light bulbs. For one week, the news showed images and footage of these engraved celebrations of love, or nicknames and dates that were in Chinese and Korean characters, although plenty were in Spanish, Italian and English, as well. The defamation of these almost sacred living cellulose tubes stretching 30 meters into the sky sent a shockwave throughout Japan, with tens of millions of heads shaking in disbelief.

The clogging of bus and train aisles with oversized suitcases has also become an accepted and daily nuisance to Kyoto commuters and housewives running errands. Tourists walk quadruple-file on the sidewalk, ignoring the ringing of bicycle bells so cyclists must veer into the street to avoid them. I have particularly observed that it's the Chinese tourists that talk loudest on the once quiet train and have witnessed the unthinkable. It was not simply rumor, but true. Sometimes Chinese tourists spit on the scrubbed pristine sidewalks outside of the Former Imperial Palace.

The polite civilized behavior and consideration of others, and the innate respect for order and purity that defines being Japanese has a lot to reckon with in this new era. The Japanese feel special. They feel highly evolved. Through the ages, having been surrounded by oceans and sometimes in purposeful isolation (re: Edo Era extended from 1603 and 1868) they have developed their culture and their traditions and woven them into a wonderful society. As mentioned before, the Japanese take great pride in their work ethic. The traditional arts and practices like flower arrangement, calligraphy, Aikido, other martial arts, and sumo wrestling are all culturally revered. There is a quietly proud notion of well-earned self-righteous superiority over the rest of Asia. I'm not the first one who's said that Japanese women are more beautiful and desirable than their regional counterparts. I've heard that having a Japanese girlfriend or partner is a status symbol amongst successful Chinese businessman.

So, the complicated geo-political dynamics along with the superiority complex, whether justified or not, naturally lead to racism here in Japan. It's not of the level that inflames and explodes into something akin to a Ferguson Riot or burning crosses on a front lawn but more like lava bubbling underneath the surface. I first heard it when I came here seven years ago when the topic of Chinese tourists occasionally came up in adult group conversation classes at the Velco schools. I would listen to some of the remarks and withhold rebuttal as it was not my place to debate. I was hired to teach English and show them a good time. At first, I thought this attitude was coming solely from the older students, but I soon realized it was also shared by the younger people. It seems a simple logical conclusion that the builders of a successful and prosperous society are proud of what it has become, and they want to maintain all that has made it so. As borders become more permeable due to social media, and all the technology of our interconnected global community, that lava bubbles up and finds a fissure or two to break through.

I remember seeing a street protest in Kyoto. Not the tear gas kind with the cops and shields we see in the West, but about 200 people with signs and megaphones being escorted by the police through the busy downtown Shijo Karasuma shopping area. It was an anti-Korean rally (a.k.a. *demo*). The protest march of common citizens with a chip on their shoulders was loud, but it would be considered polite and non-disruptive by any American standards. The message could have been broken down into the "importance of maintaining the purity of Japanese culture and society."

There is also a small but very vocal and loud right-wing, nationalist movement in Japan. The "right-wingers," as I've been told they're referred to by my students, are a little more serious and, frankly, a little intimidating. They drive around big cities in vans covered with Japanese flags and oversized loudspeakers in the middle of the day blasting out World War II era fight songs sung by men's choruses. Over dashboard microphones they yell impassioned slogans that I don't quite understand, all the while being very observant of traffic rules and proper driver decorum.

For four years I worked at Velco's Osaka branch school. Every Sunday after a one-hour train ride it was a 12-minute walk from Yodoyabashi Station to the school across bridges on both the Dojima and Nakanoshima rivers right past Osaka City Hall. And every single week in front of the closed government buildings there were about ten large vehicles parked in the street. These were not the cars of shoppers but were black painted converted buses and vehicles, the likes of which I'd never seen before. They looked like urban warfare vehicles, hybrids between Humvees and monster trucks, everything painted in menacing flat black, even over the windows. A few dozen militant right-wingers were milling about in small groups preparing for the day's activities. which consisted of driving those black convoys through the busy neighborhoods of Osaka with the speakers cranked up to eleven blasting out those fight songs and anti-international slogans. The guys too, were dressed in black, head to toe. With their pants tucked into combat boots they looked at maps and talked amongst themselves, preparing for their day. They were way too serious for a sunny Sunday morning and more-or-less scared the shit out of me. In one sense, it looked like a tailgating-party from hell. In another, it looked like working-class dudes who weren't in weekend family mode and may have had nothing else better to do. It reminded me of a gathering of Hell's Angels without the beer and laughter raising money to deliver Thanksgiving turkeys to poor families. These guys were highly motivated politically. They never had eye-contact or gave any acknowledgment to passers-by on the sidewalk as they looked at their maps and planned their loud diesel-driven tirades through the streets of Osaka. I walked by them every single Sunday for years as I arrived in Osaka early before they deployed. Surely some of them must have recognized me. However, one time I came close to one of them when our paths crossed on the sidewalk. I smiled and gave him an *ohayo gozaimasu*, good morning, and just got a blank stare in return. Relating the story to my students later that afternoon, I was told, "Stay away from them, they're a little crazy." As one half of an interracial couple, a white former Jewish, Buddhist reggae rock singer drummer who speaks a little Spanish and some toddler Japanese, I'd just chalked it up to the normal shit, xenophobia and racism, and nothing I could relate to.

As I'm writing, I have a runny nose and an itchy throat. That's caused by something called *Kosa*, or yellow sand. Every March, yellow sand blows in from the Gobi Desert in China carried by wind across the oceans into Japan. It's a superfine yellow powder resembling pollen that you must wipe off of bike seats and car windows. Everybody who doesn't wear those disposable hygiene masks is breathing it in everyday for a month. To add insult to injury and when the conditions are right, there are late-afternoon and evening winds that also blow PM 2.5 air pollution from industrial areas of China over Japan. This makes eyes even waterier than the normal hay fever and yellow sand double punch while painting the most beautiful hazy sunsets across the horizons in western Japan. But there is nothing that can be done about these problems, at least from this end. And even more prominently, it's the difference in behavior that exceedingly irks the Japanese. As I listened to my students in those first years in Japan, I was shocked at how disparagingly they looked down on the Chinese until I had an experience in a convenience store near a Kyoto train station late one night.

After working a long day and long night out of town, I was at Kyoto station. Adjoining the station was a small convenience store, the only thing open at 12:30 AM aside from some police *koban* (little outpost stations). The train stations along with their shops generally close around midnight. It was late, and I was hungry and thirsty. I didn't want much, just a little snack and a beer. I stood like I always did in the early days, gaping confusedly at the array of prepared food, including a dozen different kinds of *onigiri* rice balls, with the confusing labels and mystery ingredients. I wasn't quite sure which to eat. These stores are not large, sometimes tiny like this one, maybe 15 feet by 20 feet with aisles arranged to optimize the amount of food and amount of choices in as little space as possible. I stood there for a few seconds debating quietly to myself whether I'd get lucky and select something good or just go for a sure bet like a bag of unshelled buttered peanuts.

It was after midnight and the last trains had since started their empty journey out of Kyoto city back to the yards wherever they may be. The store wasn't crowded. In what couldn't have been more than an 8 second Libra deliberation I felt myself getting pushed from behind. Someone was literally edging me aside with their shoulder as they reached for something on the shelves in front of me. Was it accidental? Was it a little push that some referees would not whistle a foul on? No, it was something a little heavier, almost a shove. There was plenty of food laid out at eye-level on the shelves in front of us as these kinds of stores restock constantly. So, there was no need to lunge for the last remaining sake salmon rice ball. I was being rudely pushed aside by a middle-aged, short lady with short-cropped hair as she and her friend reached for the rice balls. I gave them a "WTF" disparaging look, but no eye contact was returned to me. It was a little weird and disturbing to me because I was now, after a year or so, totally acclimated to the unwavering politeness and good manners of my new home. Giving way to other passengers through elevator doors had become a way of life.

Then, it was time to pay for the onigiri. I stood next in line, a good meter and a half behind the person paying at the register. This was simply a learned gesture of polite respect to not encroach upon someone's space especially when money was involved. After that customer paid, in a flash these two middle-aged women marched right up to the cashier and put their food on the counter. The young female cashier gave me a helpless look of, "What's happening and what should I do?" My New York kicked in and I said, "Excuse me, I'm next and by the way there's a line!" No reaction. I said again this time with a sprinkle of Japanese and a gesture, "*Sumimasen*, excuse me. I'm first, LINE!" They turned around and said something half to each other and half to me that I didn't recognize as Japanese. It was Chinese. The two people behind me were staring them down as well as the women nonchalantly moved to the back of the line. As I walked out of that store, with the ring of a bell in my head, I remembered my students talking about the rude behavior of Chinese tourists and in general of the different standards of behavior between them and the Japanese. As a self-proclaimed colorblind, unprejudiced humanist, I had to begrudgingly admit to myself that, in this case anyway, they had been right.

CHAPTER 23

HEY BONO! BONO!

Everyone should live in New York at one point in their life but leave before it makes you too hard. I heard this said decades ago. And now that those seeds from The Big Apple have taken root in this land of exotic beauty and mystery, I couldn't agree with it more. My spirit is infused with energy, my life is adorned with intrigue and blossoming in ways I never could have imagined. It makes sense to me that it all started on the other side of the world.

Living in New York does make you hard. It toughens your skin and sharpens your tongue. It hones your survival skills. It shocks you good and bad, it beats you up, as it makes you laugh and curse at the same time. There is an instilled pride and almost snooty arrogance in anyone lucky enough to have been born in or lived in the vortex of First World culture, finance, and urban sophistication. To process, experience, and manage the diversity that extends along the principal axes of race, lifestyle and economics gives someone a leg up on winning anywhere else in the world. Forgive me, I'm not intentionally channeling Frank Sinatra and his crooning about New York. But I do believe that if you can survive and crawl out of this incubator (i.e. cross busy streets safely, endure childhood), and make your way unharmed out of the maternity ward (i.e., get a solid education in school or on the tough street corner) and get through the revolving doors of the hospital into the busy street (i.e., graduate from college or Julliard, or snag a Goldman Sachs internship) you CAN make it anywhere. It was perfectly suited and necessary training for me to do what I'm doing now. A "New York State of Mind" permeates all aspects of my new life in Japan. Sometimes I need to keep it inside or use it with caution. It might come out as a well-timed, soft-toned, self-deprecating sarcastic remark to make the staid clerks of a convenience store break out in laughter at my mistake in giving them the not-so-exact change. Or, it might be the way I strategically stand next to the old couple sitting on a packed train who I suspect are getting off at the next stop due to some unspoken cue. For example, I notice he has a cane and there is a physical rehab clinic at the next stop. They get up, I slip into a seat.

But there is something else about New York that is intriguing beyond the fact that it is the "city that never sleeps." Of course, there is Broadway, Saks Fifth Avenue, the Museum of Modern Art (MOMA), Brooklyn, the Apollo Theater in Harlem, the restaurants, and more. But it is also the fact that it is a city of extremes, severely contrasting extremes. There are the $5-million apartments on Fifth Avenue, protected behind doormen standing next to huge, fresh exotic floral arrangement greeting anyone privileged enough to enter or leave through those marbled lobbies. Elevators lead to these chunky slices of heaven that are loaded with the finest furnishings and artwork, chic and modern or more classic depending on the taste of the inhabitants who have made a hobby out of creating and recreating them. These homes, decorated with the advice and expense of the most upscale interior designers, may be a short walk to the Metropolitan Museum of Art or the Guggenheim. The most picturesque views of Central Park can be seen from them. But that adjacent green refuge, the place for morning jogs and groomed poodles' afternoon strolls turns into a dark and foreboding, forbidden zone at 11:00 PM, a land of lurking shadows that one would never enter alone at night.

Elsewhere in the city, with no physical border delineating the two, you can walk a few steps outside of the finest and most expensive restaurants in town, or perhaps the world, and your nostrils fill with the smell of curry from the smoking grill of a converted pickup truck. It must be worth standing in a line of 10 people deep to get that $6.00 large portion of curried chicken and vegetables, placed sloppily with tongs over rice in a rectangular styrofoam container with a rubber band and plastic fork, but no napkins.

Walk a few blocks too far into the trendy and thriving Williamsburg, Brooklyn arts district and you're suddenly in an enclave of Hasidic Jews. The typical hipster uniforms of oversized glasses, dull flannel shirts and beat up converse sneakers turn into orthodox Jewish traditional garb of long black robes, beards and twisting *payos* (traditional sideburns that are never trimmed) peeking out of hats just an inch or two shallower than what Abe Lincoln might have worn. Their unfashionably headscarved wives walking behind them are a universe away from the women darting in and out of the designer boutiques and vintage shops in Soho and the East Village.

Added to this multicolored checkerboard of humanity is the fact that anything can happen at any time without warning. This bigger-than-the-sum-of-its-parts combination has all that it takes to draw tourists, aspiring musicians, playwrights and immigrants, legal or otherwise, to come to New York City for a visit or to make a go there. You can feel this electricity walking down the sidewalk, even if there is no conscious recognition of the fact. Anything that can go wrong may go wrong. Or, the converse of Murphy's Law, anything that can go right could very well go right. It's that uncertainty, that unpredictability, that makes New York so exciting and scary at the same time. Frankly, that's something I miss in Japan.

That unpredictability can manifest in something dangerous. Decaying, outdated infrastructure is overburdened by a busy, demanding, growing population. Cutting-edge skyscrapers, where miles of coiled and routed fiber optic cables transmit huge financial transactions around the world in nanoseconds have bathrooms whose toilets flush into an, on average, 84-year-old sewer system, and shit happens. I remember a huge high-pressure steam pipe on Third Avenue burst open, making a crater that swallowed and killed a driver and paralyzed the city for two days. Sometimes huge, ominous construction cranes fail and precariously dangle, or fall and crash into adjoining buildings, killing people. Unless provoked by nature (i.e., earthquakes, typhoons, and more), this kind of stuff never happens in Japan where infrastructure, modernization and safety are more like religious precepts than underenforced regulations.

But New York's unpredictability can also be something as charming and serendipitous as sitting on a bench in Central Park on a summer day and you see a group of a hundred or so people walking together. The ten people who are leading that group are silent and dressed in Shakespearean costumes. They stop by a lake and perform ten minutes of *Othello* while the crowd stands around and watches. And then they finish the scene. Actors and spectators walk together a few hundred yards to the other side of the lake and continue the next act. What could be more charming than a roving Shakespearean ensemble with audience, performing as they walk around Central Park on a balmy, cloudy day?

Or, what could be more surprising than sitting in a crowded subway car and suddenly, in between stations, the door to the adjoining train car opens? Through the rush of air and deafening noise of an old subway car at full speed, five young men walk quickly and step through the door into the train car. They're wearing dirty training suits and have an air of seriousness about them, albeit softened by smiles. Which way is this sudden race onto the train going to go? You're not sure and apprehensively default to some fearful racial reflex you thought you'd purged decades ago. In those tense five or six seconds, you sense danger, that is until they break out into an unbelievable acapella version of "The Lion Sleeps Tonight" by the Tokens. By the time they get to the second chorus of falsetto, "Ee-e-e-um-um-a-weh," half of the passengers in the car, as directed by the smiling "manager" of the group, are now doing the "*wim-o-weh wim-o-weh wim-o-weh*," backing vocals in unison. It's an impromptu, two-minute party throughout the car bringing smiles to everybody's faces. It's pitch-perfect, unifying, and has a perfectly timed ending 10 seconds before reaching the next station, with just enough time for the young men to walk around the car and collect coins and dollar bills from the passengers. What could be more surprising and exciting than that? Well, maybe driving your car on Spring Street in Soho on a drizzly afternoon listening to U2's just released 2001 single, *Beautiful Day*. Out of the iconic Balthazar Restaurant and Bar, a man walks into the street looking at this phone. You almost hit him as you realize it's Bono of U2!!! It's the same guy who happens to be at that very moment singing from the CD player over your Honda CRV sound system, who you'd seen live in packed football stadiums, twisting and stomping under the jumbotrons, flashing politically poignant videos. He was the guy I watched with his band U2 debuting to the world in the Band Aid concerts in 1985, raising money for world hunger. He was the guy whose high notes I've tried to reach in the privacy of my own room, whose moves I've tried to imitate in front of mirrors, whose songs and messages have impacted millions of people across the world. He was the guy who was doing exactly what I felt I needed to do with my life. There he was, right in front of me! This short, scruffy man in a black leather jacket was Bono.

No one of right mind crosses a street in New York without looking. Unaware that he was almost taken out by a black Honda CRV, Bono was apparently more than "a few sheets to the wind." He was stone drunk as he walked in a wobbly line down the sidewalk. There was an inkling of commotion from the few patrons standing outside the door of Balthazar waiting to get in as he stumbled by them. Otherwise, on a rainy afternoon in SOHO New York City, he went unnoticed, except by me. Determined to talk to this guy, I immediately pulled the car over, leaped out, and started rapidly walking down the sidewalk. By this time, I'd been chanting for ten years and I believed there was no such thing as superficial, meaningless coincidences in life. I defined coincidence as passive, uninformed perception. This was truly a destined encounter, if I could catch him, that is. The Mystic Rhythm of the Universe, *Myoho*, put me in that location to meet my role model, my idol!

Bono was walking in a boozy, unbalanced, less than gyroscopic path down the sidewalk, hunched over looking at his phone, trying to get some information out of it. I later thought that maybe he'd been trying to call New Yorker Julian Schnabel, a great artist and director friend of his, or perhaps trying to beep his New York City marijuana delivery service of choice. I can only speculate. But, as I was closing in on him from about 20 yards away, I saw he wasn't talking on the cell phone, he was just pushing buttons and just sort of fumbling with it. At this point there was no turning back. I wasn't quite yelling, but certainly I was loud enough for him to hear in an ascending, progressively loudening tone. "Hey Bono...Bono...Bono!" But he didn't react. Either he was too engrossed in his awkward finger punching phone search or he'd learned to filter these types of sounds out of his head. But, when I got about ten yards from him, the words that came out of my mouth were a serious and polite, "Excuse me, Mr. Lennon!" This did get a reaction. He stopped dead in his tracks and turned around with a look on his face, the look of "what kind of asshole" would say the last words John Lennon heard before he was assassinated in cold blood by psycho killer Mark David Chapman? That had happened almost twenty years earlier about eighty blocks north from where we were now standing on this light rainy Sunday afternoon.

It worked! I got him. It got his head out of his phone, and he turned around and looked incredulously at me. I was then a few meters away, walking toward him, waving my hands in the air with a big smile on my face. I wasn't sure what the second act would be. But, I just thought a little New York sarcasm might work. I gambled on the fact that American Idol was so big on TV at the time, that the words just came out of my mouth and I recklessly blurted, "Hey if you try really hard. I mean, if you don't give up you can really make it someday." Then, his expression of, "What the fuck?" turned into a smile and he said in a lilting Irish accent, "You mean like American Idol? You really think I can do it?"

There I was, face to face with Bono, the biggest rock star in the world, according to Mick Jagger, and he was short just like I'd heard he was, and he was drunk, just like I thought he was. Once again, I was fishing for the perfect line. He had his telltale whiskered face, but I wouldn't call it a five o'clock shadow. I'd call it a Friday morning shadow, and it was Sunday afternoon. Replying to his line, "You mean like American Idol, you think I can do it?" With that, I just reached out, touched his face and sort of clasped his chin and cheeks in my hand and said, "Yeah, but you're going to have to shave this shit if you really want to make it."

Now I had him, stunned and speechless. I've outwitted him with the benefit of sobriety on my side. The man who a few years earlier said in a TV interview as if it was a spontaneous remark, *"Freedom has a smell...and it is the smell of the top of a newborn baby's head."* The media and the world were floored by that poetic and insightful "off the cuff" remark, although I just knew inside that he had rehearsed that line for weeks. What a performer in all realms! This was also the guy who goes to Africa in between tours to fight poverty and boldly petitioned European governments to relieve international debt that they held over a dozen African countries – and, I had him in my grasp by way of the outrageous barrage of stupid comments I'd flung at him meant to shock him into paying attention to little ole me. I was gazing into his eyes, and he didn't know what to say but just reached out and hugged me, a big, drunken bear hug and I made sure that our cheeks touched. Then he said, "Get the fuck out of here." As he was slowly pushing me away, we consummated some quick bro love through a grasping double handshake. I just looked at him and said, "I want to thank you for everything. Really, I mean it." With a smile he spun around and walked away, looking into his cellphone. About 10 seconds later I looked back and saw him mobbed by fans. So much for that phone call. Even now, years later, there's not a shred of doubt in my mind that those 20 or 30 seconds on a rainy New York sidewalk Sunday afternoon in the summer were meant to happen. Two prophetic singer-songwriters, shamans of the 21st Century, both with a huge mission to entertain and inform the masses, had just met on the sidewalk. One of them blazing through the stratosphere changing lives by touching hearts wherever he goes and sings, and the other the lead singer of the biggest rock band in the world.

But it's all the other encounters that are maybe not quite as shiny, but just as impactful that make New York so "special," for lack of a better word. "Look there's Lady Gaga getting out the that taxi cab!" Or, "Why is that skinny, drugged-out, naked woman doing push-ups on the sidewalk at noon outside the peep show on 34th Street?" Or, "Was that gunshots or fireworks?"

One hot summer evening driving home from dinner after a late-night Young Men's Buddhist meeting, as my friend Mike and I were approaching the Holland Tunnel, we stopped at a red light at about 11:00 PM. We were in that big, old Oldsmobile that my grandparents had given me, with the windows open. Suddenly through the front windows on both sides, topless hookers, big-boobed "Sistas of the Night" stuck their entire bodies, head to tits in the car and said, "Hey baby, wanna date?" Topless hookers at a red light hadn't been in our game plan for the evening! These types of things just happen in New York City. You don't plan or expect them, but they force you to think and react quickly.

Another time, in the middle of the afternoon, I was walking down 14th Street on the West Side, no gayer than any other neighborhoods in Greenwich Village. But as I was walking down my side of the sidewalk, two men were walking the other way, arms flailing in the air in animated, obvious gay flamboyance. A few steps before we passed each other, the tall, skinny, well-dressed black man reached out to hug and embrace me and said, "Hey cutie, come here, give me a kiss." Like a New York Giants halfback, I pivoted and ducked and twisted my body to get out of the way. Maybe a hand brushed over the back of my head. But, it was New York City, so nobody missed a step. They kept walking in their own direction. I kept walking in mine, in the opposite direction. Nobody looked back. It was just New York.

CHAPTER 24

HOW TO CARE FOR YOUR GARBAGE

"Not giving up - that's the only way. Once you give up, you are defeated."

- Daisaku Ikeda
(*Faith into Action, pg. 148*)

For as unpredictable and surprising as New York can be, life in Japan is often predictable, rigorously organized by mandatory practices. Handing of garbage is one of them. Woe to anyone who does not adhere to its ritual. Today's mission, ride! Ride that *mamachari* as far as it takes me to catch up to the garbage trucks. ("momma chariot" is a simple non-sporty practical Japanese bicycle with a basket, often including a kid's seat). Tuesday is trash pick-up day when speedy garbage trucks zip through the streets of Kyoto to collect mounds of neatly stacked, full translucent yellow city-issued bags. These bags must be used by everyone and are to be put out only on Tuesday and Friday mornings. It's the law. Each small apartment building or group of houses has a designated staging area where the bags of nonrecyclable combustibles are neatly laid next to each other or stacked upright on top of each other so as not to fall. A tough woven bright blue net is then spread out over the garbage. Obsession with cleanliness and hygiene transforms the Tuesday morning cityscape into a half-day long "artistic installation" version of Kyoto neighborhoods, with blue bumps everywhere and no traces of the little pieces and stories tossed into families' kitchen garbage cans. Incidentally, there are virtually no garbage cans in public places. The whole city operates on a "carry in/ carry out" honor system which I've only seen in state parks back in the states.

No garbage sitting outside overnight, along with this tear-proof netted barrier, means vermin or rogue pets have no chance of digging into the remains of last night's supper. Although, occasionally you can see incredibly intelligent and resourceful crows, *karasu*, having a pavement feast after finding a weak spot or lifting an improperly laid net. Gainfully employed garbage men get the job done quickly and properly. Their truck tires rarely come to a full stop as these gloved and uniformed Samurai surgically and athletically uncover those blue-meshed mounds, scooping up yellow bags and throwing them into the compactor in the back of their trucks.

That morning I arrived at the school late. With the Russian investigation vice starting to tighten on Trump, I got a little too involved in the *Rachel Maddow Show* and other nightly news shows on YouTube. Another two hours went by and it was time to take care of business. Atop my bike's small basket, I plopped a large, overstuffed yellow garbage bag which had barely enough slack to tie it with a knot. It stank of a week's worth of garbage from the school, which included the rotting remains of fish lunches and enough school marked stuff and bills to prevent me from considering any sort of illegal dumping, even in that single public basket near the hospital. My wife, Misa, told me years ago that the city is very strict, and they will investigate improperly-disposed-of bags. I had no choice but to get this stinking mess out of my school.

I've had this issue with missing the trash pickup before. The simple solution was a five-to ten-minute bike ride that could get me out of my neighborhood to an area where the trucks hadn't yet made it. I would head off toward the south and west. The areas where the trucks had already picked up were marked by those empty blue mesh nets strewn by the side of the road or neatly folded up and put in attached baskets. I'd haul my load until I crossed the boundaries of the "cleaned zones" and found a suitable target of yet-to-be-collected piles of bags. I'd look around to see if I was being observed, stuff my yellow city-compliant bag under the net, and quickly go on my way. I wasn't doing anything illegal. It's just that it's a little unusual to miss your trash pickup. There's a schedule and rules that define proper citizen behavior and they should be followed.

But this recent Tuesday morning turned into Tuesday afternoon. I was getting a very late start on the quest for suitable dumping grounds. I had recently been wrestling with trying to nail down a diet and exercise regimen and was looking forward to burning some calories on the bike. I only had night classes to worry about that day, so I didn't give it a second thought. I'd kill two birds with one stone.

Although I was hours behind my neighborhood's pick-up schedule, I surmised that surely in a city of 1.5 million it must take a whole day for a few dozen trucks to traverse every neighborhood. But as I rode further and further out of my neighborhood and the surrounding neighborhoods, I couldn't escape the "cleaned zone."

There are hundreds of small side streets in which thousands and thousands of homes are grouped into dozens of uniquely featured neighborhoods. After a frustrating hour and a half of cycling a beeline towards the hinterlands, I realized I was further south and east then I'd ever been by bicycle. I was thrilled that I finally got to see the famed Nishikyogoku Sports Stadium complex that I've seen on TV where the city's marathons end. I could feel that I was on the outskirts of a city that takes three hours by bike from one end to the other. But I could still see nothing other than those empty blue nets folded neatly or strewn by the side of the road. Google maps showed me that I was nearing the Katsura River. It was a sunny day a few weeks before summer became official, and by this time I was dripping wet from the heat. Beyond having broken a sweat, I'd broken a personal long-distance biking record and now I was starting to get a little desperate. Of course, I reasoned, I was bound to reach a neighborhood where the trucks haven't picked up yet. I had been toting that bright-yellow, overstuffed garbage bag in a bicycle basket that was big enough to obstruct the view in front of me. I could imagine that a foreigner riding a bicycle with a big bag of garbage, obviously out of his natural habitat, was a real eye catcher.

Would this now two-hour journey be for naught? Was I truly going to ride back to my school with a bag of garbage because I had allowed myself to be "out of rhythm" with the Tuesday garbage pickup ritual? No fucking way! On impulse, I decided to pull into the parking lot of a large apartment building.

Twin beige plastic dumpsters for the apartment dwellers, that must be the answer. But they looked too clean to be dumpsters and one had a lock on it. I opened the lid on the other one and saw old computer monitors, a printer, and a cracked TV set. It was the electronics recycle bin. I turned and saw that I was under the gaze of a woman walking her dog in the parking lot. I wasn't in downtown Kyoto where people are used to seeing foreigners of all kinds doing things and acting "differently." I couldn't throw that bag where it wasn't supposed to go. This is a country of rules and regulations, with Kyoto possibly the strictest city of all. I was also representing all foreigners. My next move might be discussed at dinner that night, or worse, brought up at the neighborhood meetings which are held every month. No go. I had to keep searching although I was starting to imagine stuffing that bag under my sink and burning lots of incense until the next pick up.

I was back out on the sidewalk weighing my options. Maybe I'd cross that river to the town of Katsura. Maybe the trucks hadn't made it there yet. I was also weighing the fact that every minute spent cycling that way meant another minute spent cycling back. I was getting my bearings on a phone that had 8% remaining battery charge while trying to memorize my hour and a half return route. Just then a cop on a motorbike stopped at a red light a few meters away from me. There's something very Robocop about Kyoto police. Their bikes are modern, as are their helmets. Their uniforms also invoke unquestioned authority, enhanced further by the fact I know they all also have black belts in karate or some another martial art form. He looked at the almost bursting yellow city-issued trash blimp in my basket and then looked up at sweaty me. For that few seconds, there were some complicated mental gymnastics going on. I was thinking that he was thinking that I was some disrespectful asshole of a foreigner about to dump a trash bag in the middle of this clean and safe neighborhood which was under his jurisdiction. I wanted him to know that I had committed the entire afternoon to this well-intentioned excursion that started way on the other side of the city, and that I was hell-bent on doing the right thing, that I believed in order, and that I deeply respected the beauty and cleanliness of our city. I wanted him to understand that I would try to do as the Romans do even if it killed me of heat exhaustion (or even if I was forced to lug that stinky bag back to my school). The light turned green and he sped off. A few minutes later, I saw that he had doubled back around, most likely to check on me and my yellow bag.

By this time, I was riding at full speed on a narrow road that ran alongside some railroad tracks in the general direction of home. I was trying to "get out of Dodge" towards the center of Kyoto, towards my hood, Gosho Minami. Then I came upon it! Abutting a small concrete wall next to the tracks was a waist-high blue-net-covered mound. A dozen delightful yellow bags perfectly stacked and stinky were waiting to be picked up and thrown into the back of a garbage truck! As I looked around, I saw that this was an anomaly. Something was wrong here. This neighborhood had already been serviced but maybe the rushing trash-samurai had missed this collection point. Their bad, my good. In a second, I slipped my bag under that beautiful blue net and sped off with my basket now empty.

Having rid myself of this burden was absolutely liberating. For one, it was easier to ride the bike and I didn't have that bag with the rotting fish skins wafting into my face. But I also I reveled in the levity of having purged the old stuff, the waste, the unnecessary and of starting anew. With the wind blowing through my hair and my UV-exposed head and overexerted leg muscles propelling forward, the profundity of this experience began to dawn on me. *Itsumo kidzuku*! "Always a realization" is a lyric from the recently finished video for my song SUGE. I didn't give up and it paid off!

On the way home, I happened on a quiet, cool, rebuilt section of Kyoto called Shimabara. I was told days later that it used to be one of the two areas of Kyoto where brothels were permitted. While riding through this partially rebuilt, *kakkoi* (cool) mysterious neighborhood, I discovered a hidden gem of a *sento* public bath, which is now on my "to go" list. Throughout the whole excursion, I burned quadruple the calories that I had set out to release and got the kind of workout needed to kickstart a serious exercise campaign to retake my slightly bulging abdomen. Once again, I felt myself in perfect, intricate rhythm with the universe, and not through passively glomming onto it. It was through making a determined, no holds barred effort to do the right thing, to turn my own stupidity (i.e. being late, lazy and missing the trash pick-up) into value. It was another chance to "change poison into medicine." Or as I have come learn, just another precious adventure in Kyoto.

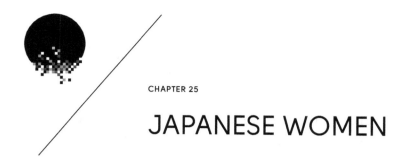

CHAPTER 25

JAPANESE WOMEN

Rob held up his tall can of beer and pointed it towards my huge flat screen TV as if it was a laser pointer highlighting a PowerPoint slide at some International Symposium of Lovesick and Heart-torn Foreigners. "Somebody had to write it," he said nonchalantly while calmly staring at the lyrics projected on my TV after I had forced him to listen to an early version of the song.

JAPANESE GIRLS

By Jay Crystall © 2015 Jay Crystall

Naoko rocks the African style, full of charm and pretty smile
Chiharu plays hearts like a toy – stalked by a Korean boy
Kaoru has some older "friends," Wears Chanel, drives a Benz
Mariko's a friend of mine – although it's been a long, long time
 Japanese Girls, they're all Japanese Girls
Maki was a lucky one, married rich and has two sons
Yuki is a cancer nurse, smokes a lot and likes to curse
Chikako's rich but no romance, wears kimonos goes to France
Sadly, Haruka lost her Dad, who knows how many boys she's had
 Ay Yo! Okoranai (Don't get angry)
 Kira ku ni iko (Take it easy)
 Are o mite kawaii (look over there, so cute!)
 Oboe toitte abunai (let her into your heart...watch out!)
 o-oo-o-o-o-o-o-o, they're all Japanese Girls – Don't try to
 understand, you`ll never understand

Writing original music is a time-warping and all-consuming calling. Conceiving of lyrics that express everything from your deepest most personal meditations to pure, accidental rhyming bullshit can be debilitating and uplifting at the same time. Then, marrying them with melodies that you hope are "original" and not contrived from or easily associated with something you've heard before becomes a throbbing, multi-layered obsession that tints every neural light pulse until the song is finally written. Tuning the guitars, playing the instruments, untangling and connecting cables, searching for samples, tweaking the arrangements, and producing it in a way that highlights the thematic and aesthetic intent, feel and message of the song is a dozen 40-hour work weeks, at best. Singing the song as if your very existence and future depended on it becomes a way of life that is both ecstatically fulfilling and emotionally eviscerating. Then engineering it, recording it while working around software bugs adds another full human expenditure into the equation. If you do finish it to near satisfaction, it's then time to make a music video. Why you may ask? Because humans of the 21st century cannot accept aural stimulation without video. Our antennae are desensitized and need what they need. I've taken great pride in and have lived and died a half-dozen times making all my videos, excepting "NANANA" and "Joy of Loneliness," using an iPhone and some cool apps, usually created in trains during commutes or in bed from 1:00 AM to 5:00 AM. Will I always be a one man show? Will I always have to do everything by myself? Did I not create enough fortune in my life that someone or some company will assist me? Do I need to exert myself even harder and change more karma, so I can meet a Sherpa or at least a donkey that will assist me on my ascent up Mount Kilimanjaro?

For example, I had all but abandoned the song I wrote about Japanese women, Japanese Girls a year and a half ago. Life in all its complexity and some whizzing curveballs had distracted me once again. There were other songs that bumped it to the back of my "to do" list. I felt I had allowed JGirls to become too heavy. I over-produced it to sound "cool," and it had too many beats and changes which blatantly violated the "less is more" credo. But after finishing my video for SUGE! last week, it was time to revisit it and finally get it done. This book was nearing completion and the song's theme tied directly into it.

So, after a year and a half of disassociating myself from it on all levels, I started to listen to it again. Once again, I immediately began to obsess on assembling the nuts and bolts needed to finish this absolute masterpiece. I was convinced that it had to "drop" as soon as possible onto the airwaves to keep the Earth from warbling and spinning off its axis. Could a good night's sleep be more important than explaining this epiphany of mine, this spoken narrated insight into the complexity of the Japanese female gender set to a cool alternative dance track? Absolutely not! That's how this semi-retired engineering brain is wired. Like roadkill on the highway of my brilliant dreams, this song twitched back to life, opening an eyelid and wriggling towards the side of the road, ready to sprint towards the woods of the alternative music charts and some semblance of financial ROI (return on investment). That is, until the devilish functions in the universe crashed my Macbook Pro hard disk AND my back up external hard drive within two months of each other. The song and all its elements, the culmination of hundreds of hours of musical sweat and spiritual reflection disappeared into the ether. It died along with thousands of files of music, some unfinished masterpieces, videos, photos, worksheets, PowerPoint presentations, school documents and everything else that I had put myself into for the eight years of my life that I lived with and loved in that MacBook Pro. The unrecoverable efforts of countless late nights and long days converted into ones and zeros by a collaboration between Steve Jobs, Bill Gates, dozens of programmers, developers, and me were now gone. That, my little pretties, is life. Whether human, botanical, planetary, digital or otherwise, it takes shape as a wave forms and begins to rise as it approaches the beach - protruding and expressing itself evermore until reaching its tipping point where it crashes down, splashing and churning up sand, before receding back into the ocean, only to splash up again on some distant shore. My song, JGirlz now exists as an unfinished mp3 version in my Gmail sent box. Perhaps I will redo it someday. But at that moment, at 10:00 PM with Rob a year ago, my somewhat traumatized, love-scarred Canadian friend was right when he said, "somebody" had to write the song. It was me.

I've always been enthralled by and impressed with Japanese females. Since moving to Japan, I have become utterly mystified, confused, and sometimes even shocked by them. I felt that for the sake of my own sanity, and as the voice of all foreigners who live or have lived here or who have had a long-term relationship with a Japanese partner, (both men and women), I had to reveal the truth about them to the world. And that was the song. One important strand of my life's mission is to dispel the notion that the monolithic stereotypes of a subservient, bending wife walking obediently behind her husband or a mindless, purring sexual kitten is the reality of the modern Japanese woman. Not by a long shot. Those of us who have experienced up close and personal the power, unpredictability, and quirkiness of Japanese women (and lived to tell about it) realize that this does not comport with reality. At least, not in today's culture. When compared to America, it is true there's clearly a much larger proportion of stay-at-home moms, and by New York City standards even more so. It's also true that a large segment of the workforce is comprised of millions of OL (office ladies) fulfilling their frequently routine roles under the stern, watchful eyes of borderline harassing, micro-phallic managers. I remember seeing an article on the "not fake news" CNN channel that ranked industrialized countries in terms of the percentage of women who hold business executive or political positions. Japan ranked second to last, just above the United Arab Emirates. This statistic is certainly changing, but perhaps too slowly. The Mayor of nearby Otsu City, Naomi Koshi, received her law degree from Harvard. The feisty and controversial governor of Tokyo, Yuriko Koike, holds her own amidst the scandalous and bickering "boys club" of politicians in the capital city. (editor's note: the first "#MeToo" rally was held this past Spring in Tokyo). I have seen first-hand the power of Japanese women beyond the bruises on my ego and scars of having been married to a Japanese woman from Kyoto. I witness it every day amongst the millennials I teach at Doshisha University. It's generally the female students who seem to lead the conversations. I gleefully keep my lips zipped as I watch them deftly emasculate their male counterparts, in sarcastic second language English during classroom practice debates.

It's the women that I hear laughing louder on the train than the men, especially the Osaka *obachan* (women aged 50-70 years) whose good-natured cackling and colorful sweaters are legendary throughout Japan. I observe in playgrounds and overhear in restaurant booths that it's the sisters in the family that have bigger balls than their brothers. It's as if the rubber-band which has been stretched in the direction of women being dominated and unempowered for hundreds of years is snapping back. Don't get me wrong. Women have always been respected here, even revered, way beyond the bounds of other male-dominated societies, including many Arab countries. For me, being as much of a feminist as my biology allows me, I not only delight in their growing profile and influence, I am downright relieved. History has taught us that whenever you have too many men working together deciding things unchecked, weird things happen, whether it's in the Catholic priesthood, the military or in the Penn State University football locker room.

Teaching the Doshisha University English circle was part Oprah Winfrey and part going back to my days as a youth division Buddhist leader in the SGI-USA.

Japanese wives don't overtly petition and fight for control of their family. Rather, they use clever and finely-honed tactics of soft-power to let the men THINK they are leading. Through outwitting their husbands by, for instance, cooking well-timed favorite meals (or not cooking at all), doling out monthly entertainment allowance to their husbands, or preparing hot baths and offering them neck massages, they are able to pull the strings and configure a life that is comfortable and enjoyable for themselves and their kids, which then extends to their hardworking husbands. I'm reminded of a song called,

"The Women are Smarter," that I played with Kansai Rocks! in bars in Osaka. I first heard the Grateful Dead sing what I know now is an old calypso song written in the late 1940s by Norman Span. It goes like this:

> *Let us put men and women together, see which one are smarter.*
> *Some say men, but I say no, the women got the men like a*
> *puppet show. It ain't me, it's the people that say men are leading*
> *the women astray. I say, it's the women today, smarter than the*
> *men in every way. That's right, the women are smarter.*

So, the times they are a changing in Japan. Estrogen is slowly chipping away at the rock-hard, sperm-formed institutions of male dominance in 21st Century Japan – and, we're all better off. There's a lot of lost ground to make up. The key to the future success of Japan may lie in harnessing the largely untapped power and spirit of Japanese women, in all their unacknowledged and unrecognized diversity. This change is inevitable and coming fast, and just in time. I'd like to give a few examples of some women I have had the privilege of observing, teaching or becoming friends with who are, in their own way, at the forefront of this revolution.

Honestly, I thought having lived and grown up in the New York Metropolitan area with occasional jaunts to California, Florida, Philadelphia and Chicago I had seen everything. Right? America is the original "melting pot" of international cultures and gurgling in the center of the pot is New York, where myriad lifestyles churn and bubble off into new ones. The gay rights movement can be traced back to the riots at the Stonewall Tavern in the Summer of 1969. My home city was the incubator of the American leg of the punk rock movement, and of trendy haute cosmopolitan culture and fashion. I had been through Big Apple boot camp and was certainly more than prepared for immersing myself in the comparatively tame culture of Japan. What could it be but a few variations and extensions of the basic Japanese character and lifestyle I'd become accustomed and endeared to? Boy was I wrong! It took only a few seasons of living here to witness some of the "extreme lifestyles" that I mistakenly thought might only exist on the fringes of Japanese society. In between the boundary stakes of workaholics, cultural traditionalists, binge drinkers and kinky hedonists lies a thousand different gradations that meld into that red circle on the white background.

Take, for instance, what I saw a few years ago. I was walking to the train after finishing an evening company teaching gig in the southern Fushimi area at 10:00 PM on a Thursday night. Although I was tired and didn't have much money on me at the time, I was compelled to stop and check out a tiny reggae-themed Indonesian izakaya opened by my friend, Dede, a few months prior. Rumah Café was crowded that night, which meant there were no more than twelve people there. Two young girls, obviously sisters, sat at the bar engrossed in a smartphone game with their backs turned to the lively acoustic duet performing. By young, I mean they were probably in the late stages of their Elementary School careers (4th - 6th grade). A "hippified" husband and wife, dressed in gauzy tropical garb, were singing in beautiful harmony to a lively reggae number in Japanese. He strummed a guitar and she shook maracas as they stood two meters away from the bar in the middle of the floor. I soon put it together that the inattentive girls at the bar were their daughters. Dancing, swaying mommy was careful not to shake the maracas too close to the bulging sling she wore, the reason being that it contained a young, sleeping infant. It took a few blinks of my eyes and a shake of the head to process what was happening. Mommy and Daddy's gig in this small, smoky Indonesian reggae club was on a school night. And I thought all Japanese mothers stayed at home on a school night, bathing the kids and getting them into bed early so they'd be fresh the next day as they are sent off to school with a homemade bento lunch box. I'm still not sure if what I witnessed that night was beautiful and natural or a completely irresponsible display of childrearing. Maybe there was no *obaachan* (grandmother) at home and nobody hires babysitters in Japan. But I know one thing, it seemed normal in a Japanese sort of way. The boundaries are different here. The deeper you dig the more you realize that there is no such thing as a typical Japanese woman.

Another example of this gender revolution is Mari. Although it's been almost two years since we last saw each other, Mari is one of my oldest and dearest friends in Japan. I met her during the second English lesson I ever taught. It was at Velco School's Umeda branch in Osaka. She was a woman in her early 60s, elegantly dressed, and walked boldly into the school on that Sunday afternoon. Greeting her with warmth and a big smile, I pulled out a seat for her at the big oval conference table and asked her if she needed tea before we proceeded with the group English conversation class attended by four other students. From the outset, Mari was smiling and spoke confidently. She had an air of worldly experience about her, for lack of a better word. Dressed to kill in Chanel on a Sunday afternoon in an English school, with short-cropped black hair, she slung an orange Hermès Birkin bag over the arm of her chair. All of us knew that the purse alone would cost as much as a very nice car. Mari was the heir to her father's real estate fortune and owned buildings in the Osaka area. Being the *Shacho*, or President, of the company, she just went there a few times a week to "show her face." She spent most of her days bouncing back and forth between medical clinics and department stores. Evenings were devoted to entertaining family, friends and business associates unless of course, she impulsively decided to fly to Saint Petersburg for a few days of dining and shopping by herself. She was funny, mildly sarcastic, and had hundreds of stories to tell about living in Vancouver and her world travels. In terms of life experience and English nuance, she was light years beyond the other students in the class. We all enjoyed bantering back and forth, which is exactly what's supposed to happen in an advanced English conversation class. Over the course of the next few months, she and I hit it off even more. We were both, in a sense, living on the edge. I was living on the edge as someone who just sacrificed an entire career and moved to Japan to start a new "career." That meant working twice the hours as I did in New York for half the pay, all the while trying to keep my family together and pursue my dream in music. Mari, on the other hand, had been fighting illness for a long time and her super-slender body showed it. An immunodeficiency disease and a lavish, indulgent lifestyle likely contributed to the swirling array of age on her smiling face. She had a bright sun of wit, a huge heart and confidence from a privileged life that shone through her, making her just gorgeous. She wouldn't hesitate to mention out loud, with a smile on her face, that her doctor suggested she speak English often to fight off or slow down the creeping onslaught of senility. Japanese and English are completely different linguistically, and grammatically they are more-or-less opposites. The mental mechanics of putting thought into two spoken languages in real time, make the neural connections between two opposite sides of the brain's language center spark like crazy. It's like training for a mental decathlon and was just what the doctor ordered.

It was at her family home during one Christmas that it really sunk in to me that Japanese families can be just as colorful as any I had experienced or heard about in the States. I'm surprised I remember the finer details of that extravagant evening which centered around an impeccable dinner cooked by Mari's husband. He was also in his 60s, with long, chemically-bleached blond hair that fell halfway down his back. Bustling about ten feet away from me in that open-air kitchen, he stretched his skinny, tight black-leather-pant-clad body toward the stove. Lanky in an orangish-maroon, oversized sweater, he was wearing a black metal-studded belt and a matching black metal-studded wrist band. He looked totally 1970s punk, like one of the Ramones. Now that I think about it, he was a spittin' image of Iggy Pop. The alcohol didn't just flow, it gushed. Appetizers were whisked onto plates along with a ceremonious champagne toast, Dom Perignon, 1988, which was followed by some superb Italian white wine. Mari's husband was putting on a stellar show, creating dishes like Wild Salmon Tarts and Parmesan Encrusted Mushrooms, all the while sipping his champagne. Mari had confided in me that he had basically been mooching off her for decades and doesn't contribute much to the family beyond those dishes, and how her lawyer had advised her that she might as well stay with him because a divorce would be much too expensive at this point. But, she certainly ate well! Over the course of the evening, we drank, and she bragged about the aged Italian red wine, French beers, Kronenbourgs, and Bloody Marys made with fresh juiced tomatoes and vodka that she had picked up on that recent trip to St Petersburg. It was a total blast, a once in five years meal for me that I suspect was a way of life for the family. By the end of the meal, I flashed back to something that Ellen DeGeneres said in an interview a few years ago "If you think money can't buy happiness, you're wrong, it can." This was a happy home. If you don't believe me, you can ask the Yorkshire Terrier that was sleeping in a fur bed near my feet as I ate dinner and drank those elixirs. Relaxed, I lost track of time. At one point, I glanced at the clock. Startled by how close to midnight it was, I raced out the door and ran a very crooked line to the train station, which was five or six minutes away, desperate to catch the last train. Breathless, I made the train as the doors were closing. Before I fell asleep on the train, I thought if I ever had the desire to write a sitcom pilot I knew where to start, and it wasn't in America.

> *Kayo moved to Tokyo – drinks red wine plays the koto*
> *Miyuki's art is wild and free she hangs objects from a tree*
> *Miki lived to tell the tale of life and love like a fairy tale*
> *Yuuko she tried suicide   three or four times...still alive*
> *o-oo-o-o-o-o-o-o, they're all Japanese Girls Don't try to*
> *understand, you`ll never understand---*

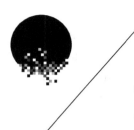

CHAPTER 26

WHY LOVE (SIC)?

What a powerful word love is. We ponder it, we yearn for it, and sometimes we lose sleep over it. When we have achieved it or think we have a grasp on its meaning, it can slip through our fingers like a fistful of wet sand we've picked up on the beach. We think we might understand what love is through spirituality or religious pursuit. God loves me. We trust in Him, so we feel a real sense of purpose fighting to do His work on His behalf – and, it feels good! Maybe Jesus loves you, but he's not *in* love with you. Love. Love. Love. Fuck! Has there ever been a word that has been more overused, misunderstood, misinterpreted, whispered in the ear or texted with two fingers crossed behind the back? There's making love, which half of all English speakers say is synonymous with fucking. There's breaking love. There's broken love. There's faking love, and there's loving chocolate. But through Japanese ears, the word love means no more, no less than romance and intimacy. I remember decades ago Misa reading my email reply to my ex-coworker, Kelly, who had mentored me and suggested we should have lunch sometime. I said I'd love to have lunch. It took two weeks to convince Misa that I wasn't having an affair with Kelly and that loving to do something just meant really wanting to do it.

"Thanks, and praise to the rain, for it makes the sun feel warmer. Thanks, and praise to the pain, so we celebrate the smallest joys. With the push and the shove, your capacity to love grows stronger every year."

- Perfectly Fine
– Jay Crystall
(Kansai Rocks!
Changing Poison into Medicine)

217

Lovesick. Merriam Webster defines it as "in love or missing someone you love so much you're *unable to act normally.*" Unable to act normally... hmmm? I wonder if the honorable Ms. Webster can expand on what's meant by "acting normally?" Regarding use of the word love, might there be some room for interpretation there, too? What kind of love makes us sick? Let's get real and admit that most people act "abnormally" when they're in love or they think they're in love. That abnormal behavior is even more pronounced when the love that they feel exceeds the love they have for themselves.

There's a fantastic and important video that I first saw on Facebook of a bearded Rabbi explaining his concept of what he calls *fish love*. In calm, elegant conviction, he illustrates this concept through the following story: A boy is eating a fish. An old man looks at him and asks, "Why are you eating that fish?" The boy replies, "Because I love fish." The old man says, "You love that fish so much that you pulled it out of the water, killed it and ate it!" The Rabbi then explains that we often interpret love as what utility or purpose something or someone serves us, or what "holes" inside of us can be fulfilled by things that lie outside of us. A woman loves a man because he can provide for her and make her feel secure and maybe give her a happy family and a home to live in. That's valid and wonderful. A man loves that woman because she cares for him, makes him feel like a man and fulfills him sexually. She cooks him dinner and raises the kids. That's why most of us love somebody; because they provide us with those things that we want and need. They are the long sought-after solution to our own specific equation. That's *fish love*. But the Rabbi then proceeds to explain another type of love, that love that we have inside of ourselves that we want to extend into other people and things. When we give that love to other people, we give a part of ourselves to that person and it lives in them. Then we acknowledge and recognize that part of ourselves in them and love them all-the-more. We try to nurture that love in them through our actions.

To me, following this logic backwards, it means that the most important thing is to develop that inexhaustible wellspring of love that is innate in all of us, Original Good. In my chosen outlook, Nichiren Buddhism, this is nothing other than the accessible but difficult-to-mine "Buddha Nature" which has always existed in the depths of our lives. Tina Turner, a fellow

Buddhist, called it in her autobiography, *I, Tina*, "the Christ-like nature in all of us." Call it what you will but realize it's there. The challenge is not to seek love and satisfaction outside oneself through the perfect relationship, or the perfect house with the perfect terrace on the perfect lake or the perfect job with the perfect salary or, if it works for you, the perfect woman with the perfect breasts. Don't get me wrong. All those things are great, and we want, need, and strive for them, especially the perfect breasts. But they come and go and like the wilting, falling cherry blossoms they are transient. The perfect terrace with the perfect view of the sunset can be blown away in a hurricane. Perfect jobs can be deleted in an instant from an org chart by a take-over from another company. The perfect breasts eventually succumb to gravity. The perfect relationship can be ended through sickness or death or through meeting Angelina Jolie on the set of *Mr. and Mrs. Smith*. Then ten years later after that, the hard fought for next level of perfect love ends. How?! Even George Clooney was shocked that somehow Brad Pitt and Angelina with their precious posse could not work things out.

So, like all the streams and rivers of the world returning to the sea, it all eventually goes back to you and what you think of that person looking back at you in the mirror. I'm not talking about just loving yourself. George Carlin did a routine about having a quiet romantic, candlelit dinner for one. Mostly he was referring to masturbation and not just "using" yourself. But I, as usual, take it further to mean it's about respecting and truly and profoundly appreciating yourself, and that includes all your flaws and shortcomings. All of us in the civilized, privileged world look at ourselves in the mirror all the time, sometimes naked, sometimes just our faces, sometimes judging our good points and bad points. Are you too embarrassed to admit that you have kissed yourself in the mirror? Even once? Even if just for practice when you were a teenager? Loving yourself in all kinds of ways is crucial for happiness but also has severe limitations. Why? Because the "self" changes from moment-to-moment and situation-to-situation. A nasty remark from somebody can change your entire perception of self-love. A disfiguring car accident, a bad mood, or the wrong drug can upend you. But if that self-love is deeply rooted in something more fundamental; oh, let's just say the primordial instinct of life to sustain and promote itself, then that kind of love becomes unshakeable and enduring. Think about the father Emperor penguin freezing and almost starving to death but providing warmth to its yet-to-be-born chick for two months waiting for the mother penguin to return from the sea. Think of the unwavering single-purposed sperm cell swimming against the torrent of multiple orgasms to promote its DNA imprint in a future being. There's the way the tall grass in your backyard you finally got around to mowing grows back the next day and sprouts forth fresh, young, green shoots determined to never give in to those rotating lawnmower blades. These are expressions of the all-encompassing drive toward sustaining life, the opposite of *fish love*. They're like the love expressed so eloquently in a published letter from American Civil War officer Sullivan Ballou, written on the battlefield to his wife who was at home with the kids. He was willing to boldly sacrifice his life and love of his family for a cause greater than himself.

> *Sarah, my love for you is deathless. It seems to bind me to you*
> *with mighty cables that nothing but omnipotence could break*
> *and yet my love of country comes over me like a strong wind*
> *and bears me irresistibly armed with all these chains to the*
> *battlefield. I shall return to my loved ones unharmed,*
> *God willing. If I do not, my dear Sarah, never forget how*
> *much I love you. And when my last breath escapes me on the*
> *battlefield, it will whisper your name.*

Whew! Put aside the fact that people just don't express themselves like that anymore. You can gasp at the utter passion and honesty in which he conveys the sacrifice that led him to the battlefield, confessing that his love for wife and family may be exceeded by his love for country. Now that's what I call *real* love. Give me some of *that*!

The lead character in the movie *The Life of David Gale*, written by Charles Randolph and directed by Alan Parker, was a college professor lecturing to University of Texas students. He told his students that almost out of habit we set goals for ourselves and strive to achieve those goals. He went further to explain that these efforts are in a sense for completely self-serving reasons. We get things, we accomplish goals, we feel good...period. He closes the lecture by exclaiming that the only truly meaningful life is one of service to others. That is not *fish love*. This deeper well of love resides inside of us but must be directed and radiated outward. The Greatest Love of All, that Whitney Houston sang about has little to do with better pocketbooks and golf clubs, great vacations, and sleeping next to someone who flicks all your switches. What I'm getting at is that if you base your life on focusing your quest to express and materialize *this* kind of love, you travel further, and the ride is more exhilarating. If you, in *your own way* "Mother Theresa" your life to save countless orphans, "Bob Marley" your life to write the perfect lyrics to express the struggle for freedom and the pain of love, or "Martin Luther King" yourself to give voice to the oppressed and eradicate injustice, you tap into the *Realm of Eternity* and *Absolute Value*. That's another way of saying you are now of the "living enlightened." You are a Buddha! Our life-force can be boundless and timeless if we allow ourselves to manifest it. We can all free ourselves from what Buddhism describes as *"the Four Sufferings of birth, sickness, old age and death."*

It's not a huge stretch to realize that it's possible to love somebody more than they hate you and, because of that, you are both more likely to win. Hopefully you come to realize that even if you can't buy a stairway to heaven, you can build a tower that extends high into the sky. You, and you alone, must build it brick-by-brick with your own detailed plans. The mortar that holds it together is the perfectly proportioned mixture of the sands of difficulty and struggle, wetted by tears of pain and delightful tears of joy. In time, the mortar cures, hopefully quickly. Do you build enough of that tower every waking hour of your day to improve it and connect to Original Good? Do you make it extend high enough and fast enough today to keep yourself juiced? What if you can't climb it quickly enough to enjoy the view before the sun goes down, or even revel in the magnificence of millions of shimmering stars? What if you also can't help other people build their towers or at least help each of them see that it lies in their own tears, sweat, and struggle? Or, what if it doesn't happen fast enough or with the people you wish it to happen with? Then it burns in your heart and can make you lovesick. I am lovesick, but blissfully so.

At this writing, my marriage to Misa is barely hanging by a thread that's woven in yen, financial need, something I want to change but feel powerless to shape because of the ravages of time and distance between us. Love often isn't lost all at once. Sometimes it's just chipped away in tiny, unrecognizable pieces until the mosaic no longer fits together. Right now, we might be that unrepairable mosaic. Time could pull us farther apart. On the other hand, there's a Japanese tradition of repairing broken pottery called *Kintsugi*, "golden joinery" or "golden repair." Broken pottery is dusted with lacquer or mixed with powdered gold, silver or platinum. Cracks or missing pieces are filled, and these fillings become part of the piece's history, rather than something to discard or disguise. The piece's damaged areas are illuminated to profile its lifetime, with all its imperfections. Kintsugi relates to the previously-mentioned Japanese philosophy, *wabi-sabi*, which embraces the flawed or imperfect in life because of its wear and tear, not despite it. So, time could be our Kintsugi wabi-sabi and pull us together in some shape or form, perhaps something other than, or even grander than, marriage. Maybe. Maybe not.

Looking back, I remember moments after our tiny daughter, Mimi, was born and she was placed in my arms. For ten minutes in a warm, quiet room in Lenox Hospital, New York we stared at each other. She was a delicate, five-pound baby barely blinking her eyes and her father, hardly able to contain my tears, held her heart close, with a tractor-beam locking our souls together. In that moment, I felt all the collective love that has ever existed in the universe, all the struggles every father has ever made to protect their daughters and provide them with a life better than they've had, and to work tirelessly so that they can have ease and comfort in their lives. I knew I would eventually scrutinize every boy or man that came into her life and interrogate them to ensure they were deserving of a daddy's precious little princess. The truth is, I'd give anything now to relive that walk along the Kamogawa River in the beautiful season of cherry blossoms with Mimi in between Misa and me, swinging Mimi in those big giant steps like we used to do in Central Park in New York, and then sit down in a restaurant and get mad at Mimi for looking at her iPad. Can you guess the shape that I just folded my napkin into? Bing Bong, you're right! It's a squid.

CHAPTER 27

DOG JOY, YAYOI,
AND SARDINE CLOUDS

ccording to the Chinese Zodiac, or Sheng Xiao, 2018 was the Year of the Dog. Along with ramen noodles and most kanji characters, Japan has adopted many aspects of Chinese culture. So, 2018 was also the Year of the Dog in Japan.

Last January, I was asked to speak at a Buddhist meeting which was attended by about 50 members of *Gosho Yumae*, my local chapter of the Soka Gakkai. Abandoning any sort of doctrinal references or doing any research, I prepared by chanting a few extra hours after my New Year's Eve hangover wore off, which naturally led to some timely kick-off-the-new-year-right reflection. I just spoke, in simplest terms, about how much we can all learn from dogs. They instinctively behave in ways that if employed by humans, can significantly improve and advance our lives. In fact, dogs embody many of the principles of Original Good. Whereas I can turn an unfamiliar body of water into a cerebral, inner deliberation of whether it's too cold or the bottom's too slimy to swim in, a dog, without dipping a paw, will just jump into the pool or bound into a lake and have the blast of a lifetime.

Dogs have an inexhaustible appreciation for living simply, giving uninhibited face-licking and gratitude to their loved ones. It doesn't matter whether their owners are simply returning home from work or walking in through the door after a two-year tour in Afghanistan, it's cause for huge excitement. A dog will wag its tail and relish every bite of the same food that it's been eating for its entire life. Something as simple as being let outside into the backyard or walked around the same block in the same neighborhood for its ritual poop and pee also prompts unabashed enthusiasm. Dogs have an exuberance for life, unjaded primal appreciation, wonderment and awe for what is repeatedly there right in front of them. Frankly, for a dog, there's probably nothing worse than the torturous boredom of a quiet house when nobody's at home, waiting patiently for their owner's return while holding their "business" inside. But, maybe it will be his lucky day. A piece of grizzle cut from a steak might be thrown off the counter in his direction. Or, on his daily walk around the block, he could run into that cute, friendly Yorkie whose smell drives him wild. Every time he sniffs her butt, it sends him into the highest planes of ecstasy. At that Buddhist meeting, with a little help from Google Translate, I spoke of that dog-like sense of simplicity and joy at the privilege of just being alive and having a routine. It seemed natural to connect that to the bold and beautiful simplicity of a black handmade teacup, a la Chojiro (that Robert talked about). Next, I acknowledged the absolute "benefit" and privilege of having been born with two arms, two legs, ten fingers and toes, and being able to go to work. There should be profound joy in knowing that one has good health and doesn't have to schedule dialysis into their weekly regimen or struggle with cancer treatments.

One day in September, I decided I had to go see a Yayoi Kusama exhibit in Kyoto. After a half a day's work on a beautiful Sunday afternoon, I rode my bicycle through the Gion district, the traditional geisha district of Kyoto, through throngs of Japanese and Chinese tourists wearing kimonos. I wove down those narrow side streets on a lone journey, as bittersweet as it was exciting because the crowds that I wove through on my bicycle were families on vacation, and my wife and daughter were far from me, living in Tokyo. It had been four months since they'd relocated to Tokyo, and I was alone. But even if they had still been in Kyoto, I knew that I wouldn't have been able to talk them into going to the exhibit anyway. However, I was inexorably drawn to the work Yayoi had done in fabric, ceramics and sketches. So, after paying 700 yen (about $6.50) I found myself staring at sketches and prints that she made 40 years ago in the 1970s. Prior to making them, Yayoi Kusama had been homeless and mentally ill by her own admission. After many years of relentless dedication to her vision, at eighty years old, she's now internationally renowned, if not the most famous and influential Japanese artist alive today. As I stood in the middle of Yayoi's sketches and prints, I stared close up at butterflies in vivid colors with wings that were comprised of hundreds or thousands of simple, repeated oval fish scale patterns that she had drawn meticulously, probably for weeks at a time. Then, as I pulled back and tried to perceive it as an entire work of art, as opposed to the sum of its myriad thousand parts, it pulsed, vibrated, moved and breathed. I began to hallucinate. I'm not sure if I was trippin' because I was completely entranced and hypnotized by Yayoi's vivid depictions of the complexity and simplicity of life in her works or if it was just due to one too many of those Grateful Dead concerts. But, I was most certainly neurologically displaced, elevated to another consciousness. The thought in my mind was, "Thank God I'm alive and have eyes to experience this! I wished, yearned in a sense, that blind people could experience what I'm experiencing right now. How lucky I am to be here in this moment!"

I left the exhibit changed and inspired and rode my bicycle back through those crowds of tourists. My thoughts through what I was witnessing through tear-filled eyes were, "What could be a greater contradiction than people in traditional Japanese kimonos taking smartphone photos with selfie sticks in front of old wooden tea houses that stand next to Starbucks?" It was as shocking as it was farcical, and as realistic as a dream can get. A "Psychology Today" article might call what I'm going through at this stage in my life a midlife crisis. But, I call it "an awakening", an absolute liberation of my spirit and justification of my very being in all I've done to get me to a point where I'm cosmically melding with Yayoi Kusama prints and absorbing and resonating with all the colors, sounds and possibilities that surround me.

That day, I finally escaped the grip of the crowded streets of Gion and made it closer to the Kamogawa river, where a sometimes paved, sometimes earthen path leads along its edge. Out of the bustle and the traffic lights, I was grateful. Lovers sat along the embankments of the river, arms around each other, and I heard conga players in the distance. I stopped my bike to take it all in because there was no need to rush. Yeah, I needed to get back to my school and vacuum it, complete my song SUGE with the great Spanish horns on it, and finish writing this book. Catherine would probably be waiting for me to send this last chapter. But, I had five minutes of eternity to pause and breathe. As I looked up, I saw an amazing sky overhead, covered in clouds. These weren't intersecting vapor trails. There's no airport in Kyoto, and it isn't under any flight paths. These weren't your run of the money cumulus, cirrus or stratocumulus clouds. Above me, there were thousands of rounded, triangular patterns extending for miles in every direction. Blanketing the heavens out beyond the horizons in every direction, they resembled the luminous scales of a sardine. They're called *Iwashigumo*, Sardine Clouds. Gazing up at them, I realized that's exactly what I'd seen breathing and pulsating in the backgrounds of Yayoi Kusama's butterfly wings, fish and pumpkins.

Peddling further on my bike, I gasped for air. I felt my heart pumping, physically taking up space in my chest, drawing blood from the tips of my fingers and toes through my body. I felt so alive! It wasn't a state of heavenly bliss, but a tectonic shifting in the depths of my life and complete connection to the past, present and future, meeting right there, swirling around and inside me. I stopped my bike once more. I looked around and noticed I was under a weeping cherry tree. A small fraction of the leaves was beginning to change colors, taking on hues of red and orange. The end of September was approaching with a slight chill in the air. How could I contain my joy? How could I help from smiling as it dawned on me that I was weeks away from experiencing another gorgeous Autumn in Kyoto? This is my life, and my new home. Is it possible to feel a higher level of love and appreciation for being here in this place, during this time, and in this body? I can't imagine it. All I know is it makes me feel perfectly, joyfully, and irrevocably in love with life. Eat too much spicy food and you may get a bellyache. Love too much and you may get "lovesic."

EPILOGUE

SUGE! (pronounced soo GAY') means amazing! *Sugoi* (soo GOI) is the most direct translation of amazing, but Japanese love to have fun with words and playfully mispronounce them to sharpen the edges. Sometimes a cartoon-like facial contortion forms as the mouth exaggerates the word, sprinkling a little pepper on it. My newest song, SUGE! is an expression of the importance and possibilities of multiculturalism, my calling, emanating from the deepest depths of my being. It's sung in English, Spanish, and Japanese and captures all facets of my "crystall." It's mischievously philosophical, maniacal, but grounded. Stylistically, it's alternative rock that will hopefully shake up a dance floor.

What fortune I've had to have drawn the few precious souls into my life who have contributed to its creation. SUGE's foundational track was made by my "little brother," Jay Mohamed, on a laptop in a small house in the commercial marijuana fields of Humboldt County, California. Guitar work comes from James Mongan (the other half of my '90s band Orchid Room), emailed from the mountains of Woodstock, New York. More guitar was contributed locally by Shoji, a loner, two-pack-a-day-smoking, skinny, leather-clad Kyoto-ite whose diagnosed "dissociative identity disorder" mind is as distorted as his guitar feedback. (His last text to me after our four-month musical love affair was "my psychiatrist says we shouldn't talk together...bye.") Piano instrumentation is provided by Julian, an impeccably well-mannered and refined Brit who runs an English school dangerously close to the WAVE. Ichi-Go, a talented Japanese multi- ethnic percussionist, plays the "Jew's (or mouth) harp," that I effected heavily. His name in kanji means "every encounter is a deeply profound opportunity." Backing vocals are sung by Rasstar, a ridiculously talented, soulful singer from Ohio who has been making music and breaking hearts across Japan for 20 years, through two divorces.

At this moment, SUGE! feels as though it's my life's work. It may be the best chance I'll have to break through a lifetime of barriers to reach that elusive goal of earning money by making original music. The lyrics, rhythm, and music are my lifeblood, splashed like Sumi ink on a scroll, released on the internet and stored in ones and zeroes for eternity. I've just uploaded its video made entirely on my iPhone which is the best I can do under time and budget constraints. Although I've listened to it a thousand times, I still like it enough that I want it to be played and danced to at my funeral! Will this song be the advent of my life on Earth? Or will it be the *next* song? Will others feel the exhilaration I feel as I grab my bag, jump on my bike on a cold sunny day with SUGE! blasting in my earphones? It must be played loud! Its fast tempo turns the five-minute ride to the subway station into a "radio-friendly" three minutes and 45 seconds. And that's just enough time for the song's final echoed horn blast to propel me three steps at a time down the stairs to catch the train to Doshisha University.

SUGE!

By Jay Crystall © 2018 Jay Crystall

We got soul, we got funny

We gonna break it in two

We gotta spend a little money to make a lotta money

We got places to meet and people to do

We got so much honey............we got bee envy

 We got a life of luxury in a cardboard box

We got the lime and the coconut– we drink it all up

We got love (yeah, we got love)

Ima ga subete (Now is everything)

Itsumo Kando suru (I'm always so moved)

Yakedo Nandemo ii (but, anything is fine)

Itsumo kidzuku (in every moment comes a realization)

SUGE! Por que no, porque no, porque no no lo entiendo

(Amazing! Why not? I don't get it)

SUGE! te estoy vigilando portate bien

(I'm watching you, so behave yourself)

SUGE! OMG, OMG Ponle donde quieres, ella dijo

("Put it anywhere you want," she said)

SUGE! Y antes de morirme quiero verlos felices y seguridad

(And before I die I want them to be happy and secure)

Kokai kokai kokai shinai (you won't regret it)

Ima ga subete - Everything is Now...EVERYTHING!!!

[Watch at: https://bit.ly/lovesicinkyotosuge]

ACKNOWLEDGMENTS

As an expatriate, musician, language teacher, and jerk of all trades, I've learned firsthand the power of collaboration and communication and how it builds bridges between people and fosters stronger communities. This book was a collaboration in the best sense of the word. I could not have done it without the support of others, particularly my co-author, Catherine Lenox, whose tireless energy, communication, and vision helped bring this book to fruition. Her belief in my story and music spurred me on. Thanks also goes to Sonja Gerard of Oei Graphics for creating the beautiful imagery in the book. Sonja believes in the power of visuals and music and has conveyed that belief in these pages. Special thanks to Ethan Yarbrough of Iron Twine Press for his expert proofreading and support. And, to Robert Yellin and all the wonderful friends, relatives, and loved ones mentioned in these pages. Our adventures and learning experiences were many, and for this joy and growth, I thank you. I thank Misa and Mimi who are forever a part of me. Finally, deepest appreciation goes to Sensei, Daisaku Ikeda, and to the Soka Gakkai International organization and its many members. It is there that I was taught how to tap into personal happiness, courage, wisdom, and compassion to better the world around me. This book is an abundant outgrowth of that practice.

ABOUT THE AUTHOR

Author/musical artist **Jay Crystall** lives in Kyoto, Japan. As founder of the WAVE Center for Language and Culture, he combines English training and cultural immersion to foster learning through a uniquely interactive, multimedia learning experience for both kids and adults. Jay also teaches English language at Doshisha University and at hospitals and companies throughout the Kansai area. Born and raised in and around New York City, Jay moved to Japan in 2011. An acclaimed singer/songwriter/producer who is an active Buddhist and purveyor of multiculturalism, he has been described as a "New Renaissance Man." Jay's first Kyoto-based band, Kansai Rocks!, produced the CD Changing Poison into Medicine, (available on iTunes and most other platforms). He continues to release his music and perform live as a solo artist throughout the Kansai area. His music is a universal blend of sound and true international collaboration. *Lovesic in Kyoto* is his first book. Follow Jay at: Instagram - @Jay.Crystall, Facebook - @LovesicinKyoto, and Twitter - @LovesicInKyoto.

ABOUT THE CO-AUTHOR/EDITOR

Owner and founder of Write Contact, author **Catherine Lenox** ghostwrites creative non-fiction, articles and blogs. She lives near Seattle, Washington. A former radio news reporter and writer/editor for numerous magazines, newspapers, corporate and government publications, she enjoys helping others tell their stories. In 1974, as a student ambassador through the Lions International Club, she lived with a Japanese family in Kyushu, Japan and fell in love with its people, the land, and culture. She's been an ardent Japanophile ever since. *Lovesic in Kyoto* is her debut as a co-author.

京都物語

CPSIA information can be obtained
at www.ICGtesting.com
Printed in the USA
FFHW011116200319
51141283-56604FF